HOW THEY MADE IT

TRUE STORIES

OF HOW MUSIC'S BIGGEST STARS WENT FROM START TO

STARDOM!

by DAN KIMPEL

HAL•LE

Photo Credits:
Cover:
John Mayer–Photofest; OutKast–Courtesy of Arista Records; Alanis Morissette–Photofest; Jewel–Photofest; Brian McKnight–Courtesy of Mercury Records; Christina Aguilera–Photofest; Maroon5–Courtesy of Octone Records; Norah Jones–Photofest; Phil Vassar–Sandy Campbell

Interior:
1 Yariv Milchan; 6 Ross Harris; 11 Photofest; 16 Photofest; 26 Guzman; 36 Photofest; 41 Dan Winters; 46 Marina Chavez; 51 Photofest; 56 Per Breiehagen; 61 Photofest; 66 Photofest; 71 Sonya Farrell; 76 Clay McBride; 81 Ann Summa; 86 Courtesy of Octone Records; 91 Retna; 96 Autumn De Wilde; 101 Photofest; 106 Courtesy of Mercury Records; 111 Kate Garner; 117 Photofest; 122 Photofest; 126 Neil Zlozauer; 130 Chris Cuffaro; 135 Retna; 139 Courtesy of Tsunami Entertainment; 144 Justin Jay; 148 Photofest; 153 Sandra-Lee Phipps; 158 Photofest; 163 Timothy White; 173 Photofest; 178 Sandy Campbell; 183 Photofest; 188 Courtesy of Epic Records; 193 Matt Barnes

ISBN-13: 978-0-634-07642-8
ISBN-10: 0-634-07642-6

Published by Hal Leonard Corporation
7777 W. Bluemound Road
P.O. Box 13819
Milwaukee, WI 53213

Library of Congress Cataloging-in-Publication Data

Kimpel, Dan, 1952-
  How they made it : true stories of how music's biggest stars went from start to stardom! / by Dan Kimpel. -- 1st ed.
    p. cm.
  ISBN-13: 978-0-634-07642-8
  1. Musicians--United States--Biography. I. Title.
ML385.K555 2006
781.64092'273--dc22
  [B]

                      2006011927

Printed in the U.S.A.

First Edition

Visit Hal Leonard Online at **www.halleonard.com**

CONTENTS

INTRODUCTION

The mythologies of popular music boast of chance encounters, of eagle-eared scouts scouring the hinterlands for potential stars, of penniless waifs discovered singing on street corners, of bands plucked from obscurity and elevated to unfathomable riches. Alluring as these fables and fairytales might be, they are media fodder. While the true stories might be less sensational, they are certainly no less compelling. Today's stars of modern music possess undeniable determination, the motivation to create opportunities on their own, to enlist invincible support networks, and to captivate massive audiences with the power of real music.

Over the past decade, the record business has undergone cataclysmic shifts. The monolithic mega-labels, rendered immobile by their very power, have been knocked down by the rise of the Internet and the accessibility of free music via file sharing. Consequently, CD sales have teetered precariously. Still, more than ever, music is ever-present in our world—in films, on television, on websites, ringing from mobile telephones, and transmitted by satellite signals. Fans don't download music simply because it's free, they download it because it is a necessity.

A leveling of the playing field has given rise to independent labels and artists in niche markets that could have never existed a mere decade ago. In past decades, record companies were talent-development resources. No longer. Instead, record labels bank on bands and artists who have already proven their worth. They want enterprising, energized entities who have taken control of touring and merchandising, who have constructed a fan base through the global span of the Internet, who have experienced regional, national, and even international touring and spread their message through good old word-of-mouth, artists whose music is similarly connected to, and driving, trends.

COMMON THREADS
In the profiles of the artists, bands, and producers in this book, it is evident that, despite their marked diversity, many similarities exist.

Economic and social background
Although some of the profile subjects are from middle-class families, virtually none of them grew up as children of privilege. Moreover, many of the artists came up with harsh backgrounds: poverty, broken homes, and families with all manner of dysfunction. It might be rationalized that this is simply a mirror of our culture at large, but it also indicates an ability on the part of the artists to rise above their birth caste with the extra added impetus to create something of lasting value while surpassing adversity and balancing out emotional emptiness.

Early Ambitions

Peter Cincotti was studying piano at age four, Alicia Keys soon thereafter. Christina Aguilera and Alanis Morissette were both child stars. Revealed in the early sagas of the profile subjects is their earliest proclivity for their art. These were not children who needed to be cajoled into studying or prodded to perform. They yearned for the power of self-expression that only their self-created sounds could provide. For many of these current stars, performing arts high schools and community-based arts education provided primary incubators.

Location, location, location

There is a truism in the music business: "You have to be able to make it happen where you are, or travel to where it is." As hopefuls in the business, many of the profile subjects took major leaps of faith, spending long, soul-searching nights in seamy motels, crashing on friends' couches, walking the mean streets of unfamiliar cities, touring the hinterlands in rusted-out vans. Country music aspirations, in particular, lead to only one signpost—Nashville. And Music City respects longevity and endurance, as Lee Ann Womack's story of a decade spent working behind the scenes and Phil Vassar's rise through the clubs will illustrate.

Growing up in a major recording capital is no guarantee of success, but it is clearly a bonus. Ozomatli, Linkin Park, Beck, Los Lobos, Maroon5 and Black Eyed Peas are Los Angeles natives, Cincotti and Keys from New York City. L.A. and The Apple are the obvious epicenters, but other, lesser-known locales also emerge. Atlanta, GA, the music capital of the New South, is home to a thriving hip-hop industry, fueled on the success of songwriter/producers who develop and nurture talent. Home to the duo OutKast, it is the adopted home of singer/songwriter John Mayer who famously asked, "Why Georgia, Why?" Virginia Beach, VA, fairly equidistant to New York and Atlanta, is home to The Neptunes and Missy Elliot. And one historic music city, Philadelphia, has forged new generations of musical creators who clearly pay homage to those who came before them, such as Jill Scott and Pink, who both absorbed and reinterpreted the Seventies soul of Gamble and Huff.

Local Motion

Those who weren't blessed to be born in major music capitals, and didn't relocate to them, share an ability to tap into a local scene that blossoms into national, and international prominence. REM came up in a sleepy college town, but early on realized that there was a rich network of similar locales where they could perform. Deathcab for Cutie and Nickelback rose up from secondary music cities—Seattle and Vancouver, respectively

Even though she emerged from Nashville, Gretchen Wilson came out of an alternative scene, joining the disaffected denizens of a local bar dubbed the "Muzik Mafia." And Jason Mraz and Jewel both built up strong local followings in the coffeehouses of San Diego, previously not a hotbed of musical activity, but a mere two-and-a-half-hour limo ride away from Los Angeles. No Doubt lived even closer, in Orange County, and enticed their fans to help them with their promotional mailings by offering free pizza.

Born to the Business

Only a handful of our profiles are products of successful musical families. Most notable among them: Rufus Wainwright, both of whose parents are well-known singer/songwriters; Norah Jones, whose father is Indian sitar master Ravi Shankar (who was not present in her life until her teens); and Beck, whose father, David Campbell, is an established string arranger and whose mother is a local hipster celebrity of sorts. There are deeper musical through-lines: Jimmy Jam's father was a musician and a bandleader, both of Jewel's parents performed, and Gretchen Wilson's father played in a family band. Sibling similarities emerge in No Doubt, pairing Gwen and Eric Stefani (although the latter left the band to become an illustrator before their huge success) and the Kroeger brothers from Nickelback.

Some of the bands might well have been brothers: Billie Joe Armstrong and Mike Dirnt of Green Day lived together as kids, the primary band-mates in Linkin Park attended elementary school together, and the principal players in Maroon5 and Los Lobos were young classmates as well.

Resilience

The music business is a food chain of rejection. Songwriters are rejected by publishers, publishers rejected by A&R execs at labels, A&R execs rejected by label hierarchies, label hierarchies rejected by radio and popular tastes—or lack thereof—ultimately rejecting the end results. Many of the artists and bands profiled in this book experienced crushing rejection, usually in the failure of an initial recording project or, in some cases, in the dissolution of a record deal or the disintegration of their record label. Maroon5 were an entirely different band, Kara's Flowers, a signed act with an unsuccessful CD. Missy Elliott was a member of a girl group whose first release was shelved permanently, and Sheryl Crow's and Melissa Etheridge's first expensive recording projects were scrapped altogether. Rufus Wainwright noodled away for three years in the vastly overpriced halls of a major L.A studio, recording everything he'd ever written since his teens, while Avril Lavigne worked on both coasts until clicking with L.A.-based song-writer/producers Clif Magness and The Matrix. Signed to Eazy-E's Ruthless Records, Atban Klann, later known as Black Eyed Peas, saw their music languish in the vaults; they were unable to release it or even perform, since they didn't even own their own band name.

Sideways Segues

Writing jingles and recording them might not seem like a path to a career creating meditative New Age music, but composer and pianist Jim Brickman learned vital lessons about connecting with people-pleasing music by penning commercials. Queen Latifah, Jill Scott, and Missy Elliot all guest-starred with and wrote for other artists; Sheryl Crow sang back-up for a globe-spanning Michael Jackson tour and Michael W. Smith was the bandleader for superstar Amy Grant. All three of the production teams—Jimmy Jam & Terry Lewis, The Matrix, and The Neptunes—have crossed the borders from band members and musicians to platinum production teams. Songwriter/artist Jeffrey Steele has the best of both worlds—his smash hits for country artists allow him to maintain an independent career as a recording and touring artist, doing what he loves best. In this age of American Idolization, only Joss Stone emerged from a competitive television show, England's *Star for a Night*. Both Alanis Morissette and Christina Aguilera went down to defeat on the Eighties show *Star Search*.

Indie Action

The momentum gained from independent, DIY (Do-It-Yourself) ventures propels successful artists forward, especially in these fiscally-cautious times. Beck recorded for a series of local, Los Angeles-based labels, and it was an across-the-board acceptance of his indie projects by radio that directly led to a signing with a major. Green Day, at the time signed to an indie label, Lookout Records, informed Rob Cavallo, the label executive who signed them to a major, "We are fully confident that we are going to do it on our own, anyway." REM and Nickelback had their own careers fully up and running before a major came aboard. Death Cab for Cutie recorded for a local label, Barsuk, delivering a series of well-received albums before being wooed by Atlantic Records.

Timing

OutKast may have been hip-hop stars, but they didn't cross over to huge audiences until hip-hop music became the dominant musical force. In the late Eighties, their west coast counterparts, Black Eyed Peas, with their positive, upbeat rap, were anomalies amongst their Uzi-toting gangsta compadres. Norah Jones, with melodic sensitivity, was a true alternative to the alternatives. Pop music is cyclic. What goes around comes around, be it emotive singer/songwriters, sullen rebels, choreographed boy bands, or wailing divas. All of the profile subjects in this book experienced a breakthrough as a result of crucial timing.

Is it Live?

A strong live show was key to the signing of many of the artists. Jason Mraz and his bandmates crammed themselves into the cab of a tiny Mazda pickup truck, drove thousands of miles, rented their own P.A., and performed for concert fans in parking lots. Nickelback logged interminable miles across the bleak Canadian prairies to build a loyal fan base. Green Day wasn't content simply to be local stars around their northern California community; instead, they set off across America in a refurbished bookmobile, crashed on fans' floors, and predicated their own success one town at a time. No Doubt built their enormous fan base as an opening act for major artists. Some artists built their own momentum. Phil Vassar even owned his own nightclub in Nashville, where he performed.

Support Networks

Without exception, someone had to believe in each of these artists. In some cases, it was a family member. Alicia Keys' mother worked a second job so her daughter could study piano. Brian McKnight's brother Claude was the co-founder of the vocal group Take 6. Christina Aguilera's mother facilitated her audition for Disney, and Jewel's mother and Pink's father both assumed management duties.

Having a strong supporter already in the business is another notable attribute. Manager Bill Leopold dragged record executives to unfashionable Long Beach, CA bars, where they were the only males in attendance, to witness the power of Melissa Etheridge. Executive Jeff Blue put his own career on the line to champion Linkin Park. Warner/Chappell executive Judy Stakee figured into two careers—Sheryl Crow and Jewel—and Matchbox Twenty captured the attention of radio programmers and DJs on local stations.

CODA

One fundamental truth unites every single subject in this book: they all continue to create enduring music that touches souls. I hope their stories will inspire you, too.

—Dan Kimpel
Los Angeles

Christina AGUILERA

The Diva's Drive

They called her "The Little Girl with the Big Voice." Belying her diminutive size, Christina Aguilera is immense in every other way—sound, influence, and divadom. At the time of her emergence into the rarefied circle of pop stardom, she was already a lifelong veteran of the stage and studio, with a tumultuous backstory of intrigue, deals gone sour, broken promises, and triumphs.

Christina Aguilera grew up in the Pittsburgh suburb of Wexford, PA, where her family settled after living in various locations around the globe. It went with the territory. Her father, Fausto Aguilera, is a U.S. Army sergeant of Ecuadorian descent, and her mother, Shelly Loraine Fidler (now known as Shelly Kearns), is a Spanish translator from Newfoundland, Canada. Aguilera's parents met while Fausto was serving at Earnest Harmon Air Force Base in Canada. During Christina's early years, the Aguilera family followed her father's assignments to Florida,

"I was blown away. I thought I was listening to a little black girl from the South. When I saw her, I was like, 'Wow! This is the little package that was singing like that? Incredible.'"

—Michael Brown

Texas, New Jersey, and Japan. After having another daughter, Rachel, the Aguileras separated around 1986. The following year, Shelley Aguilera moved with her daughters back to her hometown of Wexford. After her mother remarried, Aguilera's family included siblings Casey, Robert Michael, and Stephanie. For several years after the divorce, Aguilera had very little contact with her father.

Early on, singing was Christina's lifeblood as she performed at block parties and in talent competitions, besting her opponents with little effort. Bolstered by her mother's support, she appeared on the televised talent show *Star Search* in 1990, singing Ella Fitzgerald's "Sunday Kind of Love," but failed to win. She returned home and appeared on Pittsburgh's KDKA-TV's *Wake Up with Larry Richert* to perform the same song again. (Later on, she would sing Mariah Carey's "Vision of Love" and astonish listeners by hitting every riff and note, including Carey's trademark high notes.)

In Francis Scott's Key

As a local phenomenon, Aguilera sang "The Star-Spangled Banner" before Pittsburgh Steelers football and Pittsburgh Pirates baseball games on a regular basis. At an open audition in Pittsburg for Disney, she impressed the casting directors, but they declared her too young for their forthcoming project. They held onto her audition tape, however, and in 1993 she joined the cast of the Disney Channel's variety show *The New Mickey Mouse Club*. Her co-stars included Britney Spears, Justin Timberlake, JC Chasez (who went on to join *NSYNC), and Keri Russell (who later became the star of *Felicity*).

Michael Brown and Bob Allecca are a New Jersey-based writing/production duo who have worked on a range of projects including SWV, Foxy Brown, Toots and the Maytals, and The Misfits. They couldn't help but be impressed when one of SWV's promo people called in 1997 and held up the phone so they could hear a teenage girl sing the national anthem. Her name was Christina Aguilera. "I was blown away," marvels Michael Brown. "I thought I was listening to a little black girl from the South. When I saw her, I was like, 'Wow! This is the little package that was singing like that? Incredible.'"

The next day, the pair arranged for Christina and her family to travel to Lodi, NJ. This inaugurated a two-year period of songwriting, production, and career development to launch Aguilera. For months at a time, Christina moved in with Allecca and his wife while Brown and Allecca arranged international showcases in Japan and Romania and shows in Florida and New York so Aguilera could support her family. They both were convinced this girl would be a pop star.

Dancing Queen

The major component was the songs and production. "We didn't want to make her into a Mariah, because she had a similar approach, feel-wise," recalls Brown. "We wanted to take that and put it into more of a dance deal which wasn't so much of a threat. In that form, people accept things and it doesn't step on anybody's feet. Larry Flick at *Billboard* did a very nice review of the single 'Just Be Free' when we initially released it. The record started to move. She also did a show-case at The Motown Cafe in New York City and she did the May Fair Festival in Coconut Grove, FL with Power 96 radio, on the bill with The Blues Brothers. It started to make a lot of noise." Christina traveled to Japan where she recorded a duet, "All I Wanna Do," with Japanese pop star Keizo Nakanishi, appeared in the video, and toured. Later that year, the young show-biz veteran almost caused a riot at the Golden Stag Festival in Transylvania, Romania when she waded into the crowd of 10,000 while performing her two-song set on a bill which included Sheryl Crow and Diana Ross.

Signed for management to Steve Kurtz, on her return to the States in early 1998, Christina was invited to audition to record "Reflection" for the Disney animated film *Mulan.* The studio's search for a powerful voice with a wide vocal range quickly ended. They needed someone "who could hit a high E above middle C," according to Christina. At Kurtz's suggestion, Christina cut a one-take demo on her boombox in her living room, singing to a karaoke tape of Whitney Houston's "Run To You." The demo was sent Disney via FedEx. Within 48 hours, Aguilera was in a Los Angeles studio recording "Reflection." The same week, Ron Fair at RCA signed Aguilera to a deal.

"At that point, we suddenly had a problem with her management," Brown recalls. "It was the manager and lawyer, a father and son team. The father I'd known for 25 years. The son had been my attorney for 13 years; he's the godfather of my son. We were very close, I thought, but greed or something got in there and they figured out a way to move ahead without Bob and myself."

The Magic Lamp

Songwriter David Frank remembers the moment when he and his co-writer, Steve Kipner, first heard Christina Aguilera sing "Genie in a Bottle." "Our jaws almost dropped off," he laughs. David Frank is in an enviable position. He can deliver songs based on a guarantee that his song will be first or second single from an album. So when record executive Ron Fair called him about this new artist, Frank was not entirely thunderstruck. "He told me she had been on Disney and I was like, 'Oh yeah, great.'"

"Then I listened to 'Reflections' and I thought she was a wonderful legitimate singer. We wrote 'Genie in a Bottle' not specifically for her, but we had a short list of singers and groups and she was on it. But until she came over and sang it, I wasn't sure she was the right artist."

Co-writer Steve Kipner confirms Frank's description. "With 'Genie,' we knew we had a very good song, and we wanted to find the best artist to record it. Several artists wanted to record the song, but Christina Aguilera's A&R exec, Ron Fair, was very persuasive. Ron said he had to have the song. The next thing that happened, Christina came over to David's house, and she sang 'Genie' for us. Christina sang it great, and it was obvious that we should produce it on her."

It was a lucky break for the third writer, Pam Sheyne. "A girlfriend said to me, 'The next time you go to L.A., you've got to work with David Frank,'" Sheyne recalls. "I called him and we had one day to put in. I said, 'If we've only got one day, we really should get another writer so we can nail a song.' I like working two ways, but sometimes three ways is better to get it all together." Frank invited hit songwriter and collaborator Steve Kipner, also his neighbor down the road in L.A.'s rustic Topanga Canyon, to join the writing session. "We wrote the song in a day, and I went back the next day and did my loop with David. Within a week, we had a few artists fighting over it."

Not everyone was thrilled with the song's success. Michael Brown recalls, "One thing led to the next. We heard 'Genie in a Bottle' on the radio and I know Bob almost had a car accident right then and there. It was a pre-meditated thing. We made enough noise for her to get enough attention and they were able to entice RCA, which wasn't that hard, because I had already had a relationship with people there. No fault of RCA, they were misled from the beginning on our involvement. They went on to sell all those records and she found out the manager/lawyer team was doing something wrong and she sued them first. That vindicated our position, that's what we were saying. 'How can you do this?'"

On October 13, 2000, Aguilera filed a Breach of Fiduciary Duty lawsuit against Steve Kurtz for improper, undue, and inappropriate influence over her professional activities, as well as fraud. According to legal documents, Kurtz did not protect her rights and interests. Instead, he took action that was for his own interest, at the cost of hers. The lawsuit came about when Aguilera discovered Kurtz used more of her commissionable income than what he was allotted, and had paid other managers to assist him. She also petitioned the California State Labor Commission to nullify the contract.

In addition to the writers and producers who created "Genie," Ron Fair assembled a winning team of Los Angeles-based hitmakers. "What a

Girl Wants" was produced by Guy Roche (Brandy, Cher, Dru Hill, Aaliyah, K-Ci & Jo Jo); "Blessed" was penned and produced by Travon Potts (co-writer of Monica's chart topping "Angel of Mine"). Meanwhile, Carl Sturken and Evan Rogers (*NSYNC, Boyzone, Brand New Heavies) contributed a pair of tracks, the soul-flavored "Love for All Seasons" and the rousing "Love Will Find a Way." Hit songwriter Matthew Wilder produced "Reflection" and master tunesmith Diane Warren wrote the smash "I Turn to You."

At the 1999 GRAMMY Awards®, Aguilera pulled an upset win over Britney Spears to claim the award for Best New Artist. At the time of the award, Christina's album had been out only a few months, so most people expected Spears to walk away with the GRAMMY®. Aguilera herself appeared shocked at getting such recognition mere months after her album's release. The following year, she claimed her second GRAMMY Award®, this time from the Latin Recording Academy, for her Spanish-language release *Mi Reflejo*. Although she had to record the album phonetically because she did not speak Spanish, Aguilera looked at the experience as a chance to reconnect with her father's side of the family. The album was a major success and sold over three million copies in the year after its 2000 release. That year, Aguilera released another platinum-selling album, *My Kind of Christmas*, a collection of holiday standards.

Producer and A&R executive Ron Fair, who engineered the signing of Christina, says "Christina is remarkable, but it didn't happen overnight for her. It wouldn't have happened at all if she didn't work at it. I don't know of anyone who's successful in this business who didn't work very hard at it. Those stars usually start long before they make it big." Fair insists that the path forged by Aguilera is the perfect road to follow: "Do everything you can, sing everywhere you can, like Christina. When she was 12, she was singing the National Anthem for all her hometown games. She was singing at every block party. She was going on every possible audition she could find out about. Her mom was cooperating. She was really dedicated to this ever since she was eight years old."

RECAP: Road to the Dotted Line

CHRISTINA AGUILERA

- Began performing at local events
- Auditioned, and became a cast member, for a television show
- Made a successful transition from child star to teen vocalist
- Hooked up with management and producers

BECK

ROCK LEVITATION

"I was encouraged to be curious. If I had an interest in something, there was nobody telling me 'No, don't do that, that's stupid.' It was okay to explore."

Iconoclastic, imaginative, unpredictable. When he rocketed seemingly fully-formed onto the music scene in the mid-Nineties with his song "Loser," it was apparent that Beck—Beck Hansen, or Beck (sometimes spelled "Bek") David Campbell, his birth name—was an artist of auspicious vision and more than a smidgen of attitude. A jumble of images reflected a polyglot of influences: hip-hop, punk, skater culture, and art rock. Clearly, Beck was a product of a media-overloaded age, and he could have emerged only from his Technicolor marvel of a hometown, Los Angeles.

Beck was born to a show-biz family. His father, David Campbell, is a noted Hollywood string arranger who has worked with artists ranging from Alanis Morissette to Leonard Cohen. His mother, Bibbe Hansen, is a post-graduate of the Andy Warhol art scene. She was only 13 years old when she appeared in Andy Warhol's film

Prison with Edie Sedgwick. She also appeared in Warhol's first *Restaurant* film in 1965 and two other Warhol films which, at the time, were referred to as *10 Beautiful Girls* and *10 More Beautiful Girls.* In 1964, she made a recording on Laurie Records with Jack Kerouac's daughter Janet, as part of a band called The Whippets. A scenemaker of the first order, Hansen's father, Al Hansen, Beck's grandfather, is a visual artist and an early proponent of the FluXus movement. In the Sixties, Al Hansen also published the underground magazine *Kiss*—"the paper you read with one hand"—which featured contributions by Andy Warhol and various Factory superstars, including Ondine and Brigid Berlin.

Though his parents split soon after his birth in 1970, Beck was raised around a coterie of hipsters and art types. Bibbe recalls taking him, at age seven, to The Masque, a notorious punk hangout in the Seventies. For Beck, it all seemed normal. "It was just being around people who were interested in things, in life. It wasn't passive," he says. "It was a family where you could sit and talk about history or film or politics for five hours. That environment is pretty rare." It was also conducive to his emerging artistry. "I was encouraged to be curious," he says. "If I had an interest in something, there was nobody telling me 'No, don't do that, that's stupid.' It was okay to explore."

And explore he did, but his higher education wasn't necessarily in the classroom. School and Beck did not agree, and he relates that although he attempted to get into one of L.A.'s performing arts high schools, he wasn't accepted. He dropped out at age 14. A voracious reader, he nonetheless pursued his self-education by watching French New Wave films, absorbing the sounds of ancient blues masters gleaned from second-hand LPs, and learning the guitar by studying seminal folk singers like Leadbelly and Woody Guthrie. The influences of his neighborhood—Latin rhythms, emerging hip-hop culture—shaded and sharpened his blossoming imagination, as did his immersion in all manner of pop media.

Passports and Parameters

In 1987, Beck further expanded the parameters of his growing artistry with a visit to Germany to spend time with his grandfather. Upon his return to Los Angeles, he made the fateful decision to take a bus trip to New York City. By all accounts, Beck's first foray into The Big Apple was less than auspicious. The girlfriend with whom he traveled across a continent ditched him, and he crashed on many a seamy couch.

At that time in New York, a new acoustic movement was springing up in Greenwich Village. Dubbed "Anti-Folk," it included future indie luminary Michelle Shocked and John S. Hall of King Missile. Here, Beck found a sympathetic scene. He performed in Manhattan clubs and coffeehouses and made his first low-fi recording, *Banjo Story*. But the frigid Manhattan winters could not compare to the balmy palm-shaded climate of Los Angeles. Returning to L.A., Beck made do with a string of mind-numbing day jobs—video store clerk and hot dog vendor among them—while performing anywhere and everywhere he could at night.

It was a fertile time for acoustic music in Los Angeles as a "caffeine circuit" began developing in hipster coffeehouses scattered across the sprawling landscape. One such venue, Highland Grounds on Highland Avenue, one of Hollywood's main arteries, became a regular stage for Beck. In 1990, Bibbe Hansen and her new husband, Sean, opened the Troy Cafe in L.A. The establishment became an important hangout and showcase venue for young new talent until it closed in 1995. During that time, Bibbe also co-founded and played rhythm guitar for the band Black Fag—"the best-hung band in rock and roll"—with lead singer Vaginal Davis. Beck performed at the coffeehouse regularly, sometimes with props and masks. The creative community embraced Beck and his art-informed songs, and he joined other musicians like Carla Bozulich of the Geraldine Fibbers and Ethyl Meatplow, and Martha Atwell (with whom he had a short-lived Carter Family/Louvin Brothers cover band called Ten Ton Lid). He also became friends with Joey Waronker, his future long-time drummer and brother of That Dog's Anna Waronker, children of Lenny Waronker, a longtime music industry executive.

Streets of Silver Lake

Even in a city of unusual neighborhoods, Silver Lake is unique in Los Angeles. Named for a reservoir that occupies its highest points, it is an inexplicable jumble of expensive homes, low-rent businesses, artsy enclaves, and gang-infested side streets. In the late Eighties, a two-day summer event was formulated to bring all of the elements of the area together. Named for the intersection of Sunset and Santa Monica Boulevards, Sunset Junction Street Fair embraced all of the communities and became an eye-popping event where tattooed hipsters, time-warped hippies, harnessed leather daddies, and multi-generational Latino families could spend three days in the streets—eating, people-watching, and listening to live music together.

Rob Schnapf, a co-founder of the small, local label Bong Load Custom Records, dropped by the fair and caught a performance by Beck, who was appearing on a stage sponsored by a local rehearsal studio, Hully Gully. About a week later, Schnapf's partner Tom Rothrock independently checked out a show at the Jabberjaw Coffeehouse and witnessed Beck commandeer the stage in-between billed bands. Schnapf and Rothrock saw unlimited potential in the ragged, energized performer. Rothrock is credited with introducing Beck to Carl Stephenson, a producer for the Geto Boys and mastermind of the diverse musical project Forest for the Trees. Both Beck and Stephenson shared a concept for a hip-hop/folk hybrid style. One day in the studio, Beck rapped a typically sarcastic jibe at slackers with a Spanish chorus. The duo added a Dr. John sample and a slide guitar riff, an intriguing sonic mix, but the song, "Loser," sat dormant for a year.

Minor to Major: Bongload, BMG, Geffen

Meanwhile, in 1992, Beck traveled to Olympia, WA to record for Calvin Johnson's K label. He also inked a publishing deal with BMG. Recording continued with Carl Stephenson on possible *Mellow Gold* tracks (as Beck's official debut was eventually titled), but tiny Flipside Records released "MTV Makes Me Want to Smoke Crack," a song that later appeared on a B-side to the "Loser" single.

The miniscule Sonic Enemy label released a very limited edition cassette, *Golden Feelings*, in January. Finally, Bong Load pressed 500 copies of "Loser" and distributed them to a small number of radio DJs across the country. The label was overwhelmed with requests for more pressings. Sonic Youth's Thurston Moore, who raved about Beck after seeing him perform at a backyard party, was a staunch ally. Beck agreed to sign with Geffen Records in November, on the condition that his contract would allow him freedom to release work on independent labels and to make what was deemed "uncommercial" music. He finished *Mellow Gold* by August, yet label negotiations and haggling stalled the release. By the end of the year, Beck continued working with Calvin Johnson and Scott Plouf (later of Built to Spill) and produced an unreleased mix tape for his mother's birthday, *Fresh Meat and Old Slabs*.

In March 1994, Geffen finally released *Mellow Gold* and reissued "Loser" on a national level. Instantly labeled an anthem for the so-called slacker generation, the song was a sensation, climbing into the Top 10 and hitting #1 on Billboard's modern rock chart. Ironically, the hard-working Beck, driven by creativity and less-than-ideal socio-economic conditions, had never been a loser or a slacker. Since his early teens, he had absorbed and distilled every influence around him—visually, musically, aesthetically.

Bong Load won the rights to put out the record on vinyl, but the consolation-prize nature of the compromise was the beginning of a years-long tug-of-war between labels. Reaction to *Mellow Gold* was critically positive, and the musical diversity of the album helped to eradicate the idea of Beck as a one-trick pony with a goofy novelty hit. Nonetheless, the "slacker" label persisted. The album's vivid hallucinatory lyrics led some to question the influence of drugs on his work, but with three other Beck full-lengths there was no doubt of his prodigious output.

Stereopathetic Soul Manure was released in February on Flipside, with a sonic jumble of recorded impromptu street performance and hallucinatory comedic narratives that garnered a confused, lukewarm response. Fingerpaint Records put out a 2000-pressing 10-inch vinyl, all with original artwork, called *Western Harvest Field By Moonlight*. Finally, the folky *One Foot in the Grave* was released on Calvin Johnson's K Records. With his fan base growing exponentially, Beck was cryptically skeptical about the speed of his newfound fame. "I just mistrusted; I didn't take it seriously," he reflects. "I said 'Uh-huh, they'll be on to something else in two months.'"

In 1996, Beck's masterpiece *Odelay* won him Artist of the Year with the Record of the Year for *Rolling Stone* and *Spin* magazines. In 1997, Beck received two GRAMMY Awards®, one for Best Alternative Music Performance ("Odelay"), the other for Best Male Rock Vocal Performance ("Where It's At") He also garnered a Brit Award for Best International Male, an MTV Video Award, and most improbably, a VH1 Fashion Award. He continues to be one of his generation's most original, baffling, and compelling artists.

RECAP: Road to the Dotted Line

BECK

- Born to a musical family
- Dropped out of school, became self-educated, and traveled
- Relocated to NYC and became part of a scene
- Continued to develop his own scene and sound in Los Angeles
- Performed at every possible venue
- Recorded for small indie labels
- Was intent on creating a diversity of forms including "uncommercial" music

BLACK EYED PEAS

Slow Cooking

Los Angeles has been famously portrayed as a city of exclusion, separated along ethnic lines by monolithic freeways that effectively marginalize and divide. With an African-American, will.i.am; a white woman, Fergie; Taboo, who is Latino; and a Filipino, apl.de.ap, hometown band Black Eyed Peas is clearly a band of inclusion.

Will.i.am grew up in East Los Angeles, but was bused to an exclusive Brentwood Elementary school on the west side of Los Angeles. The band's genesis harkens back to the days of high school, when will.i.am and apl.de.ap became friends as two compo-nents in Tribal Nation, a break-dancing crew. Apl.de.ap, adopted by the father who had supported him long distance from the Philippines, recalls, "Will asked, 'What did you do in the Philippines?' I said, 'I learned to dance.' I showed him this dance and he started laughing." The two and their break-

"Disco is hip-hop, rock is hip-hop. You ask me if it's the dominant world music? The only reason I say yes to that is that hip-hop is the only form of music on the planet that takes from every other form."
—will.i.am

dancing buddies performed in parking lots prior to concerts by A Tribe Called Quest.

The duo met Taboo, born and raised in East Los Angeles, in a break-dancing circle at Ballistics, a Los Angeles club, hosted by actor David Faustino, Bud Bundy from the TV series *Married...With Children*. Taboo relates that his form of physical expression wasn't appreciated in his barrio. "Break-dancing wasn't cool back then. It was kind of forbidden for Mexicans to be down with the blacks." Style was a big part of the bonding experience, and Taboo was embraced by will.i.am and apl.de.ap for his individuality.

Will had learned all about computers, mastering an Apple in elementary school. As he embraced the emerging sampling and beat-driven technology, the break dancing group evolved into rappers and DJs, spinning playful rhymes over jazzy samples under the name Atban Klann (in homage to their roots, an acronym for "A Tribe Beyond a Nation").

Meanwhile, from the mean streets of south central Los Angeles, Gangsta Rap was rising in popular consciousness. Eric Wright, known as Eazy-E, rich with profits from various nefarious street level businesses, formed Ruthless Records with businessman Jerry Heller. He created the rap group N.W.A. with Ice Cube, Dr. Dre, MC Ren, DJ Yella, and Arabian Prince. The group's second release, *Straight Outta Compton*, and its title track were smash hits, generating untold millions for Wright and Heller.

From the outset, the emerging West Coast rap phenomenon was rife with violence and bloodshed. It was an ironic, then, that the upbeat music of Atban Klann, recorded while the trio was still in high school and available only through underground tapes and word-of-mouth, came to the attention of Jerry Heller by way of his nephew. In 1992, the group was signed to Ruthless Records and they recorded a debut album. But it was never released and for three years, until the death of Eazy-E, the album sat in storage.

Ruthless Records owned more than just the group's music. It also owned their name. Unable to perform or record as Atban Klann, the trio regrouped as Black Eyed Peas, adopting the name of Will's production company with his former partner. They added back-up vocalists Kim Hill and Taboo and performed to pre-recorded DAT tapes all across Los Angeles.

Colleges booked the band. Will credits the students who were interning at record labels with creating the initial buzz and enticing the label execs to come to the shows. Colleges also figured into the equation when the band met a fledgling video director who was studying at Loyola Marymount University. As a class assignment, he produced a video, "Fallin' Up," for the band. Additionally, the whole crew recorded tracks at night in a studio at Loyola, including "Joints and Jams," "Head Bobs," and "Positivity."

Says Will.i.am, "At the time when we first started BEP, the record company didn't want to sign us because they said, "Well, you guys have a band, and the Roots don't sell records, so why do you think you guys are going to?" We couldn't play hip-hop clubs because we didn't use records, and I hate performing off a DAT. It's like microwave food. The only place we could play was rock clubs and your traditional Hollywood sunset strip clubs, and colleges—every single college around our area. Colleges are the world to come. You have a lot of interns that work at record companies that end up being vice presidents, heads of A&R or heads of marketing someday. If you want to do anything, go to colleges. That's where the hunger is. There are very talented people in computer graphics who will kill every single person that's on the Cartoon Network because they are inspired by that and they want to take it to the next level."

Their performances became major events when they added a live band to the shows. The record labels, informed by their interns, took note. Black Eyed Peas signed with Interscope Records in July 1997. With Will and keyboardist Brian Lapin at the controls, BEP recorded 50 songs at a Los Angeles recording studio from July 1997 to February 1998. Those 50 were narrowed down to the 16 that appear on *Behind the Front*.

While the nascent peas were cooking, Stacy Ferguson was working as a child star, albeit off camera. In 1983, it was only her voice that was heard as the character of Sally on the cartoon *The Charlie Brown and Snoopy Show*; she was eight years old. She also lent her voice to two other Charlie Brown cartoons, *It's Flashbeagle Charlie Brown* (1984) and *Snoopy's Getting Married, Charlie Brown* (1985). Her next appearance was in *Be Somebody or Be Somebody's Fool*, an educational video in which Mr. T and members of New Edition tell kids how to do the right thing. Her big break came when she was cast in the television series *Kids Incorporated* alongside another future celebrity, Jennifer Love Hewitt. She appeared on the show until 1989.

She took time off for normal kid stuff and in 1997 reconnected with Renee Sands and Stefanie Ridel from *Kids Incorporated* to form the pop band Wild Orchard. They released their self-titled debut album in 1997.

In 1999, Stacy, along with her bandmates, made her way back to Saturday morning television on a series called *Great Pretenders*. They co-hosted a show in which the audience voted for the contestant who did the best job at lip-syncing a song. The band began to lose popularity, however, and in 2001 their record label refused to release their third album. Wild Orchard dissolved and Ferguson worked as a dancer in nightclubs and sang back-up for bands. At this juncture, she met will.i.am and was enlisted to perform back-up for the band in 2001 and 2002. In 2003, she joined the band as a full-fledged member.

For will.i.am, it's all in the timing. "People finally see, and trust, my interpretation. And that's all it is, how you like to hear music. I can't say I'm the greatest pianist or drummer. In comparison to our drummer and keyboardist, I'm pretty horrible. Why did I get the gig? Interpretation. Vision. It's the only way it makes sense."

Will.i.am shares his take on the origins of the music that forms the rhythmic firmament of the Black Eyed Peas sound. "Disco is hip-hop, rock is hip-hop. You ask me if it's the dominant world music? The only reason I say yes to that is that hip-hop is the only form of music on the planet that takes from every other form. I heard a Led Zeppelin song and as soon as someone started rapping over it, it was hip-hop. Hip-hop is all because of technology, because they cut some fucking school program in New York, so someone started teaching music on a turntable. When there's a boundary and they put borders up, you go around it and get things done. Hip-hop is a culture of not having; to one day obtain by other means. There would be no hip-hop if they hadn't cut school funding for music, so there will always be hip-hop."

He continues, "Since 1991 when I signed with Eazy-E, I've been dreaming. A lot of times the record company might say, 'You're not tired? We're not overworking you?' and I'd say, 'No.' Sure, it hurts to be away from the family and it's hard on the body but I'd rather be doing it than dreaming about it at home. This is what everybody's been asking for. This is what we wanted. We didn't get signed shopping a demo. We didn't get signed 'cause we were down with such and such camp. We didn't get signed because we had a hit song on our demo. We got signed because we played around L.A.—at colleges and rock and blues clubs because we couldn't play hip-hop clubs with a band."

Fashion, fate, funk and future. After a decade of ascension, will.i.am clearly relishes the band's phenomenal success. "We always had the people who liked our music and to us that was great to be able to sell out the House of Blues in L.A. or SOB in New York, the Jazz Cafe in London, Metro in Sydney. That was dope. We were happy traveling. But now, comparing the monstrosity of it all, it's different. We couldn't go to Philippines, Brazil, or South Africa and play to 30,000 people. Back then, we couldn't go to Warsaw or Lithuania. Now, we can be anywhere on the planet and people know our music."

RECAP: Road to the Dotted Line

BLACK EYED PEAS

- Embraced technology and street culture
- Connected with live audiences
- Were part of a larger cultural entity
- Had to wait until positive music could emerge from the hip-hop subculture
- Established a multi-cultural identity that included a wide audience

Jim BRICKMAN

Building a Career Brick by Brick

"It's important, whatever path you're on, that you be who you are as much as possible."

It certainly would seem that composer/pianist Jim Brickman has a penchant for accomplishing many tasks with equal velocity. From his beginnings as a jingle composer to his celebrated career as an acclaimed song stylist with a string of gold and platinum releases, his knack for the thematic—coupled with his endearing trait for touching public sensibilities with very personal music—has made his recordings for Windham Hill some of the label's best-selling releases ever. Most recently, his *Simple Things* and *Love Songs & Lullabies* have enthralled audiences worldwide. Known especially for his collaborations, Brickman has recorded with Michael W. Smith, Martina McBride, Donny Osmond, and Olivia Newton-John, to name a few. His popular holiday albums are best-sellers. In addition to writing and performing music, Brickman also hosts his own weekly radio show, *Your Weekend with Jim Brickman*, that brings listeners the best in adult contemporary music and lifestyle issues, with interviews and the latest news in entertainment, health, money, and relationships. In its five-year run (and counting), Jim has interviewed celebrities ranging from Bill Clinton and Tom Cruise to J.Lo and Jennifer Aniston. In addition, he has authored best-selling essay collections, and contributes regularly to public television.

Unlike many of the subjects in this book, Brickman was in his third decade before he broke through as a recording artist. "I was 33 when I got my deal," he begins. "I didn't have this 'recording artist' thing. I was a jingle writer and was writing songs for other people. I thought my career was as a songwriter, writing hits. But I always loved the piano, and in 1994 I discovered there was a niche I could capture, writing romantic songs." It was the era of Windham Hill and New Age Music, and Brickman's concept was to contemporize the genre, make it more like pop, "which were the only kind of songs I knew how to write."

The results have been dramatic. With a career that spans ten albums (four of which have been certified gold, one platinum), a string of sold-out concerts and sales in excess of ten million units worldwide, the Ohio native has accumulated an intensely loyal following for whom his distinctive piano playing is the quintessential expression of his romantic spirit. In turn, he has garnered a GRAMMY® nomination, a pair of SESAC Songwriter of the Year awards, a Canadian Country Music Award, and a wide television audience for his acclaimed PBS specials, as well as regular appearances on *The Today Show*.

Buckeye Beginnings

Jim Brickman was born on November 20, 1961 in Cleveland and grew up in the Shaker Lakes area of the city. He didn't grow up with music in the house, he says. "No, none whatsoever. That's why destiny is such an appropriate concept for me. Beyond that, historically in my family, music is nowhere to be found. Nobody was singing or caroling or playing a lot of records when I was younger." His first keyboard wasn't very impressive: a long piece of green felt with notes drawn in with a magic marker. By age ten, it was time for his first real piano, a beat-up Yamaha upright that he still owns. He began writing songs as a teenager and discovered that his gift was one of imitation; he could formulate an original Elton John, Carly Simon, or Beatles song. "First of all, it's not a choice, it's not a decision. What happens is you sit there and play other people's stuff and you start going, 'I wonder what would happen if I played this instead of that or this chord. I wonder why they didn't go to that note?' It's inherent. It's the same as writing. You learn from reading, and you learn from imitating, and you learn stylistically how to form certain structures of the way things should be. And all of a sudden your voice takes shape." While Jim has said he never thought he would grow up to be a performer, he and childhood friend Anne

Cochran were in a band together while they attended a Cleveland high school. (Cochran still performs regularly on Brickman tours and has guested on his CDs.) He also carried his dedication to music with him into his college years as he studied composition and performance at the Cleveland Institute of Music. Prophetically, he was taking business classes at Case Western Reserve University at the same time.

Can You Make it More Commercial?

Even though his own career as a recording artist was late in developing, music was Brickman's entire life. His first career, and his first taste of success, began while he was still living in his college dorm room. At 19, he was hired by Jim Henson Associates to write tunes for *Sesame Street*. Eventually, he combined his love for music with his business training and opened Brickman Arrangement, his commercial jingle company. It was advertising, writing jingles, and even giving motivational speeches on creativity that paid the bills.

He wasn't shy about selling his talents. In 1987, he presented a jingle package to local station WLTF. The station bosses deemed it unsuitable for the station, but noted that one cut, "Turn on the Night," sounded like it might be a perfect jingle for the station's love song show, "Lovelite." At the station's request, Brickman rewrote the jingle to say "Turn on the Lovelite," and it became one of the most popular love song jingles in adult contemporary radio. During his jingle phase, he wrote for McDonald's ("Food, Folks and Fun"), Coke ("Just for the Taste of It"), Flintstone's Vitamins ("Ten Million Strong and Growing") and General Electric ("We Bring Good Things to Life").

Jim then put his business training and determination to work for himself a second time. He moved to Los Angeles in 1989, figuring the city would give him more options regarding what he could do. He figured if he wrote and performed "pretty" music, someone was bound to like it and buy it. He wrote six songs, booked some studio time, cut a six-song demo, and then traveled across the country meeting radio station program directors and doing market research. When it came time to pitch his concept to record companies, he says most of them thought he was "nuts." It was Windham Hill that finally offered him a deal, liking the music and finding the concept interesting.

Trunk Songs

Not surprisingly, Brickman never relied on a record label to make him successful. After the *No Words* album was recorded, he filled his car trunk with CDs and hit the radio station road tour once again, this time to actually get the music played on the radio. "I did it by myself at the very beginning, meeting radio station DJs just like Elvis did," he told the Berkshire, MA *Eagle*. "That's the way it used to be, and it kind of surprises me that it's not the typical way anymore, because you still have a product that you're trying to get people to hear." During the radio road trips, the solo pianist focused on adult contemporary radio stations at a time when playing an instrumental song was practically unheard-of in that format. After breaking into adult contemporary radio, he chose country singers to do the vocals on his songs, with "Valentine" and "The Gift" becoming huge hits.

"My career has always been about bucking the system, breaking molds and challenging the staid and obvious," Brickman notes. *No Words* produced one Adult Contemporary hit song, "Rocket to the Moon." While the song never placed on *Billboard* magazine's charts, it was played on radio stations across the U.S. and appeared on adult contemporary charts in publications more intently focused on an adult radio programming audience.

Instinct and inspiration are two touchstones of Brickman's song-writing craft. He explains his notion of creative immediacy. "There's not a lot of second guessing. I'm not the kind of writer who goes back and pushes myself to tinker all the time. I figure it is what it is, and if it came naturally, it's what it's supposed to be. I don't believe in too much drama. It's about the overall feeling and the message. My lyrics are conversational, like I'm talking to someone or sharing a thought."

Brickman testifies that these contrasting arcs in his career lead to one destination. "It's the same basic persona and concept of what I do. None of it is real foreign. It's all a natural extension of my music career, to be more well-rounded in a media way. I like to write songs, but I don't envision myself like a lot of my friends where all they do is write. I'd go out of my mind because I'm not disciplined that way. But I feel I'm a good writer, and I enjoy the collaboration experience. I don't have a lot of patience. I like to get with it. My writing happens more in my head while I'm living my life. My songwriting process is more a culmination of the thinking in my mind as I walk around the world."

Revealing his Midwestern roots, Brickman offers this solid guidance: "The best advice to any aspiring musician is to just get out there and play. So many people say, 'You know, if I just lived in L.A. or something, I would be discovered,' but it's not true. It's really just getting out there. And the problem is that now with things like *American Idol*, people think that it's a contest rather than just getting out there and doing what you love to do. The more you do it, whether it's a wedding or a smoky bar or whatever, you get better and better at it every day that you do it and you get better in front of people. You get more experience and it's really a matter of just getting out there. It's not who you know, it's just working hard and showing people what you can do in any situation you can find."

"And," concludes Brickman, "it's important, whatever path you're on, that you be who you are as much as possible."

RECAP: Road to the Dotted Line

JIM BRICKMAN

- Studied business in college
- Established himself in one division of music before moving to the next
- Relocated to Los Angeles
- Did his own market research
- Invested his own money in his projects

PETER Cincotti

88 Keys and the Passion

The island of Manhattan is afloat on music, from the bustling streets of Alphabet City to the halls of Lincoln Center. If one sound is synonymous with New York City, it would have to be the sound of jazz. Although the birthplace of America's most emblematic musical style is far below the Mason-Dixon line, it was in the heated incubator of Harlem, Birdland, and The Village where the form caught fire. Peter Cincotti is a product of Manhattan, a young artist with an urbane musicality shot through with youthful exuberance.

For young Peter, growing up in Manhattan afforded a wealth of musical influences and opportunities. When he was three, his grandmother bought him a toy piano and taught him how to play "Happy Birthday" on it. It sparked an interest and Cincotti began picking up melodies and playing them by ear. His mother Cynthia, a real-estate broker and former *Good Housekeeping* art director, and his father Fred, an attorney

"The more I learn, the more I listen to it all and bend genre lines. It all comes together. I try to use the freedom that is so much a part of writing music and it proves to be fulfilling in the end. No rules. That's what I like about jazz and music in general."

who died of a heart attack when Cincotti was 13, decided that he was old enough for formal instruction and purchased a Baldwin. At age four, Peter began taking formal lessons. His mother instructed the teacher not to make him play anything he didn't want to, insisting that the lessons remain fun, not an exercise in drudgery. Although the teacher was primarily classically based, she acquiesced to this request and allowed Cincotti to play everything from movie songs to *The Phantom of the Opera* to the theme of *Jeopardy*—whatever appealed to his ear. His mother never insisted he practice, but she didn't have to; Cincotti would rush home from school and sit down to play with his book-laden backpack still attached. The family was musical and listening was a part of their lives. They favored mainly older music such as Ella Fitzgerald, Nat King Cole, and selections from the Great American Songbook.

Cincotti's father died young and unexpectedly. "It happened when I was 13, and I was between sets at a club here in New York," he says. His dad was the victim of a heart attack and his son saw him die. "It puts things into perspective," Cincotti says. "The music is an outlet for me. Other people have their outlets, sports or writing or whatever it may be. But I know now that anything that comes my way, whether it's death or heartbreak, I can use the music as an outlet. My father always made the best of a situation."

Boogie-woogie and the incendiary Southern piano-pounding Jerry Lee Lewis made Cincotti view his instrument through different ears. "Jerry Lee was a major influence. He gave me goose bumps. When I was five years old, I bought a Jerry Lee tape and tried to copy his style. Boogie-woogie, too. There was so much to explore, but Jerry Lee first got my ears up."

Cincotti's family was well aware of Peter's prodigious talents. According to family lore, Cincotti's sister, Pia, then ten years old, cadged her way to meet Harry Connick Jr. backstage at the Village Vanguard, bringing him flowers and an audio recording of her brother. The family had planned to introduce Peter to him backstage, but Peter was sick and couldn't attend. Nevertheless, the tape made an indelible impression and Connick invited the budding virtuoso to sit in with him at a show at Bally's Grand in Atlantic City, NJ.

Peter's studies now included classical piano at the Manhattan School of Music and advanced private studies, but his tastes were becoming increasingly well-rounded. By his mid-teens, he was adding vocals to his musical mix and also began writing songs. At 16, he performed at Switzerland's Montreux Jazz Festival.

Four Sets a Night

While still in high school, he began performing professionally in clubs and restaurants in New York, most famously a regular gig at the jazz club/steakhouse the Knickerbocker Hotel. At one of those performances, he was approached by the producer of the off-Broadway show *Our Sinatra* to join the cast of that revue, a positioning that led to press and media attention in New York. He met manager Mary Ann Topper, who began directing his career. "Right away I thought, 'This is the package,'" Topper told *Pollstar*. "He had a great voice, wonderful phrasing, was very mature for his years. I found him very sincere about his talent, his need to perform, and his honesty about his music and what he wants to do with his life. That's not always the case, even with great talents. Sometimes, there's an ambivalence."

In jazz, where the stars (with the exception of singers) and the managing powers traditionally have been male, Topper has built a formidable niche. By refusing to acknowledge jazz's glass ceiling for women, she has pushed through it to become one of the jazz Pygmalions of the 21st century music scene. She has done so at a time when jazz record companies have had less success with new artists than they have with the repackaging of their valuable catalogs. Although jazz sales have grown recently, the spike has been aided by the success of some acts that are only loosely jazz-related, such as Norah Jones and Steve Tyrell.

Aware of the importance of this kind of star power, Topper maintains a small roster of acts that she feels have strong breakout potential. "Personal management is an enormous responsibility," she says, "for careers, for lives, for talents. We're not just talking about performance bookings and recording deals. We're talking about insurance policies, health insurance, homes, cars, children, their education—all of this surrounding a decision that you may or may not make with that artist, and for that artist."

Topper's involvement reaches into the creative arena as well. Trained as a musician with a master's degree in music literature and vocal performance from the University of Michigan, she takes an active, in-the-trenches role with every aspect of her clients' career. In addition to having Topper's management expertise, Cincotti is also affiliated with a powerful jazz agency, Ted Kurland Associates.

Cincotti chafed at the arty ageism he figured would await him in the industry. "You know, years ago, when some of the all-time greatest jazz singers started out, like Billie Holiday, they were young and nobody complained."

Another powerful New Yorker, promoter Ron Delsener—who has produced shows, tours, and events with luminaries including Bette

Midler, Liza Minelli, and Elvis Costello—took notice of Cincotti's arcing career, and booked him into one of Manhattan's premier venues, Feinstein's (owned by pianist/vocalist Michael Feinstein) for regular Monday night gigs. He invited a select roster of industry heavyweights to see the shows, including Phil Ramone.

Ramone Alone

There are a handful of legendary record producers who can walk an artist into a label and land a deal simply on the power of their commitment. Phil Ramone is at the top of this rare breed. With 30 GRAMMY® nominations, 12 GRAMMY Awards®, an Emmy, and numerous honors and accolades to his credit, Ramone's musical acumen and his use of audio technology are unmatched among his peers. Phil Ramone's impeccable list of music credits includes collaborations with such diverse artists as Billy Joel, Frank Sinatra, Paul Simon, Ray Charles, Quincy Jones, Madonna, Carly Simon, Gloria Estefan, Luciano Pavarotti, Natalie Cole, B.B. King, Paul McCartney, Sinead O'Connor, George Michael, James Taylor, and Jon Secada.

Ramone has a particular affinity for New York artists. "There's a lot about New York that is unique and there's always a culture and a subculture existing everywhere. You get a tremendous emotional contact with New Yorkers. It's 10 or 15 countries in a 20-mile radius. It's amazing." Ramone has rarely offered to work with an artist after hearing him only once, but has claimed, "I just fell in love that night. It was so good, it was like a Hollywood ending. I walked over to him and I said, 'If you haven't signed a deal and you would like to, I would like to help you.'"

All Aboard for Concord

Producer, agent, manger, and promoter—all of the pieces were in perfect formation. Ramone choose to approach Concord Records, a prestigious jazz label with impeccable credentials, for his newest artist. Concord Records is a standard-bearer for the most celebrated forms of American music, jazz and traditional pop. Act III Communications, owned by film and television veterans Norman Lear and Hal Gaba, acquired Concord Records in 1999. Lear recalled, "It was about five years ago, my partner Hal Gaba, who is a great jazz aficionado, came to me one day and said 'This remarkable label with a remarkable history is for sale.' We had been in theaters, film theaters, we had a chain, and he'd built a group of television stations. We were out of these businesses, we had sold, and now he was looking at Concord. I said 'Go.' I heard Mel Torme and Rosemary Clooney and these great names were listed, but his excitement was enough."

Peter Cincotti fits Lear's criterion of a Concord artist to a proverbial T. "I think the definition of a Concord artist is unsurpassable talent and a good-guy quality. This is a small company, more or less a boutique company. It hopes to grow, get larger, but never past the point of good people wanting to work with others, passionate people wanting to work with other's passions. That's who Concord is."

Under the auspices of Phil Ramone, the music that had enthralled New Yorkers in the intimate cabarets and hotel rooms found expression in the studio. Cincotti has continued to win new fans, young and older alike, with his winning combination of instrumental reverence filtered through a fresh approach. Songwriting has been increasingly important to him and his sophomore debut contained more self-penned songs. Above all, he professes a desire to grow musically. "My collection of music includes Eminem, Miles Davis, Jeff Buckley, and Ella Fitzgerald. It's interesting because my collection wasn't like that five years ago. The more I learn, the more I listen to it all and bend genre lines. It all comes together. I try to use the freedom that is so much a part of writing music and it proves to be fulfilling in the end. No rules. That's what I like about jazz and music in general."

RECAP: Road to the Dotted Line

PETER CINCOTTI

- Began formal music studies at age four
- Balanced musical education with real-life experience
- Lined up a manager, a promoter, and an agent before pursuing a record deal
- Embodied a timeless lineage of non-trendy music that appeals to all ages

Sheryl Crow

MIDWEST FLIGHT

"I knew that I was going to have to make the leap and pursue the dream, or resign myself to not pursuing it. I felt that was such a heavy weight to have to live with, wondering what would have happened."

Folksy, funky, and fun. Through loose-limbed grooves and quirky lyrics, Sheryl Crow was introduced to the record-buying public with her infectious song "All I Wanna Do," a narrative that displayed the singer swilling beer to cop a morning buzz next to a carwash somewhere amid the asphalt and palm trees of urban Los Angeles. For Crow, the record deal was both an affirmation and a bittersweet affair, but there was no denying the success of the formula and the potency of the songs.

The rise of Sheryl Crow directly coincided with the birth of the AAA (Adult Album Alternative) radio format. Crow, in her early thirties, was older than many of the new artists of her era, but for baby boomers, she was a sonic touchstone to the music they'd grown up with and a bridge to the new video channel, VH-1.

Sheryl Suzanne Crow was born on February 11, 1962 in Kennett, MO. Both of her parents had performed in swing orchestras, her father on trumpet and her mother as a singer. Her mother continued musical pursuits as a piano teacher, and all her daughters learned the instrument beginning in grade school. The picture that emerges of Crow's childhood appears idyllic. She was an attractive, popular girl—active in athletics, choir, and school plays—but she has said that she felt on the periphery of the cool group. The yearbooks that chronicle her four years at Kennett High, from 1977 to 1980, bear out the golden girl image: drum majorette, a member of the Pep Club, Future Farmers of America, and the National Honor Society. She was also Freshman Maid, Senior Maid, and the Paper Doll Queen.

Sheryl penned her first song at age 13. In college at the University of Missouri at Columbia she majored in music education with a concentration on piano. Her goal was to teach music to youngsters. More tellingly, she joined a cover band, Cashmere. Playing covers every weekend for the local frats and sororities, Crow performed songs like Heart's "Barracuda," Diana Ross and Lionel Richie's "Endless Love," the Doobie Brothers' "China Grove," and Nena's "99 Red Balloons." The band got Crow onstage, singing and playing keyboards in front of the public, and revealing her first overt sign of an ever-deepening drive to perform.

Teacher's Pet
College ended, so did Cashmere, and so did the abbreviated performing career of Sheryl Crow. She moved to St. Louis, lived in the Georgetown Apartments in Webster Groves, and worked for two years teaching music at Kellison Elementary School in the Rockwood District in St. Louis County.

At the time, the clean, modern, brightly-lit school in Fenton served roughly 700 students in kindergarten through sixth grade. Crow worked as a vocal music teacher and taught the special chorus for the fifth and sixth grades.

But performing stint with Cashmere had awakened something in the elementary school teacher. An acquaintance suggested she contact Jay Oliver, a St. Louis musician who had made a name for himself as a producer of commercial jingles, industrial themes, corporate music, and demos. Oliver, who now lives in Los Angeles, ran a thriving recording studio in the lower level of his parents' home in Creve Coeur. He invited Sheryl to his studio. He remembers "a really sweet, very innocent girl" with effortless charm, good looks, and a brilliant smile. Although Oliver found her too undeveloped as a singer and musically naïve in terms of the roots of rock 'n' roll, the two shared a jazz background and immediately hit it off. Under Oliver's tutelage, Crow threw herself into an intense learning period. Within months, she had improved so rapidly as a vocalist that Oliver began using her as a singer on jingles. Her first was a back-to-school commercial for Famous-Barr clothing stores.

Although Sheryl enjoyed the experience of teaching children, she considered her day job merely a temporary one. She asked Oliver if it was a smart move for her to quit her teaching gig and do music full-time. He answered affirmatively. She worked eight hours a day for months on nearly every aspect of her craft—learning music history, perfecting her voice, performing with a local band (P.M., signed to Warner Bros.), and recording a number of jingles for the Oliver's clients, including McDonald's and Toyota.

A Ticket to Tinseltown

Crow took a brief break in her career to visit a friend in California who lived about 45 minutes from Los Angeles, in the beachside community of Redondo Beach. She returned to St. Louis with a plan to relocate to the West Coast. In 1986, when Crow was 24, she headed for Los Angeles. "I knew that I was going to have to make the leap and pursue the dream, or resign myself to not pursuing it," she says. "I felt that was such a heavy weight to have to live with, wondering what would have happened."

The city held immediate lessons for the small-town girl who moved four times in six months. She finally settled into a $500-a-month apartment. Crow might have arrived naïve, but she was not unprepared. Jay Oliver had helped her put together a professional demo tape of her commercial-jingle work. She acquired a list of all the top session music producers in Los Angeles and pitched them with tapes and photos. It was a pro package, and Crow was relentless in marketing her talent. If people wouldn't take her calls, she'd deliver her tape in person. She landed her first gig and made connections in the tight-knit session-contractor world. Eventually she was doing four or five jingle sessions a week. It was during one such studio session that she overheard the news that Michael Jackson was auditioning for back-up singers for his upcoming 1987-88 *Bad* world tour. Crow, who knew none of the industry rules, crashed the audition and won a slot.

She's Bad

The tour was a high-profile gig that took Crow around the world and kept her onstage for 18 months, done up in towering blond hair and engaging in several bump-and-grind duets with Jackson every night. It landed her on the cover of the *National Enquirer* and similar tabloids, linked romantically to Jackson, with news that she was carrying the singer's love child. The tour introduced Crow to the music industry and acclimated her to high-stakes back-up work, which she continued with artists including Sting, Rod Stewart, and Don Henley.

Producer Robert Kraft was enlisted to produce Crow as a solo artist. She also made a powerful ally with music publishing executive Judy Stakee at a 1988 lunch meeting when Kraft ask Stakee to suggest songs for the project. After lunch, Sheryl went to Stakee's office to continue the meeting. It is Stakee who is credited with encouraging Sheryl to write her own songs and to develop her signature sound. The two quickly became fast friends. Stakee took an executive position at Warner/Chappell Music, and signed Crow to a publishing deal. As her friend and publisher, Stakee devoted an exceptional amount of time and energy into promoting her career. "I was her champion, and I was also like a mom, a teacher, and therapist," explains Stakee. "She didn't have a manager yet, so I was helping her in this role, too. We would meet almost every morning at Hugo's restaurant on Santa Monica Boulevard for coffee, and we would map out our strategies. This was a partnership. We were going to do this together."

Stakee compiled a five-song demo tape of Crow's music and began playing it for labels. There was definite interest, but the breakthrough occurred when David Anderle, head of A&R for A&M Records, heard the tape, based on the recommendation of producer Hugh Padgham. Anderle recognized Sheryl's potential as an unique singer/songwriter, and subsequently signed her to the label where A&M President Al Cafaro was also a strong supporter. "A&M was fabulous. They were total believers in Sheryl," said Stakee. "They knew she would become a great artist, so they gave her the time and support to fully develop her artistic identity and sound."

Hugh Padgham took Crow into the studio in 1991 to record her debut album, but his slick pop expertise resulted in a ballad-laden record that didn't reflect the sound she wanted. A&M was not impressed and the album was shelved. Sheryl sank into a depression that lingered for nearly a year-and-a-half. However, her boyfriend Kevin Gilbert, an engineer who'd attempted to remix her ill-fated album, introduced her to a loose group of industry pros that included producer Bill Bottrell, David Baerwald, David Ricketts, Brian MacLeod, and Dan Schwartz. Dubbed the Tuesday Night Music Club, it was a hip collective that met once a week at Bottrell's Pasadena recording studio to drink, jam, and work out material. In this informal, collaborative setting, Crow was able to get her creative juices flowing again. The group made its newest member—the only one with a record deal—the focal point. Sheryl and the collective worked out enough material for an album. With Bottrell serving as the producer, she recorded her new official debut, *Tuesday Night Music Club*, in tribute to the environment that had inspired her.

A Good Beer Buzz Early in the Morning

A&M released two tracks before deciding on "All I Wanna Do," a song partly written by poet Wyn Cooper, as a single. Success came with a heavy price. In 1994, Crow was invited to perform "Leaving Las Vegas" on *Late Night with David Letterman.* In an interview segment, Letterman asked if the song was autobiographical, and Crow offhand-edly agreed that it was. (In actuality, the song was mostly written by David Baerwald, based on the book by his good friend John O'Brien that had also inspired the film of the same name.) Having been burned by the industry, some of the Tuesday Night Music Club took Crow's comment as a refusal to give proper credit for their contributions. Baerwald in particular felt betrayed. O'Brien committed suicide not long after Crow's Letterman appearance, but O'Brien's family stepped forward to affirm that the singer had nothing to do with the tragedy. In 1996, the chasm deepened when Sheryl's ex-boyfriend Kevin Gilbert died in Los Angeles.

Crow was a big winner at the GRAMMYs® in early 1995, taking home honors for Best New Artist, Best Female Rock Vocal, and Record of the Year (the latter two for "All I Wanna Do"). Her stunning sweep propelled *Tuesday Night Music Club* into a genuine blockbuster, with sales of over the seven million mark. After a decade, Sheryl Crow was center stage.

RECAP: Road to the Dotted Line

SHERYL CROW

- Created a career as a demo/jingle singer
- Parlayed studio connections into L.A. gigs
- Hooked up with like-minded collaborators
- Built industry recognition through back-up gigs
- Created a new style of music that had retro roots

Death Cab for Cutie

Indie Band Speeds to New Destinations

Rain-shrouded, introspective, coffee-infused, Seattle is a city with a hard-rocking musical legacy and a vibrant scene. Physically isolated from the cultural mainstream, it is an historic locale for bands that flourish with originality and independence. Death Cab for Cutie qualifies on both counts. A gleaming link in the city's sonic chain, the band's music is atmospheric and orchestral, with sweeps of guitars painting expansive sound-scapes, shadowing emotional, eloquent lyrics wrapped in an undeniable pop sensibility and rendered through Ben Gibbard's distinctively honest voice.

Kid Stuff

Gibbard doesn't feel his childhood was dissimilar from most kids. "I find there's a similar story: somebody stole a tape from their brother with The Descendants on one side and Bad Brains on the other when you were 13, they brought it to school and everyone freaked out. But it was the beginning. There was other

"I feel like we're an exception to the rule in so many cases. When people have come to me saying, 'Hey, somebody just came to our band. A major label wants to sign us,' or even some band that we're friends with that Atlantic's been talking to, I feel like I need to always qualify that we're a very special situation in this whole major-label world.
—Ben Gibbard

music out there in 1990-91 up to the Nirvana explosion. Stone Roses, Charlatans UK, bands from Manchester. I was a huge fan of Low, and Afghan Whigs."

And he didn't feel particularly marginalized. "There were no jocks beating up punks. I don't know if I went to a large or small enough school, but everyone had their group, no one messed with us. We'd hang out with kids who were into music and spend our weekends skateboarding and go to the house of the one guy who lived in a valley and could get the college stations and listen to the radio and bullshit. I had an innocuous kind of life."

Deathcab for Cutie had its origins in Bellingham, WA, a college town where Gibbard and guitarist Chris Walla bonded as students at Western Washington University. It started out as a solo project when the engineering student and committed indie rocker turned a freshly-broken heart into nine songs that he wasn't embarrassed to share. To record, he recruited fledgling four-track producer (and fellow Teenage Fanclub fan) Chris Walla and bassist Nick Harmer, the most amiable (and comic-book obsessed) musician on campus. After a cassette-only release, *You Can Play These Songs with Chords* became a local hit and Death Cab for Cutie became a full on band. Their name was purloined from a song title by a Sixties cult band, The Bonzo Dog Band. Gibbard explains, "I saw the Bonzo Dog Band in the Beatles' *Magical Mystery Tour* film. I was a huge Beatles fan. I'd never been a fan of the Bonzo Dog Band, they were pretty grating. But after seeing that movie in college I thought, 'You know, if I ever start another band, I'll call it Death Cab for Cutie.' And I've cursed myself ever since because journalists always ask questions about the name."

Refining the Straight Job

Prior to Death Cab for Cutie's ascent, Gibbard worked a straight job. He'd graduated from college with a degree in Environmental Chemistry and during his school days, he'd had an internship at an oil refinery. When he graduated, he was employed to do environmental testing. "It was a dangerous job, and I knew I wasn't planning on doing that for the rest of my life. In the early years of the band, by the time we started going on tours, I was making $14 an hour; that's when I was paying $250 a month for rent. I'd go to my bosses and say, 'I'm leaving on tour for a month. You can fire me if you like, but you know it'll take a year-and-a-half to train someone to be where I am now.' So I had them by the balls. Everyone has those jobs. I thought, 'I could do this the rest of my life or the foreseeable future, and live and exist, but it doesn't make me happy.'" And, of course, there was the pungent smell of the refinery itself: "You could smell that shit for miles."

The straight job was soon history. Relocating to Seattle, Death Cab for Cutie recorded their full-length debut, *Something About Airplanes*. Generating a Seattle-area buzz, they became a proper band, releasing their official debut in 1998 on Barsuk Records, a burgeoning indie label.

Independence Days

Barsuk Records began as a venture by Josh Rosenfeld and Christopher Possanza to release the album by their band, This Busy Monster. Taking its name from the Russian word for "badger," the label, based in Seattle, is home to Jesse Sykes and the Sweet Hereafter, Rilo Kiley, Nada Surf, and many others. "We used to accept unsolicited demos," says Rosenfeld. "We got too much stuff. It's harder now than it was 10 or 15 years ago. It's so easy now for someone to make music with a home computer. There's so much, it became overwhelming. We started the label because we were in a band and we couldn't find a label who wanted to put out our music. I remember thinking at that time as I looked at the rosters of labels I admired, that it seemed cliquish: 'Oh, of course they signed you because you know the guys in that band.' I've come to realize exactly how that functions over time. The one huge place where we find music we like is when bands on the roster are on the road, play shows, bring us a CD back and say, 'This band is really good.' I share a taste in music with bands on the roster, so there is a lot of overlap. It's not a clique. That's how I hear music I like."

After the band's debut, they began touring. More albums were tracked, including *We Have the Facts and We're Voting Yes* (2000) and *The Photo Album* (2001), each more successful, in content and sales, than the last. The band is distinctive for a cast of rotating drummers. Good left the band just prior to the release of *We Have the Facts*, replaced by drummer Michael Schorr, who first appeared on *The Forbidden Love* EP, released in fall of 2000. The following year, another LP was released, entitled *The Photo Album*. Limited editions of this album contained three bonus tracks, which were later released separately as *The Stability EP*.

Seattle Sonics

Gibbard says that Seattle has a number of geographic factors that make its popular culture distinctive. "It's always been a nurturing, community-minded place as far as music and art go. People aren't holding hands and running through the streets, but this place requires a level of humility. Back in the day, bands wouldn't even come here to play because it's so far off the beaten path. You come from San Francisco to Portland and Seattle, and then you've got to drive two days to get to anywhere else worth playing. The most important thing for us is, we can come home, hold our heads high in Seattle and realize we came up through the city."

Having created a substantial body of work as a band, Death Cab for Cutie took an extended hiatus. Chris returned to his first love, producing, working on widely-hailed releases by The Decemberists, The Thermals, Nada Surf, and Travis Morrison. Ben spent some time in the L.A. neighborhood of Silver Lake, recording electropop songs with his friend, producer Jimmy Tamborello, singer Jen Wood, and Jenny Lewis from the band Rilo Kiley. This little side project, called The Postal Service, yielded an album, *Give Up*, that has, to date, sold over 600,000 copies with no tours and no promotion. "We made the record because it sounded like a fun project and it turned into a far larger entity," he says. "We don't play shows, promote the record, or do interviews. The record quietly continues to sell and people are into it. Jimmy will send me songs and I'll work on them in my own time. He's down there and I'm up here. He'll send me a fragment of a song he's working on and we'll put the pieces together, make a song out of the parts, just a kind of playing a video game." Gibbard stayed with Tamborello for a spell, in his residence down the street from the club Spaceland. "It's the epicenter," notes Gibbard. "It seems that for every band who's trying to make it big, there is another band who is purposely trying not to do that."

In 2003, refreshed and renewed by their time apart, and inspired by the recruitment of ace drummer Jason McGerr, Death Cab recorded and released the rave-spawning *Transatlanticism*. Milestones began to fall like dominos: sales that doubled those of any previous release, successful tours of Japan and Australia, magazine features, TV appearances (including a memorable spring 2005 performance on Fox TV's *The O.C.*), and a personal invitation to join Pearl Jam on the Vote for Change tour. Death Cab's 2004 *Transatlanticism* tour is documented on the DVD *Drive Well, Sleep Carefully*, directed by noted filmmaker Justin Mitchell. *Transatlanticism* received critical praise and also became the band's top-selling album, with 225,000 copies sold during its first year out. In addition, tracks from the album appeared in the soundtrack of *The O.C.* Other television shows, movie trailers, and feature films brought Death Cab for Cutie and Postal Service to international audiences by utilizing both band's songs on air.

In the fall of 2004, Death Cab for Cutie inked a worldwide deal with Atlantic Records. Leaving their long-time label Barsuk Records and the rank of indie record labels, Gibbard stated on the official website that nothing would change except that "Next to the picture of Barsuk holding a '7,' there will be the letter 'A' on both the spine and back of our upcoming albums."

The band's label debut, *Plans*, was released in August 2005. The notably indie band had arrived at a crossroads. Ben Gibbard explains, "When things started shaping up really strangely, not only for us, but obviously in relation to Postal Service and all these weird cultural things—the *Garden States* and *The O.C.s*, and just this weird kind of rebirth of indie-rock culture on a much larger level the last couple years—we found ourselves being able to go back to some of the same labels that had sent people sniffing around seven years before, or five years before, with basically the same list. Atlantic looked at it via the lawyers; obviously there's more to it than that, but in a nutshell, they looked at the same list and said, 'Great, we can do this.' The record just came out, so we're still in the honeymoon phase. I don't know where this is going; time will tell whether this was the right thing for us to do, but I think the most important thing for me now is that I feel incredibly comfortable. And while it's not a family the way Barsuk is a family, I certainly really like the people that are in charge of things for us at Atlantic. It doesn't feel like that slimy corporate machine that so many bands get ground up in."

"But also, and I certainly don't say this to toot our own horn," Gibbard continues, "I feel like we're an exception to the rule in so many cases. When people have come to me saying, 'Hey, somebody just came to our band. A major label wants to sign us,' or even some band that we're friends with that Atlantic's been talking to, I feel like I need to always qualify that we're a very special situation in this whole major-label world, I think, because of where we've come from and what we've done on our own with Barsuk."

RECAP: Road to the Dotted Line
DEATH CAB FOR CUTIE

- Principal members united in an underground sensibility
- Came up in a college town
- Relocated to a larger community and progressively larger audiences
- Signed to an indie label
- Built a grassroots following by endless touring

Missy Elliott

Supa Dupa Success

"People are going to call you names because you're aggressive in what you want. But you can't be weak in this industry, because people will see that and they will run all over you."

Missy Elliott is more than just a magnetic performer and a multi-platinum recording artist. With a list of production credits that includes Whitney Houston, Janet Jackson, Christina Aguilera, Justin Timberlake, and Destiny's Child, she is one of the rare women who enjoys an equal amount of success behind the scenes as both a song-writer and producer. As the head of her own record label, The Goldmind, Inc., Missy launched the successful career of platinum-selling R&B star Tweet. In addition, Elliott has created a unique joint venture with famous athletic company Adidas for a line of clothing, shoes, and accessories under the moniker Respect Me.

Born Melissa Arnette Elliott in Portsmouth, VA, the future star's early years were turbu-lent and traumatic. An only child, she has acknowledged publicly that her father was relentlessly abusive to her mother. "The low point in my life was growing up in a house where my mother and father would fight all the time," she recalls. "My mother was battered, so it was hard as a kid, because I never wanted to go places because I was scared my father would be beating up my mother. I never had that perfect childhood like a lot of kids do. But I overcame it. Just by watching my mother be strong made me strong and prepared me for this business."

As a creative child, Melissa retreated into her own private fantasy world of performance and music. She wrote daily letters to Michael and Janet Jackson, with the resolute belief that one of them would come to her school, whisk her away, and make her a star. Songwriting came easily and naturally to her. By junior high school, she was already penning love songs, forming girl groups, and winning local talent shows.

Creative Alliances

Since the Nineties, the state of Virginia has emerged as an R&B music center. A favorite vacation spot for New Yorkers who live a mere six hours distant, it is also a quick eight-hour trip to Atlanta. In Portsmouth, there was a lively scene of other rappers and producers creating beats and songs. One promising scenester, Melvin "Magoo" Barcliff, introduced Elliott to his partner, an up-and-coming producer named Tim Mosley.

"We always got music real late," Elliott explains. "New York would always have the hot records, but by the time we got them they would have already moved on to the next thing. Everything was late coming to Virginia. We were very far away and very closed off. A lot of the kids were probably forbidden from even listening to R&B music because down South they're more into church music. They're very spiritual, you know. Go to church Sunday, go to church Tuesday, go to church Thursday," she laughs. "I don't think we did it consciously, but because we didn't have the music to listen to, we became creative."

In high school, Elliott, LaShawn Shellman, Chonita Coleman, and Radiah Scott formed an R&B group called Sista, for which Elliott served as a singer and songwriter. With Mosley as the group's producer, the quartet began cutting demo tracks. Relentlessly ambitious, when they heard that the popular vocal group Jodeci was planning an appearance in their town, the girls purchased matching outfits, cajoled backstage passes for the show, made their way to Jodeci member Devante Swing's hotel room and, as the story goes, sang their hearts out with *a cappella* versions of Jodeci songs. Swing had his own custom record label, Swing Mob Records, under the aegis of Elektra Records. Based on their demos with Timbaland, he signed the group to a record deal. Sista moved to New York City, and Elliott took along Mosley (whom DeVante re-christened Timbaland), and Barcliff.

New York News

Twenty-plus members of the Swing Mob, including future stars such as Ginuwine, Playa, and Tweet, all resided together in a single two-story house in New York, where they were often at work on material both for Jodeci and for their own projects. It was an intense and fruitful time for the enterprising Elliott, who contributed songwriting duties, both credited and uncredited, to the final two Jodeci albums, *Diary of a Mad Band* (1993) and *The Show, The After Party, The Hotel* (1995). "DeVante had forbidden us from listening to the radio and from watching TV. There were a lot of things we couldn't do. But it's crazy because, out of a situation like that, I think we learned more creativity. We didn't get a chance to see what was hot, what videos were hot, and to end up mimicking it. We ended up having to create our own style."

Timbaland and DeVante produced a Sista LP, *4 All the Sistas Around the World*, which was completed in 1994 but was shelved and never released. By 1995, Swing Mob had folded and many of its members dispersed. Elliott, Timbaland, Magoo, Ginuwine, and Playa remained together, however, and collaborated on each other's records for the rest of the decade.

After leaving Swing Mob, Elliott and Timbaland began working together as an independent songwriting/production team. The two of them crafted hit singles for a number of artists between 1995 and 1997. Among these acts were SWV ("Can We?") and 702 ("Steelo" and its remix), but the most notable of them was Aaliyah. Elliott and Timbaland wrote and produced nine tracks for Aaliyah's second album, *One in a Million* (1996), among them the hit singles "If Your Girl Only Knew," "One in a Million," "Hot like Fire," and "4 Page Letter." Elliott also contributed background vocals and/or guest raps to nearly all of the tracks she and Timbaland worked on. When *One in a Million* went double platinum, it made a name for the hard-working production duo.

Rhone Alone

As a solo rapper, Elliott began her career as a featured vocalist on MC Lyte's 1996 single "Cold Rock a Party," which was produced by Sean "Puffy" Combs, but she wasn't yet signed as an artist. Then a full-figured woman, it was dictated to Elliott in the earliest days of her career that she should stick to songwriting because she didn't have the right look to make it as an artist. Puffy Combs disagreed, and hoped to sign Elliott to his label, Bad Boy Records. But it was Sylvia Rhone, the Elektra Entertainment Group chairman and CEO who had the insight to sign Missy as an artist and businesswoman. Says Rhone, "In this fiercely competitive business, you have to earn respect. Missy has developed into one of contemporary music's most original stars, without succumbing to negative stereotypes or sexual clichés.

She's opened many doors for other African-American female artists and executives. In an unprecedented move, Elliott was also given her own imprint, Goldmind, for which she would record as a solo artist. "Identifying superstar talent is a visceral process," says Rhone. "You could recognize instantly that Missy possessed star potential."

Missy held fast to her earliest hometown alliances. For her debut, Timbaland was again recruited as her production partner, a role he would hold for every Elliott solo release. Defying the conventional standards for beauty, Elliott also emerged as a cultural icon, challenging limited assumptions about black and female beauty. In her collaborations with Hype Williams (who directed videos for mega hits "The Rain," "Hot Boyz," and "She's a Bitch"), she appeared with exaggerated lips, a bald head, and blue-black skin, in blow-up neon suits and as a cartoon character. Dismissing the notion that female artists must be diminished to size four to be successful, Missy paved the way for curvaceously healthy artists. It was a long way from the days when full-figured powerhouse Martha Wash of The Weather Girls had to watch skinny girls lip-sync her songs in videos.

Although female producers are rare in any pop music medium, Elliott says that she didn't feel shut out. "I think after the first record, people kind of could tell, 'OK, she has something here between her and Timbaland, they have their own style.' Fortunately, I didn't have to travel over hurdles to get here. As an artist, that's a different story, 'cause as an artist I didn't have that so-called look or image people were used to seeing on TV, to see a heavy-set girl come in the rap game. People understood Biggie Smalls being a heavy-set male, but you know, the girls are supposed to be in little tops and little panty outfits. And to see me coming and I got this big plastic bag on, that was hard for people to accept. But then I think once they saw the video, they said, 'Hey, she's got something kind of different here, so maybe let's wait until the second single to see if we're really ready for the heavy girl to come here and try to get on and sing like that.'"

As for the subject matter of her songs, she states, "A lot of the songs I have got from situations around me. They're not necessarily all Missy problems. Basically, what I want people to know Missy for is that I'm very original, creative, and futuristic. You're not gonna see Missy doing what everybody else is doing. You'll see me with a bald head in my video, but no other female would have the courage to do that."

Being a woman in a male-controlled business requires fortitude, she acknowledges. "People are going to call you names because you're aggressive in what you want. But you can't be weak in this industry, because people will see that and they will run all over you. Females should not back down. I don't feel like you have to have a negative attitude, but I do think, in this male-dominated world, you have to come in strong-minded and just do what you gotta do."

As meteoric as her career appears, Missy Elliott is quick to recognize a higher power. "If you listen to all my records, you know I always take time out to give thanks. In this business, you're always going to have to engage in a lot of things you might not want to, but it never takes away from my spirituality. No matter what happens, that will always be there."

RECAP: Road to the Dotted Line

MISSY ELLIOTT

- Formed groups while still in high school
- Hooked up with a musician with his own label
- Maintained creative relationships with a hometown producer
- Established herself as a songwriter first
- Guested on records she produced
- Crafted an undeniable visual image

Melissa ETHERIDGE

Rocking Woman

Formed in 1963, in an era when the very idea of women playing their own instruments in rock bands was unheard of, Goldie and The Gingerbreads—recognized as the first all-female rock band—played just as well as they sang, but never excelled beyond cult status. The role of women in rock music throughout the liberated Sixties was mainly that of pop divas until the emergence of the San Francisco sound and Grace Slick's stratospheric incantations and Janis Joplin's bluesy wailing gave birth to a new era of straight-up female rockers.

Melissa Etheridge is the next logical link in this musical chain. But emerging in the Eighties, she owed more to the roots-based male rock of Tom Petty and Bruce Springsteen than to the multi-octave chanteuse style of Pat Benatar, the Hollywood hustlerette vibe of The Runaways, or the quirky pop aesthetic of the Go-Gos. Upon her emergence, Etheridge

"I never did write any songs that were specifically about women. I wanted the big picture, singing about passion and desire, and love of any kind."

was clearly the real deal—an anthemic songwriter and a galvanizing performer who could inspire arenas of listeners, a flat-out rocker from the plains of America.

It was a long road—from the Midwest to Boston, back home for a spell, and then to the West Coast where she performed in women's bars for almost five years. The story of Melissa Etheridge is one of potential, perseverance, and pride. Notably, she is the highest-profile rock performer ever to proclaim her sexual orientation as a lesbian.

Born in Leavenworth, KS, the young Melissa was fascinated with her family's portable Philco 45 record player. By the time Melissa was eight, her father realized she was serious about music. He bought her a six-string Stella guitar, and enrolled her for lessons with a jazz guitarist, albeit one with missing fingers, who ran Leavenworth's only music store. "He was real strict about timing," says Etheridge of her stern teacher, Don Raymond. "He tapped his foot really loud on an old wooden board. He's the reason I have really good rhythm."

Early on, songwriting was a part of the equation. She wrote her first song at age ten. Music and lyrics were a way of expressing her feelings in the Etheridge household, where emotions were contained. Her parents, both of whom came from alcoholic homes, avoided emotional upheavals. As Etheridge explains, "All they wanted was to forget their past, so I grew up in a house where everything was just fine. I was not abused. If I needed something, I had it, but there was no feeling. There was no joy; there was no sadness or pain. And then if there was pain, it was just a nod."

Local Notions

At age 11, Melissa won a local talent contest. Soon, she had become a fixture in Leavenworth at supermarket openings, bowling alleys, even playing at the Leavenworth prison. She joined a country band part-time at age 12; the group performed at Parents Without Partners dances and at bars, where she would play the first hour, then go home to bed. As a teenager she would bring along her guitar when she accompanied her father to his National Education Association teachers' conventions. Etheridge's father generously offered to chauffer his daughter to gigs, including churches. By junior high, Etheridge was playing drums, saxophone, piano, and clarinet, but she preferred the richer, jangling overtones of the 12-string guitar, the instrument that would figure into her sonic equation for many years to come.

After high school graduation, Etheridge enrolled in Berklee College of Music in Boston. Between classes, in a time-honored tradition, she busked for extra money by playing at the occasional subway station. More lucrative was a cover gig at Ken's by George, a club on Boylston Street, where she could earn about $50 per night, five nights a week, for playing multiple sets, while earning much more in tips from a crowd of inebriated businessmen.

With its academic jazz orientation, Berklee was not an exact fit for Etheridge and her rootsy, emotionally-charged style of songwriting and performing. She dropped out after her second semester and worked as a security guard at a hospital in the Boston area to support herself while performing in local clubs. In 1981, she moved back home to Leavenworth with a plan of performing in locals clubs until she earned enough money to buy a car; she would then depart for Los Angeles. Onstage at her gig at the Granada Royal Hotel, she performed cover tunes, soft rock, more requests until she finally left for L.A. on her 21st birthday.

All Roads Lead West

In the early Eighties, the vitality of the punk scene was smoldering embers, and musical tastes were increasingly dominated by "Hair Bands"—macho, rooster-coiffed denizens of the Sunset Strip, such as Poison and Motley Crue. It was not the most welcoming scene for a single woman in a flannel shirt with a 12-string guitar, no matter how strong her songs and earnest her intentions.

Just south of Los Angeles, the city of Long Beach is a rough-and-tumble shipyard community, home to a large gay and lesbian population. Etheridge, as a gay woman, felt at home socializing in the city's clubs. It was a logical extension of her bar-performing background that she would soon find a home playing in the women's bars that existed in the gritty seaside community.

Women's sports teams, regardless of their member's sexual orientation, congregated regularly at women's clubs to quaff brews and celebrate victories. Karla Leopold, the wife of music business manager Bill Leopold, was one member of a women's soccer team who regularly hung out in the club. After hearing Melissa regularly for a year, she introduced her husband to the young singer, who made a striking impression. Eventually, he signed her for management.

But there was really little to manage. By now, Melissa had moved to a regular gig in Long Beach, performing five nights a week at Que Sera. Record company response was decidedly cool. Etheridge had earlier sent a demo to Olivia records and, she recalls, "They weren't interested. I played some women's music festivals, but I was always rock-and-roll whereas their music was always quieter, more folksy." Although performing almost exclusively in women's bars, her songs were not Sapphocentric. "I never did write any songs that were specifically about women. I wanted the big picture, singing about passion and desire, and love of any kind."

In 1984, Melissa auditioned for the TV series *Fame*. The producers thought that she was terrific, but hired Janet Jackson instead. Although the labels were not yet impressed, Melissa's songwriting had evolved to a point where a publishing company was. Don Zimmerman of Capitol records financed a few demos and John Carter produced them, but the label didn't sign her. A&M also passed over her. But Leopold hooked Etheridge up with Lance Freed, son of legendary rock DJ Allan Freed, and the president of Almo-Irving, a music publishing company affiliated with A&M Records. He signed her to a publishing deal and she received a regular stipend to create.

One Man Is an Island

Armed by now with some industry credibility for his client, Leopold began inviting L.A. A&R execs down to Long Beach to hear Etheridge in her native habitat, the bars where she was a local star. It was into this improbable showcase that he brought Chris Blackwell, the legendary record executive who had championed the careers of everyone from Traffic to Bob Marley. Blackwell heard her there and immediately surmised the enormous appeal of the unvarnished Melissa Etheridge. Since he was the head of his own label, everything was very simple. There were no months of negotiations and, as befits a new artist, no big advance, either.

Reveals Blackwell, "To me, the first and always the most important thing is talent. I go with my gut instinct, like the first time I saw Steve Winwood play in a pub in Birmingham, or Melissa Etheridge. I knew these were artists who could really deliver, and would grow. Both of them were passionate onstage, and that's what people respond to, to a great extent. Without commitment, all the talent in the world won't be enough. You have to have drive, and total focus on wanting to make your music heard by as many people as possible."

By all reports, Etheridge's first album, made on the kind of huge budget that was standard in the heady Los Angeles Eighties, buried her passionate vocals beneath layers of arrangement and frothy production. Chris Blackwell hated it, fuming, "That's not the girl I saw in a bar in Long Beach. It was terrible. I didn't want a group image, I just wanted to hear her." Blackwell taped the album cover photo to the wall of the studio and told her to "make the album that goes with that picture." Lance Freed also avowed that the first attempt had been "too pop."

Still, Blackwell believed. Given creative freedom, Etheridge chose her own musicians and her own producer, Niko Bolas, a recording engineer and producer, who booked four days of studio time at Cherokee Studios in West Hollywood, commencing on October 19, 1987. Some of the songs she tracked were older and had accompanied Etheridge throughout her club years, but four of them were brand new. Among the older songs in the repertoire was "Like the Way I Do." Melissa recalls, "I wrote 'Like the Way I Do' in the mid-Eighties, a couple of years before my first album came out. It was my show-closer even when I was playing the bars. I have to play 'Like the Way I Do' last or everything will pale following it. I play that, 'Piece of My Heart,' and 'Meet Me in the Back.' Those three songs were the last 30 minutes of my set in the women's bars in Long Beach and Pasadena. It was also the first original song that someone requested. Usually I would hear people in the audience say 'Play that Stevie Nicks song,' or 'Play that Bruce Springsteen song.' That reaction gave me hope that if I ever got a record deal, maybe someone would want to hear my songs. 'Like The Way I Do' has turned into an opus. Even when I played it solo, I would do a big, long rhythmic guitar solo. When I went into the studio to record the first album, it was hard to do a little four-minute version of it. That's why we just faded it at the end. But my fans know when they see me perform there's another 15 minutes of the song."

The record, self-titled, was not an immediate smash, but Blackwell's faith in Etheridge's live power was confirmed when a Los Angeles radio station, KMPC, began playing tracks recorded live at the Roxy in L.A. for a promotional CD. With a trend-setting powerhouse station behind her, Melissa was on her way to unparalleled rock stardom.

In 2004, Etheridge endured a bout with breast cancer. At the 2005 GRAMMY Awards® ceremony, she appeared shorn of hair to deliver a roof-raising rendition of Janis Joplin's "Piece of My Heart." It was evident to all that Etheridge had won her toughest battle.

RECAP: Road to the Dotted Line

MELISSA ETHERIDGE

- Began performing locally while still a young teen
- Attended a major music school
- Relocated to Los Angeles
- Made her name doing local gigs
- Never compromised for the sake of safety
- Was signed as a songwriter first
- Was championed by a manager

GREEN DAY

PUNK'S POP PRINCES

"I'll never forget when Green Day said to me, 'We're going to be a great band.' And they knew it. They knew what it took to be successful in the music business."

—Rob Cavallo

With endless adrenaline, Green Day is a super-charged alternative band who handily crossed over from the punk underground to solid acceptance in the pop mainstream. Jaded critics griped that the youthful band were mere punk revivalists, rehashing the frenetic energy of punk-pop songs. Sure, the music wasn't particularly innovative, but they brought the sound of late-Seventies punk to a new, younger generation of malcontents. What Green Day has is endless, appealing personality, as embodied through lead vocalist and guitarist Billie Joe Armstrong. "The butt of my generation," is a phrase Billie Joe Armstrong has used to describe Green Day's appeal. Combining the take-no-prisoners ethos of punk music and amping it up with a self-effacing, sometimes sophomoric sense of humor, Green Day invented a winning formula that has made the California band one of the biggest groups in rock music.

Green Day is both a band and a tight brotherhood extending back to when the band members were all in their early teen years in Rodeo, CA. As kids, Billie Joe Armstrong and Mike Dirnt became instant friends, and during sleepovers at each other's homes would play songs by the metal warhorses—Ozzy Osborne, Def Leppard, and Van Halen. In 1984 and 1985, when the two were in the seventh grade together, they formed their first band, Truant, and performed covers like "Ain't Talkin' 'Bout Love," "Crazy Train," and "Rock You Like a Hurricane." By the next year, they were writing and playing their own original songs.

"White trash and hicks" is the offhand description offered by Armstrong to describe the band's suburban hometown. Mike Dirnt's history is particularly turbulent. Born to a heroin-addicted mother who gave him up for adoption, Mike was returned to her custody at age seven upon the divorce of his adoptive parents, a Native American mother and white father. His friendship with Billie Joe Armstrong was cemented by the cancer-related death of the latter's father, an itinerant jazz musician, in 1982. (Armstrong's first song, "Why Do You Want Him?" was about his mother and new stepfather.)

At 15, Mike briefly moved into Billie Joe's parental home before the pair relocated to a squalid dwelling on Oakland's West Seventh Street that subsequently was to be immortalized in "Welcome to Paradise." It was the tarnished era of punk, and weekends were spent at local punk club, the legendary all-ages, completely volunteer-run Gilman Street Project. Here, in 1987, Dirnt and Armstrong hooked up with drummer Al Sobrante (born John Kiftmeyer) to form the band Sweet Children. Gilman Street was the epicenter of the scene, showcasing local groups like the Dead Kennedys and Buck Naked. A committee handled all bookings at the venue and show promotion was done mostly via recorded phone messages. An alleged violence-, drug-, and alcohol-free environment, it was the club's creed that they would not book or support racist, misogynist, major-label, or homophobic bands or performances.

Their first show as Sweet Children was in 1988 at Rod's Hickory Pit in Rodeo, CA, where Armstrong's mother worked as a waitress and Mike Dirnt worked as a short-order cook. A few months later, they played a high school party with the local band, the Lookouts, in a remote mountain location near Willits, CA, where two band members, Tré Cool and Kain Kong of the Lookouts, lived and attended school. Cool, born Frank Edwin Wright III, had been recruited as the drummer into The Lookouts at age 12. Only five kids showed up for the party. There was no electricity in the house, so Sweet Children had to perform using a generator and candlelight. They played, as Lookouts singer/guitarist Larry Livermore recalls it, "as if they were The Beatles at Shea Stadium."

Herbal Essence

Lookout! Records, based in Berkeley, CA, was formed in 1987 by Livermore and David Hayes. (Hayes departed in 1989 and started Very Small Records and Too Many Records, leaving Lookout to Livermore, who sold it in 1997 to former mailroom assistant Chris Appelgren.) Many of the bands on Lookout! were, like Sweet Children, graduates of the Gilman Street scene. It was Livermore who offered Sweet Children a deal. In early 1989, they recorded their first EP, *1,000 Hours*, and then decided, weeks before the EP release, to change their name to Green Day, a slang term for a day where you sit around and do nothing but smoke a certain mind-bending herb. (The band members were all alleged to be serious bong-hitters since puberty.) The band recorded *1,000* Hours in two days. The members were then 17 years old and seniors in high school. While Mike Dirnt graduated, Armstrong, in true rock-and-roll rebel fashion, dropped out one day prior to his 18th birthday.

They released *1,000 Hours* and swiftly followed it with their debut *39/Smooth* album on Lookout. They headed out on their inaugural U.S. tour. When the band found the underground scene, they nose-dived right into it, establishing their geeky, good-time approach that was right in tune with the times and their audiences. Before leaving, the prolific band recorded another four-song EP called *Slappy*. While in Minneapolis-St. Paul, they recorded a four-song EP of some of their old tunes for the local label Skene Records, and titled it *Sweet Children*. (In 1991, *1,039/Smoothed Out Slappy Hours* was released on CD, re-issuing *39/Smooth* with all the tracks from *Slappy* and *1,000 Hours*.)

After this tour, at the end of the summer of 1990, Al Sobrante left the band on what was supposed to be a temporary basis to attend college in Arcata, CA. By this time the Lookouts had become mostly inactive and Tré Cool, now 17 and living in Berkeley, began playing with Green Day as a temporary replacement. The combination worked so well that he soon became Green Day's permanent drummer.

Miles in the Bookmobile

Tré's father, who owns a small trucking company, overhauled a used bookmobile and served as the driver on three separate tours. "I watched them go from a bunch of kids to a group of musicians with work ethic," says father Frank Wright. "On their first tour or two, it was more of a party than anything else. I still scratch my head and say, 'How in the hell did they make it?' They used to practice in my living room here, a lot of the songs they did on *Dookie*. You hear it coming together, and you don't expect people are going to go out and buy it. But when it does, you just say, 'Wow, that's so cool.'" Before they ever hooked up with a major label, the band had already completed five national tours, driving in their bookmobile outfitted with bunk beds (often with Tré's father at the wheel), tooling from coast to coast and crashing on the floors of friends and fans.

During 1991, the band toured and played locally, amassing their local fan following. They also wrote and recorded their second album, *Kerplunk*, and recorded in five days on a $1,000 budget. It was released on Lookout! Records in January 1992. Relentless touring continued to establish Green Day as rock contenders, as the band played skate parks and VFW halls. They continued to tour through 1992 and 1993, ranging as far afield as the United Kingdom, Germany, Spain, Italy, The Netherlands, Poland, and the Czech Republic. By the time *Kerplunk* had dropped into record-store bins, word had already gotten around about the invigorating new punk trio. Both its albums sold in excess of 30,000 copies to break all of Lookout's previous sales records. Green Day's popularity had grown to such a degree that everyone, Livermore included, realized that the band had outgrown its record label. The trio left Lookout! on friendly terms and went in search of a label that could provide the kind of tour support and promotion needed to advance to the next level. After a short bidding war, producer Rob Cavallo signed the group to Reprise Records. (Part of the deal was that Lookout! would retain the rights to the first two albums.) Green Day entered the studio and spent five weeks, instead of five days, to complete recording on its third effort, *Dookie*, which packed 14 songs into only 39 minutes. The album hit stores in February 1994 and within a couple of months had sold more than a million copies, spurred on by copious amounts of radio and MTV airplay for the singles "Welcome to Paradise" and "Longview."

As 1994 progressed, Green Day's profile grew ever more significant. After completing its own club tour, the band joined the lineups of both the Lollapalooza Festival and Woodstock '94. Green Day's Woodstock gig was an event steeped, or smeared, in legend. A huge mud fight ensued between the band and the audience with so many fans onstage by the end of the set that one of the security guards mistook Mike Dirnt for an interloper and broke several of his teeth while attempting to haul him off the stage. Later in the year, the band pulled off an unheard-of feat when it staged an arena tour with no ticket prices set higher than $20. Throughout all these tours and festivals, fans came to rely on one thing: that Billie Joe Armstrong was liable to drop his pants at any given moment. *Dookie* was an immense hit, selling over ten million copies in the U.S. alone.

Reprise is the Beginning

Rob Cavallo recalls, "I'll never forget when Green Day said to me, 'We're going to be a great band.' And they knew it. 'We're going to be a great band no matter what Reprise does for us.' They already could draw 1,000 kids in a good 10 or 12 cities across this country, and they'd already played Europe three or four times. These kids were 21 years old. They knew what it took to be successful in the music business. They never had jobs. They made their living being a band by the time they were age 16 or 17. They were like, 'We think we need the help of Reprise to realize our potential. However, we are fully confident that we are going to do it on our own anyway. So you're going to take the record that we make and you're going to send it to radio stations for us. So when they hear it, they're going to like it and they're going to want to play it.' That was the way they thought. They didn't think like a lot of other bands that go, 'Oh, we're on Reprise now, so that means people are going to like us. You're going to get our record played on the radio because we're on Reprise.' Well no. That doesn't work at all."

RECAP: Road to the Dotted Line

GREEN DAY

- Co-founders were united while still in their early teens
- In their first incarnation, hooked up with a local label
- Toured relentlessly, crashing on fans' floors
- Embodied the ethos of the audience
- Signed to a major only when their burgeoning career demanded larger distribution

Jewel

Precious Music

San Diego, CA is the perfect incubator for developing talent. Blessed with beautiful weather and an abundance of outdoor activities, it is also home to an ever-shifting flock of college students, impressionable music fans who take their artists to heart. In addition to a lively club scene, San Diego is known for the quality and quantity of its coffeehouses, intimate listening rooms where acoustic performers can perform for attentive audiences, distracted only by the occasional whir of an overheated cappuccino machine. The Inner Change coffeehouse on Turquoise Street in San Diego's Pacific Beach district is gone now, but a decade ago it boasted out-the-door lines to catch a set by a knockout blond troubadour, Jewel Kilcher.

Kilcher, born in 1974 in Payson, Utah, was raised in Alaska. Both of her parents, Lenedra Caroll and Atz Kilcher, were musical. By age six, Jewel was accompanying them to

"Remember to blah blah blah blah and always get perfect moments stuck between your teeth."

gigs in local villages and at tourist attractions in Anchorage where she began singing in their shows as well. She also started to master one of her specialties, yodeling, with her father's help. During their "family dinner show," the Kilchers sang, presented skits, and showed a documentary of the Kilcher's pioneering home life created by Yule, her grandfather (spelled "Juel" in his homeland), a Swiss native who settled in Homer, Alaska in 1940. Jewel's mother Lenedra has "Jewel" as her middle name, and she involved Jewel and her two brothers, Shane and Atz Lee, in "creativity workshops" where they enjoyed writing poems, singing, and creating arts-and-crafts projects. One of Jewel's favorite songs was "This Little Bird," which she and her mother later reprised on Jewel's *Spirit* CD. Lenedra also taught the children a reverence for the natural world and the wisdom of indigenous people.

When the Kilchers divorced two years later, Jewel stayed with her father on an 800-acre homestead in Homer, AK. She found solace in writing prose; her early journals reflect the undeniable hurt and emotional uncertainty she felt from her parents' breakup. During her early teen years, Jewel and Atz performed together in Homer during the summers. From her father, Jewel learned how to "work a room" and to gauge audience reaction to the songs and stories. She'd travel back to Anchorage to spend the winters with Lenedra. As a tourist center, Jewel says, Homer was not an isolated outpost. "I had friends from Chile and Guatemala, Puerto Rico, Australia and New Zealand. Those people turned me on to a lot of different languages, religions, and different ways of thinking. Summer was always a good education."

In 1989, Lenedra helped Jewel polish a rendition of "Over the Rainbow" for a performance on Tom Bodet's *The End of the Road* show, a popular Alaska Public Radio series. It was during this performance that Jewel found her voice. By now, Jewel was playing guitar and performing her self-penned songs. For a brief stint, she also joined a local rap group called Le Crème, where she was known as Swiss Miss.

Michigan Memories
Clearly gifted, Jewel applied to the prestigious Interlochen Fine Arts Academy in Michigan as a voice major. Interlochen doesn't come cheap, but 70 percent of Jewel's tuition was paid for by a vocal scholarship, with the remainder of the expenses raised at what turned out to be Jewel's first solo concert. With the citizens of Homer supportive enough to cover the rest of the first year tuition, summer jobs filled the gap the next year. Jewel spent her junior and senior high school years of high school at Interlochen. Her voice matured while practicing the intricate arias of Monteverdi, Bononcini, and other classical composers. During this period, she worked as a waitress in Traverse City. At the academy she overcame dyslexia, learned to play guitar,

and began refining her songwriting skills. Jewel also talked the academy into letting her participate in the drama program, which wasn't allowed at the time. She ended up landing the leading role in that semester's play, *Spoon River Anthology*. Theater instructor Robin Ellis remembers her as "an excellent student... intelligent, curious, energetic, eager, and fearless." Voice instructor Nicole Philibosian had even more vivid memories of the young singer. She still recalls the first time she heard Jewel perform off-campus. "Jewel was just getting ready to leave Interlochen and she said, 'I'm going to sing in Traverse City tonight. Do you want to come hear me?' She was singing at Ray's Coffee House, playing her guitar. Jewel just blew me away. I just sat there with tears running down my cheeks."

Into the Van

After high school, Jewel went to San Diego to stay with her mom. Following a brief sojourn to Colorado, she returned to San Diego, the city she now calls home. When a series of dead-end jobs led nowhere, Jewel took up residence in her VW van, existing on a diet of carrot sticks, peanut butter, and songwriting. She performed at the local coffeehouses, including the Inner Change, and made friends with the local folkies—Steve Poltz (lead singer of the Rugburns), his fellow Rugburn members Rob Driscoll and Gregory Page, and area musicians including Joy Eden Harrison and Byron Nash. Steve Poltz and Jewel maintained a collaborative songwriting relationship, creating the catchy "You Were Meant for Me" that appeared on her debut album.

Although the early shows were sparsely attended, Jewel's magnetic performances began packing them in. "A good buzz got started," Jewel recalled, "and in a relatively short amount of time, a bunch of limos started coming down and I'd get flown off to New York. I'd be eating carrot sticks and peanut butter in my van, then fly off to New York and have these huge dinners, and then be plopped back in my pumpkin bus." (The later shows were reportedly so packed that she often had to walk across tables to get up to the stage.) Audiences could witness Jewel's rambling stories, endless guitar tuning, and improvised set lists. It didn't matter, because the emerging songs were compelling. Inevitably, Jewel would forget to bring a guitar pick, and when someone from the audience offered her one, she'd complain that it was either too thick or too thin. When anyone would get up to leave (or go to the bathroom), she'd ask, "Are you leaving?" and if so, she'd have everyone in the audience say goodbye.

Jewel played long sets, often up to three or four hours, debuting songs she'd just written and stumbling through the lyrics or making them up as she went along. She also drank water from a large jug, while making jokes about someday receiving a corporate sponsorship from a water company. (She still found it unreal that people had to pay for good drinking water.) She ended every show by saying "Remember to blah blah blah blah and always get perfect moments stuck between your teeth."

Jewel's mother, Lenedra Caroll, no stranger to the music biz, managed her daughter's career. (Jewel is now signed to industry powerhouse Irving Azoff.) Eventually there was much to manage. One of Jewel's earliest industry fans was Judy Stakee, the Warner/Chappell publishing executive who had championed and signed Sheryl Crow. "Judy Stakee in our creative staff was onto Jewel 18 months before she had a hit. We still couldn't close the publishing because the lawyer saw the excitement in the rest of the industry and realized that all he had to do was wait a while and he could make a better deal," recalls Les Bider, then the head of Warner/Chappell Music Publishing. Eventually Jewel signed with the firm and, with a powerful publishing entity in her camp, was ready to firm up a lucrative deal with Atlantic Records.

All this added exposure continued to draw crowds to the Inner Change, which first added a second show, then upped the admission price to five dollars. On July 28 and 29, 1994, a sound crew descended on the Inner Change to record four live sets of Jewel. All the live recordings on *Pieces of You* come from those two sessions.

Jewel had outgrown the tiny Inner Change and began looking for larger venues. She did two shows at the Wikiup Cafe in Hillcrest. The coffeehouses were a through-line. On her first tour, the label set up a series of residency tours where she would play four different coffee joints in four different cities for four weeks, building up her fan base much like she did in San Diego.

Jewel's first officially-released recording was an acoustic version of "Angel Needs a Ride" that was released on a San Diego radio station's sampler with other local bands. This disc came out in conjunction with the 1994 May Day Festival. On this release, Jewel is already credited as being at Atlantic Records artist. The sampler also contains a track from the Rugburns' first album. Jewel, the Rugburns, and Gregory Page are the only acoustic entries on the rock release.

"My first album was like student art. It wasn't meant to be sold in galleries," says Jewel. "When it ended up being a hit, it was like an alley dog winning the Westminster dog show." The success was built on taking Jewel to the people. After the album was released, the singer toured relentlessly for about 18 months—covering, she estimates, "15,000 miles every four weeks"—before her softly glowing debut single "Who Will Save Your Soul" began climbing the charts. "It took a lot of touring," reveals Jewel. "In the beginning, a lot of radio stations said my music was unplayable, and video shows and TV stations said it was unlistenable—which was fine, because I never expected to sell a lot of albums with this one. It was just supposed to be a time capsule of where I was. I was 19 and just learning to write songs and play guitar. I know that hard wood grows slowly, and if I wanted to have a longterm career like Neil Young, it would just take touring. I grew up doing live tours and playing in bars, so it was what I love to do. I was just glad not to be living in my car anymore, so I just toured. I would do 40 cities every 30 days, four shows a day. I worked a lot. I had a really good time and got enough of a groundswell following to just keep playing. My label kept me out long enough that people couldn't ignore me anymore. Radio had to start playing the songs."

Pieces of You garnered Jewel a GRAMMY® nod as Best New Artist.

RECAP: Road to the Dotted Line

JEWEL

- Ascension paralleled the rise of female singer/songwriter such as Lilith Fair
- Came from a show biz family and began performing early
- Received formal music education
- Emerged as an artist from a pre-established coffeehouse scene with a built-in college audience
- Had over 100 songs ready to roll
- The industry came to her, not the other way around.
- Wholesome, blonde good looks appealed to MTV and VH1 viewers
- Linked romantically to Sean Penn, who directed the video for her second hit

JIMMY JAM & TERRY LEWIS

TWIN CITY MAGIC

"It always starts with your family and the values they instill. My mother was very 'do unto others.' I know how much that has impacted my life. We never forget where we came from."

—Jimmy Jam

As creators of over 100 gold, platinum, and multi-platinum albums—16 #1 pop hits, 25 #1 R&B smashes, and winners of three GRAMMY Awards® with eight nominations— Jimmy Jam and Terry Lewis are rightfully acknowledged as the most successful songwriting and production team in modern music history. Oscar and Emmy nominations, an NAACP Image Award, an Essence Award, the ASCAP Golden Note and additional ASCAP honors as Rhythm and Soul Songwriters of the Year for 1988–1992 and 1994–1995, plus Pop Songwriters of the Year in 1988 and 1992. Across a span of genres—from pop, soul, and dance to rap, gospel, rock, and reggae—their genius is distilling the purest essence of artists into luminous productions and equally stunning songs. The Minneapolis, MN natives have written for and/or produced a slate of hitmakers that includes Boyz II Men, Sting, Mary J. Blige, Elton John, Usher, Shaggy, Yolanda Adams, Herb Alpert, Luther

Vandross, Rod Stewart, New Edition, Human League, Earth, Wind & Fire, Mariah Carey, Robert Palmer, Gwen Stefani, Kanye West, and Sounds of Blackness. They guided Janet Jackson into the stratosphere of superstardom with over 40 million records sold worldwide and over 20 gold and platinum singles.

Over 30 years ago, when the two teenagers first met in an educational program called Upward Bound, Lewis was the worldly one. "He had this black and green bass," recalls Jam. "I gravitated to him because he was older and he had all the girls." Jam was from a musical family. His father was a keyboard player. His earliest musical memories include sitting at the organ, kicking it to provide a beat, while he listened to the classic Sixties radio soul. Academics were also important to Jam, especially the study of music. At age 13, he was already playing drums for his father's group, but his interest in music was growing to encompass songwriting, arranging, and playing other instruments. He recalls a counselor in school, an aspiring singer, who wrote excuses so Jam could meet him in an abandoned music room to provide piano accompaniment. Music was not only a source of inspiration, but also a source of pride.

Terry Lewis's original interests were in scholastics and athletics. As he recalls, "The ultimate break was just to be able to start playing music. That was not in the cards for me. No one else in my family played music or is musical. And just to get hooked up with some fellows who did, that's the beginning of everything, that's the genesis of it all. We were lucky enough to get a start by playing gigs around town, coming out of the music classes within the school and taking Saturday morning classes, jazz classes, with a guy named Rafer Johnson. He was one of the best teachers and the meanest teachers. He was the meanest man who ever lived. I'm going to tell you, he almost broke my knuckles!" But the lessons were learned. Lewis, because of his athletic background, already considered himself a leader. He was able to pull people together for projects, so when he envisioned a band, it was natural to convince other musicians to follow his lead. When Lewis organized a band to perform for the Upward Bound program, he enlisted Jam, who was then a drummer, as his keyboard player. "Terry really was the one who gave me my final shove into playing keyboards," says Jimmy. "We formed a band back then and we've been joined at the hip ever since."

Booking the Gig

Minneapolis is home to a distinguished legacy of music: symphonic, choral, rock, blues, and even polka. Jam and Lewis absorbed it all. Lewis recalls, "We played in bands where, in order to make the gig work for us—say, at a ski resort—we'd have to play jazz, fusion, disco, funk. It made us musically diverse and it's had a lot to do with our longevity." Jam agrees. "To maximize the number of events we could play as a local band, we had to be versatile enough in a club when someone said, 'I need you guys to play an hour of jazz while people are having dinner. Then I need you to play some hits from the radio and requests.' When you play different types of music, you appreciate how the arrangements are put together and the lyrics and songs."

Forming their own band, Jam and Lewis had no alternative but to create and promote their own shows. They convinced the owner of a run-down hotel, The Dykeman, to let them use the hotel ballroom for a show. They printed thousands of handbills, distributed them around town and, when the night of the concert arrived, over 2,000 attendees showed up—so many that they had to be turned away at the door. Jimmy Jam recalls, "Then I knew we had something. All of our gigs were generated by doing that one gig. We didn't make any money. We went into the hole to do it, but it gave us a start. Club owners would say 'Where's our crowd this weekend?' and they'd hear, 'They're all down seeing this band you won't book because they're black!' It taught us how to be entrepreneurial." Lewis concurs, "I always had to find a way to make some money because nobody was ever going to give me any."

Crowned by Prince

Jam and Lewis were founding members of the celebrated rock/soul band The Time. When their friend Prince's career exploded, they knew they had a shot at national recognition. "Prince was—I don't know if you want to say *nice* enough or *savvy* enough—to come back and grab us as The Time and get us a record deal," informs Jam. "If you look at it from a national point-of-view, getting with Prince and The Time and that being the next launching pad to the national level. The first thing is just getting around people who like music and being a part of that. The music comes first. It wasn't like we wanted to be famous first or we wanted the money first. We wanted to do music. That was all we wanted. It wasn't about anything. 'Let's do some originals, man.'" Gold records for their first two albums with The Time were testimony to their rising prominence. Most prophetically, the duo expanded into production with their first R&B hit, "Just Be Good to Me" by the S.O.S. band and Cheryl Lynn's #1 R&B track, "Encore."

Today, while Jam and Lewis continue to extend their unstoppable string of hits, they also devote their energies to the music, arts, and educational communities. Jimmy Jam serves on the Board of directors of ASCAP (American Society of Composers, Authors and Publishers) and is a trustee of NARAS (National Association of Recording Arts & Sciences). "Jimmy's the senator," explains Lewis. Jam's and Lewis's philanthropic support—much less-publicized than their hit records—is extended primarily to organizations that support music education. Explains Terry Lewis, "I'm the street guy. I want to help kids so they don't get taken advantage of, bring some people through that period so we can have some veterans around."

"Ultimately, being a nice guy is much more important than any statistics," states Jam. The duo clearly dispels the old adage that nice guys finish last. "Nice guys *finish*," corrects Lewis. "Guys who aren't nice don't care to finish. We've been endowed with gifts. We have to be responsible with these gifts, to put something in the world to help, enlighten, or make somebody's day better. We love the music and the music loves us because we love the music first."

Their ongoing legacy and hit-making destiny will continue to unfold, notes Jam, by "not being afraid of change, and embracing new technology and ideas. You have to keep looking forward and appreciating the new forms of music and the people that are making the music. Technology and talent. We'll be around to have a part in the future."

Both Jam and Lewis are committed fathers and family men. "It always starts with your family and the values they instill," Jam discloses. "My mother was very 'do unto others.' I know how much that has impacted my life. We never forget where we came from. We had a ceiling in our old studio we're going to duplicate in our new place, with musical people who watched us from heaven. Not that they've all passed away, but they're the people who came before us. You see the Temptations, Paul Robeson, and Mahalia Jackson. The visual tells us how fortunate we are, and that we have a responsibility to use music in a responsible way to uplift people."

Making connections in the music business was key to success for Jimmy Jam and Terry Lewis, not just with their peers and contemporaries, but also with finding mentors. Clarence Avnet, a Motown veteran who, at the time of Jam and Lewis' ascension was running Taboo Records, offered the duo invaluable legal and career guidance. "The norm then was to keep everyone in the dark. We can take advantage of them that way," laughs Lewis. "We kept asking and learning and kept growing and we started to reveal the answers we could find. We were fortunate to find some answers we were about to reveal. So many artists before us never found the answers."

Interestingly enough, Jam and Lewis have never had a manager or an agent, although Lewis's background includes studying business. Jimmy Jam adds, "We're not saying this is the way to do it for everyone. Common sense will get you a long way. You know the adage 'If something sounds too good to be true, it probably is.' If someone says, 'Here's a million dollars, sign here,' I don't need a manager or an agent to tell me something's wrong. So there's gotta be something in here when I'm signing my wife and kids away. Don't worry about taking it to a lawyer. There are certain things that are so obvious."

Commencing their third decade of shared creativity, Jimmy Jam and Terry Lewis continue raising new standards as songwriters, producers, musicians, entrepreneurs, and visionaries. Indeed, the duo now has its own star on Hollywood Boulevard's fabled Walk of Fame. "Not bad for two little ghetto boys from Minneapolis," concludes Terry Lewis.

RECAP: Road to the Dotted Line
JIMMY JAM & TERRY LEWIS

- Both were products of arts education
- Created their own performance venues
- Were part of an ongoing local scene
- Parlayed membership in a band to production gigs
- Launched their own company

Norah JONES

Vocal Inflections

Norah Jones crosses musical borders that are both intensely personal and innately fluid, expanding from jazz to soul to folk-based pop. Her own story is equally intriguing. Norah Jones was born on March 30, 1979 in New York City. When she was four years old, she and her mother Sue moved to the Dallas suburb of Grapevine, TX. Norah's earliest musical influences came from her mother's extensive LP collection and from "oldies" radio. She began singing in church choirs at age five, commenced piano lessons two years later, and briefly played alto saxophone in junior high school.

Her father, whom she didn't spend time with as a child, is the revered Indian sitar master, Ravi Shankar. She rarely speaks about Shankar in public. According to a 2002 article in *The Guardian*, "She saw her father a few times a year until she was nine, and then not until she was 18." When Jones was 15, she

"I'm so happy to sell all these records. The main thing that scares me about it is that I don't want my record or my name or the songs to be crammed down people's throats."

and her mother moved from Grapevine to Dallas's central city, where Norah enrolled in Booker T. Washington High School for the Performing and Visual Arts. (Soul singer Erykah Badu and trumpeter Roy Hargrove are also Washington alumni.) On her 16th birthday, Jones played her first gig, an open-mic night at a local coffeehouse, where she performed a version of "I'll Be Seeing You" that she'd learned from Etta James's treatment of this Billie Holiday favorite. While still in high school, Norah won the Down Beat Student Music Awards for Best Jazz Vocalist and Best Original Composition in 1996, and earned a second SMA for Best Jazz Vocalist in 1997. She also sang with a band called Laszlo, playing what she describes as "dark, jazzy rock." After graduation, Jones entered the University of North Texas, an institution well-known for its music program, where she majored in jazz piano. Although she always enjoyed singing, she felt that studying piano would provide a more solid career foundation. Jones recalls, "It was cool. I'm glad I didn't go all four years, because I would have burnt out a bit. I did jazz gigs around town. In college, I had a weekend gig at a restaurant, a solo thing that was the best practice I could have ever had. That's where I learned to coordinate my singing and my piano playing."

New York-born songwriter Jesse Harris and bandmates—including leader and bassist Marc Johnson, Tony Scherr, and Kenny Wollesen—were at the college for a jazz clinic. Staying at Denton's Radisson Hotel, they needed a lift to the school, so Norah Jones and her 1971 Cadillac were called into service. "That short ride from across the highway is, I guess, what started all of this," she says. Jesse Harris remembers, "The night we met we hung out and had a jam session. She sang a couple of standards. We were on a fairway. We got some drinks and some guitars and marched out onto the golf course. At night it was a good spot," he recalls.

It Takes a Village
When Jones made a summer trip to New York to take over a sublet from a family friend, she reconnected with Harris. She was soon part of a burgeoning scene centered around The Living Room, a tiny Lower East Side corner bar furnished with scroll back kitchen chairs and macramé plant hangers. (It has retained its name, but has since relocated to a more sumptuous space, albeit with no cover, a suggested five-dollar tip donation, and a one-drink minimum.) "There is a scene here for sure," avows Jesse Harris. "It's a melting pot of songwriters and musicians who aren't just rock players." Despite the aural simplicity of the new blend of music, the players who create it often have more complex reference points. "I tend to play with a lot of guys who also play in the downtown instrumental scene," he notes.

Hanging out with the local songwriters inspired Norah to begin writing her own songs. Jones relished performance opportunities with a variety of players. For about a year, beginning in December 1999, she appeared regularly with the funk-fusion band Wax Poetic (now signed to Atlantic). She sang two songs (Roxy Music's "More Than This" and "Day Is Done" by Nick Drake) on guitarist Charlie Hunter's Blue Note album *Songs from the Analog Playground*, and frequently performed live with the group.

"I played in restaurants and piano bars for about a year, using my music as my job because I'd never thought about doing anything else," Jones says. "But I was tired of the bad audiences, so I took a job as a waitress to make my living and planned on playing one or two really good gigs each week just before I signed with Blue Note."

Blue Note Devices

Jones soon assembled her own band with Harris, Lee Alexander, and Dan Rieser. In October 2000, this lineup recorded some demos. Norah used this as an opportunity to find her voice between her jazz roots, her interpretation of standards, and a new passion for songwriting. (The resulting demos were available as the now out-of-print EP *First Sessions*.) In addition to Harris, Alexander, and Rieser, guitar players Adam Rogers and Tony Scherr were also featured on the tracks. At a meeting with Blue Note president Bruce Lundvall in January 2001, Jones played him demo that included her recording of "Spring Can Really Hang You Up the Most," one of Lundvall's favorite jazz standards.

"This young kid nailed this song completely, and I said, 'How do you even know this song?'" he remembers of their first meeting, which came about when an EMI royalties department employee—who didn't know Lundvall—brought Jones to his attention. Lundvall, a legendary record man, got it and allegedly signed her on the spot.

"Blue Note has a very long history in American jazz, and it's always stood for considerable integrity," says Howard Mandel, a freelance writer and president of the 500-member Jazz Journalists Association. "They have the most commitment to the music in many of its forms. There's very little overt attempt to commercialize the music. They are very honest about their approach, whether it's Norah Jones or [alto saxophonist] Greg Osby."

Started in the 1930s by jazz enthusiast Alfred Lion, with the help of fellow German immigrant Francis Wolff, Blue Note has gone from being a beloved hobby to the darling of collectors and music critics worldwide. Stamped on most of its recordings is its longtime motto "The Finest in Jazz since 1939."

Norah began recording the songs on *Come Away with Me* in May 2001, doing preliminary work with producer Craig Street at Bearsville Studio in Woodstock, NY. In August 2001, the singer and her musicians went back to work, this time with Arif Mardin at Sorcerer Sound in Manhattan. Mardin's genius transcends genres and includes a huge roster of artists, among them Aretha Franklin, the Average White Band, the Bee Gees, Phil Collins, Hall & Oates, Herbie Mann, Willie Nelson, Carly Simon, and Barbra Streisand. Many of the songs he's worked on have become classics, from the Young Rascals' 1965 #1 "Good Lovin'" to Chaka Khan's groundbreaking "I Feel for You" and Bette Midler's GRAMMY®-winning Record of the Year, *Wind Beneath My Wings*. He has also worked on numerous Broadway cast albums and television and film soundtracks. "I was nervous at first," Jones admits. "I didn't want some amazing producer who'd done all these famous records to come in and have me be scared to tell him what I thought. But Arif is the nicest guy in the world, very easygoing. He was there to keep my act together and make sure I got a good record. Arif had great ideas."

Mardin refers to Jones as "his retirement joke." He says, "After I had retired from Atlantic in 2001, Bruce Lundvall called me and said, 'We have this wonderful singer. She made an album, but I think they went away from the original feeling of the piano-oriented demos,' which he'd loved. What they had recorded was more guitar-oriented and he wanted the original feel. I agreed. I loved the way she was singing and playing the piano, and the songs were wonderful. So I started to work with Norah. At the beginning, we had a meeting and I told her, 'You are the boss; I work for you. I bring in ideas; we talk about them. That's all.' When our journey started, we had this understanding. I'm not a producer who puts his stamp on the sound. She doesn't want synthesizers, but an organ would be fine. She doesn't want a big string section, but a duo or string quartet, maybe."

After little more than a year of work, Norah Jones released her debut album, *Come Away with Me*, the platinum-plus release that garnered five GRAMMY Awards®. Jesse Harris was well-represented on the album and one of his songs, "Don't Know Why," was awarded a GRAMMY® for Song of the Year. For Blue Note, a small label for whom 50,000 units would be a cause for celebration, selling millions of CDs was a remarkable achievement.

Jones says, "I'm so happy to sell all these records. It's of course a great thing. The main thing that scares me about it is that I don't want my record or my name or the songs to be crammed down people's throats. I don't know why it happens, but it happens. I don't want it to happen, because it's already doing well enough on its own. I don't want it to be super, hyper-marketed. I don't want people to get sick of it, because that's what ultimately happens. It happens with me. Maybe I'll like a song the first time I hear it, but then I hear it a thousand more times, just in the grocery store, and I get really sick of it. That's the only thing that I don't like about all this."

The success of Norah Jones took everyone by surprise, and Jesse Harris is no exception. "There was no way to know. I was always confident that she'd do well, but from the beginning it took on a life of its own. It was really quite bizarre. I remember thinking, 'How do people know to go and buy this album?' And every week it grew. I never thought it would be a #1 record. It still seems to be taking place in another universe."

RECAP: Road to the Dotted Line

NORAH JONES

- Was a product of an arts education high school
- Attended college to study music
- Hooked up, by chance, with a New York musician
- Relocated to Manhattan
- Created her own musical style

Alicia
KEYS

UNLOCKING THE MUSE

"I felt like I had to have these people validate me to make me mean something, and it tore me apart. You start wondering 'What's going on? When is this gonna turn into something good?'"

Accepting the ASCAP Award for Songwriter of the Year in 2005, Alicia Keys praised the power of musical diversity. "It's a lot of fun to be able to identify with so many varieties of music. My love for Stevie Wonder, Donny Hathaway, Smokey Robinson, Jimmy Jam & Terry Lewis, Prince, Nina Simone, Roberta Flack, Beethoven, Bach, Alanis Morissette, Three Dog Night—so many different varieties of music we can relate to. It makes it broader, more fun, and more understandable," she said.

Although an astoundingly successful debut, *Song in A Minor*, introduced a piano-playing prodigy to the world, for Keys, then in her early twenties, it was the culmination of over a decade of hard work. Born to an Irish-Italian mother, Terri Augello, an actress who also worked as a paralegal, and a Jamaican father, Craig Cook, Alicia was raised in the Hell's Kitchen neighborhood of New York City where she devoted herself to the piano and music. She made her stage debut as a singer in her kindergarten's version of *The Wiz*. Her mother recognized her daughter's talent and was willing to work a second job so young Alicia could study the disciplined Suzuki method of classical piano. Keys began playing piano when she was seven and learned classical music by playing Mozart, Beethoven, and Chopin, her favorite composer. She wrote her first song, "Butterflyz," at age 14. It is a tune that later surfaced on her debut album.

"My mom is definitely my rock," says Keys. "Growing up, we didn't have anybody but each other to survive in the city. She really helped me to become the type of person I am. The strong-mindedness that I have is all because of her. I don't think she would have made it if she had been a weak person who always felt like she needed somebody in order to make it. She never gave me that impression. She taught me to stand on my own two feet, and I was always presented with a lot of obstacles."

Fame and the Harlem Nocturne

As a preteen, Alicia trained with vocal coach Conrad Robinson at the Harlem Police Athletic League Community Center on 124th Street in upper Manhattan. She later enrolled at the prestigious Professional Performing Arts High School, memorable from the movie *Fame*. She and three other girls formed a vocal group and rehearsed with Robinson, who told his brother, Jeff Robinson, about the talented Keys. When Jeff sat in on rehearsals and began to talk to Alicia about her future, it was evident that he shared her vision for her music. Robinson also encouraged Keys to leave the group and to pursue a career as a solo artist.

Robinson minces no words when he talks about the rigors of the music business. "There's no longer any artist development to teach these kids the rights and the wrongs of this business. We just throw them out there and hope they get a hit on the radio, then have them run around the country for two years. But when the second album doesn't work out, you never hear from them again. Working with Alicia has been a building—constant talking to, counseling sessions, bonding, communicating, and the real meaning of artist development. She's not going to break down in a couple years. She's here for the long haul."

"Jeff has believed in me from day one," Keys says of her manager. "And through every up and down he's always been there for me, and vice versa. If I had not had his support and the support of people who really loved me, people who didn't push me into the wrong places, I wonder what I would have been convinced to do, being so young. I've always been strong-minded, but I wonder. I'd rather not have anything than be a liar."

"I like working with young, up-and-coming artists," says Robinson, who works from his MBK Entertainment offices in New York City. "The older artists are set in their ways. I want to work with those who are young and want to grow and develop. I don't believe in putting out an artist before their time."

Record Deal Number One

At 16, Keys was valedictorian of her high school senior class. She was accepted at Columbia University, but it was another Columbia that beckoned. Columbia Records, the famous record label, signed her in 1996. The label's interest was a result of a live showcase. Robinson says, "I knew the way Alicia's personality worked. She is cute, she could sing and play, and she's got star appeal. Once she's in front of an audience, it's over. It's a wrap. So I let her do her thing on the piano, no band, no background singers, just her and a piano doing what she does best. She played the piano and talked on the mic and won everybody over."

"They gave me a good deal and they offered me a baby grand piano, so how could I refuse?" asks Keys. But Columbia shelved the album she recorded. "They wanted something more easily definable," she remembers, "something not me." Finding this personalized sound was tough. Robinson and Columbia selected a roster of high-priced producers, but two years went by without anything fruitful. "The producers would be like, 'Just go in the booth and sing,' and that got her frustrated," Robinson avows. "They'd be like, 'Yo, I worked with this one and that one. I know how records should go. Just get behind the mic and sing how you sing.' I'd come in the studio and she'd be all upset, eyes all red, about to cry, ready to fight. I'd be like, 'All right, session's over. We're out.'"

"I felt like I had to have these people validate me to make me mean something, and it tore me apart. It tore me apart in a major way, and it was really hard for me to merely get up because of how much I had put into it," she says. "It killed me. That was hell. It was terrible, horrible. You have this desire to have something good and you have thoughts and ideas, but when you finish the music it's shit and it keeps on going like that. You start wondering, 'What's going on? When is this gonna turn into something good?'"

The answer came when Alicia Keys took control of her own project and began writing, singing, and playing what was in her soul. She also wrested control of the production, unheard-of for a young artist. Robinson relates, "At the time it was like, 'We're gonna let this little 16-year-old girl produce tracks?'" She began sitting in with producers and engineers and asking questions, trying to learn how to create music and the intricacies of recording. "I already knew my way around the keyboard, so that was an advantage," Alicia says. "The rest was watching people work on other artists and watching how they layer things and oh, that's why it sounds bigger and oh, you put three and four instruments doing the same line just to make it thick. Then all I had to do was figure out why a Babyface song sounds like a song and mine sounds like an idea."

Alicia recorded 32 songs for her debut. "But what I appreciate about my team—my manager Jeff Robinson, my partner Kerry Brothers, and Peter Edge at J Records—is that they all told me, 'You have to make the final decision.'" The music came together and was joined with a strong visual component in a video for "Falling," which featured searing images of incarcerated women. Later nominated for an MTV Music Video Award, it displayed Keys' multi-media appeal. But with the album nearly complete and the video mapped out, Columbia's management changed and the euphemistically-described "creative differences" arose with the new regime. "They wanted to go back to the traditional 'Sing over this loop' type thing," Robinson says.

Alive with Clive

With Columbia Records in disarray, it was possible for Robinson to extricate Keys from her agreement. That done, Robinson knew who would understand the artistry of Alicia Keys, and so he contacted legendary record man Clive Davis. Clive got it. "Did I know she was going to sell a million records?" Davis asks. "Of course not! I knew she was unique, I knew she was special. I knew she was a self-contained artist. But did I know with Janis Joplin? Did I know with Springsteen? Did I know with Whitney Houston? When you sign them, you don't know, but you feel this is something special and unique, so waiting for artistry to flower and giving them the space to do it is the thing. Then, when the album is done, you take nothing for granted."

Davis knew, as Robinson had known years before, that Alicia could be successful performing by herself in front of small groups of influential people. "Few new artists can be showcased this way and blow people away," he said. "But she can cause a hurricane onstage. So we showcased her for tastemakers. Her maturity and electricity allowed her to do it for herself." At one of these showcases, a booker for *The Tonight Show* decided to air her immediately. Then Davis personally took the "Falling" video to MTV. "When it finished playing, half the women had tears down their faces." Finally, he wrote a letter to his friend Oprah Winfrey. "I said, 'What you've done for books is well-known. In music you play established artists. How about new women in music? Why don't you put on Jill Scott, India.arie, and Alicia Keys, my artist without an album?' I'd never written to her before. I got a call the next day."

Kerry "Krucial" Brothers is a constant factor in Alicia's world. Described by Keys as her "partner" and by the media as her "boyfriend," Brothers is a prime component in a new joint venture, the company Krucial Keys, founded by the duo for the development of new talent. He is also listed as a co-producer on her projects. "We definitely love collaborating with artists," says Keys. "We pick and choose, take it kind of easy and let the vibe move us. But there is so much coming up in the future for Krucial Keys—the writers that we sign, the producers that we have and just really continuing to grow as a legacy, to really create quality and make something that is going to last the test of time. That's why we don't just go ahead and do anything and everything. We pick things that are really special and are going to be here forever, classic."

Before her album was released, Alicia did *The Tonight Show* and *Oprah*, as well as heavy rotation on MTV. The first week the album was available, her label J Records shipped 240,000 copies. The second week, word-of-mouth and television exposure was so immense that record stores demanded another 450,000 copies. "Alicia," Clive Davis says, "was her own goodwill ambassador."

RECAP: Road to the Dotted Line

ALICIA KEYS

- Studied piano as a young child, with an emphasis on classics
- Was a product of an arts education in high school
- Hooked up with a manager who hung in for seven years prior to her breakthrough
- Took control over her own recordings, despite being directed by a label
- Exited one unproductive deal and signed a second one

Avril
LAVIGNE

Pop's Petulant Princess

With an edgy sound that married irresistible pop hooks to a tough rock backbeat, the punky pop priestess Avril Lavigne struck an immediate chord with a record-buying public. Still a teenager, Lavigne was a reflection of the small-town tough girl. It was an image that could not have been manufactured. Lavigne grew up the middle child in a strict Baptist household in Napanee, Ontario, Canada—population 5,000—where her father worked for the local telephone company. Apart from a handful of old Beach Boys, Creedence Clearwater Revival, and Beatles tapes, her parents didn't listen to pop music. Lavigne always sang. She graduated from church choirs to the local community theatre, taught herself guitar, and performed Dixie Chicks numbers at country fairs. At 14, she entered and won a local radio competition. Two days later, she was onstage at Ottawa's Corel Centre in front of 20,000 people, dueting with Shania Twain, her idol.

"I'm really strong. I can deal. I can take it on."

Her first manager, Cliff Fabri, heard her singing new country songs to tracks at a Chapters bookstore in Kingston, Ontario when she was 15. "I have a very simple philosophy," Fabri recalls. "After growing up in Ottawa, Canada, I got to witness the whole Alanis Morissette phenomenon. I knew her story, inside out. I wasn't going to let Avril fall into the trap of having people tell her what to sing and what to be. This was going to be Avril's CD, about her. I didn't want her turning 20 and looking back regretting her career. I knew that Alanis found her co-writer in Glen Ballard when she went to L.A. I knew with our resources I could give Avril the same opportunity." It is Fabri who is credited with introducing Lavigne to the craft of songwriting. The most significant advice he gave to his client: never record a song you haven't co-written. (Fabri's name is conveniently left out of the official Lavigne story. According to credible sources, Fabri is forbidden—by the terms of an economic settlement with Lavigne—from discussing their split prior to the release of *Let Go*.) Says Fabri, "I got Avril writing, because publishing money provides the artist with much-needed income early and throughout a career. I knew Avril would have an opportunity to write with the best songwriters in the world. I set a very early precedent. If these writers wanted to work with Avril, she would be in the room with them and get a piece of the song.

Fabri put together a videocassette of Lavigne performing onstage and in her parents' basement and sent it out to some industry insiders. Former Universal Music Canada exec Brian Hetherman was taken with Lavigne and traveled to Napanee to meet with her and her family during the summer of 2000. In the basement, she performed Sarah McLachlan's "Adia," Faith Hill's "Breathe," and a tentative original song. "She had a lot of work to do, but I was really impressed. I looked at her as a little kid sister. I was really taken by her. I thought she was an absolute doll," says Hetherman, who followed up by sending Lavigne CDs by Holly McNarland, Blink 182, and the Matthew Good Band. (Fabri says Lavigne's shifting musical tastes were particularly influenced by the latter.)

Nettwerk Records VP Mark Jowett met Lavigne and was also intrigued by her budding talent. "I don't know if she had a clear picture of her direction yet. I think her parents liked country quite a lot, and there was a part of her that was attracted to that kind of music," says Jowett. He forwarded the tape to New York songwriter and producer Peter Zizzo. It whetted Zizzo's appetite to collaborate with Lavigne.

Avril signed a development deal with Canadian label Nettwork and made several writing trips to New York. She eventually moved to Manhattan with her brother, taking up temporary residence in a West Village apartment. Peter Zizzo is a well-placed songwriter. He has had cuts with Celine Dion, Jennifer Lopez, and Donna Summer. At the time he met Lavigne, he and his wife—songwriter Tina Schafer, founder and producer of The New York Songwriters Circle shows—were developing Vanessa Carlton. They envisioned building Lavigne's career, particularly her writing chops, over a period of time. Initially, they worked on cutting one of Zizzo's compositions, but Fabri says he pushed for his client to co-write. The result was a song called "Why." Ultimately, the track didn't make it onto *Let Go*, but it proved to everyone, especially Lavigne, that she could compose her own songs. "On the way home to Napanee, we must have played it over 100 times," Fabri says. "The parents were going 'She can write!' Her confidence just soared. From then on, she never wanted to talk about doing other people's songs."

On a subsequent writing trip, Ken Krongard, at the time a talent scout with Arista Records, stopped by the studio and was so energized by Lavigne that he arranged to bring her back to New York at a later date to perform for label boss Antonio "L.A." Reid. In the fall of 2000, Lavigne, Fabri, and Zizzo hosted the record mogul at Zizzo's studio. Avril did two of Zizzo's songs and closed with "Why." Reid thanked her for singing, told her she was wonderful, and left. Arista wanted to sign Lavigne.

The problem, Fabri recalls, was that the company was fixated on what Reid saw at Lavigne's three-song "audition" in October 2000. But the three audition songs were not what Fabri and Lavigne were interested in pursuing, even though one of the songs was Lavigne's "Why." The audition numbers had a definite New Country flavor, but both manager and artist were determined to head out in a tougher, rock-pop direction. "I think the record company was getting worried or upset," Fabri recalled. "It seemed like we were turning down everything, but even though Avril knew and accepted that we needed the help, the material just wasn't what we had decided she was going to put out."

These early recording sessions were reportedly disastrous, so Arista sent her to L.A., where she hooked up with producer Clif Magness. Magness's string of hit singles and records began in the Eighties when he had a #1 hit with Jack Wagner ("All I Need") and a Top 5 with Wilson Phillips ("Impulsive"). In 1990, Magness took home a GRAMMY® for the song "The Places You Find Love" from Quincy Jones's *Back on the Block* album. Just three years later, in 1993, Clif was nominated for an Oscar and a Golden Globe for "The Day I Fall in Love," from the film *Beethoven's 2nd*.

Despite Lavigne's love for the heavy guitar-driven collaborations she and Magness devised—among them, the title song "Let Go"—the label disagreed with this direction. Enter The Matrix, a trio made up of Lauren Christy, Graham Edwards, and Scott Spock, three industry veterans hungry for a hit.

At this juncture, Fabri was still involved and intent on making sure his artist's story wasn't lost in the sonic shuffle. "Every artist, I believe, needs to tell their own story, their life, their experience, no matter how much help they need to deliver their message. In my time with Avril, The Matrix and Clif Magness went on to co-write ten of the twelve songs on the disc, including the first four singles. I negotiated her publishing percentages, unheard of for a first time co-writer. The publishing alone, on these songs for Avril, set the foundation for her financial security for life."

"She was a disgruntled little 16-year-old girl who sat down and sulked, basically," Graham Edwards from The Matrix says. "'I don't want to do that kind of stuff.' We were open and said, 'What did you want to do?' She said, 'I'm young. I want to rock.' She played us a song that was too rocky, too thrashy, like System of a Down. We couldn't imagine that. She's so gorgeous. We thought about it and we came up with the original versions of 'Complicated' and 'SK8R Boy,' and she fell in love with them. Then we all started writing and became friends. It was the summer of fun and it's one of those albums that connected with the people. Kids loved her. It all happened so fast. Three #1s. It changed our lives."

In interviews, the Matrix has said that their initial impression of Lavigne was that her label, Arista, wanted her to be a country artist. Avril contradicts this. "No, not at all. I think they thought I was more like Michelle Branch, more pop/folk or whatever she is. But they got me right away. I went in and played 'Losing Grip' and said 'I want to write more songs like this.' They were more into writing singles."

A press quote by a member of The Matrix suggesting Lavigne's only contribution to "Complicated" was to change a couple of words and Lavigne's gripes to the music press about the L.A.-based production team's use of programming and pitch correction have revealed cracks in the relationship. Clearly, she doesn't want to be perceived as a bystander on her records. "I have ideas," she insists. "I talk to my producers and tell them what I hear, what kind of vibe I want to go for, how I want the drums and guitars and everything. The cool thing is the people I work with I trust, so I let them do their thing, but I also gave my input. I'm not trying to take away their credit, but I'd have questions about what the drums and guitars would be like."

When Lavigne signed a management deal with Nettwork, Fabri was out of the picture. He expresses that he has no regrets, but says that people often speculate about the split. "They wonder if I'm sad because I'm not on this ride with Avril. I tell them I was on this ride with Avril through some incredible times. I got off. I don't want to live in New York City or L.A. I love my life. I just discovered another young talent who I believe will do great things. This is what motivates me. What an artist does with their opportunity is of their own doing, but the steps to get to that opportunity are my doing. That's the game I love. The challenge is endless."

By December 2004, *Let Go* had sold 15 million albums and reached the #1 spot in Australia, Canada, and the United Kingdom. At that time, Lavigne was the youngest female solo act ever to have a #1 album in the UK charts, a record now held by Joss Stone. *Let Go* also peaked at #2 in the United States.

Artwork, merchandise, album sequencing. From the onset, Lavigne was intent on controlling multiple elements of her burgeoning career. "I'm so picky about everything. Right now I'm working on the album artwork. It's like, 'Send it back to me, make it a little darker here. Bring the border down, take the scratches off the photo.' I'm so into that. I'm like that with merch, too."

One of Avril's more recent songs, "How Does It Feel," includes the line "I am small and the world is big." She notes, "Sometimes I feel like I'm this little person and what I've been taking on is such a big thing." But the next line in the same song is even more resounding, as Lavigne sings, "I'm not afraid of anything." She laughs loudly as the weight of this contradiction takes hold. "At that moment I was saying, 'I'm really strong. I can deal. I can take it on.'"

RECAP: Road to the Dotted Line

AVRIL LAVIGNE

- Being a self-taught musician, found local outlets for her talents
- Heard in a bookstore by a manager who became involved early on in her destiny
- Was advised to record only her own songs
- Relocated to Manhattan while still in her mid-teens
- Changed artistic direction despite the objections of her record label

Linkin Park

In the End, It Really Does Matter

"Our Lincoln Park is in Santa Monica, CA. But when we started national touring, everyone thought we were a local band wherever we went, because there are so many Lincoln Parks everywhere."

—Mike Shinoda

In the past few years they've become an international recording and touring force, a relentless cadre blending beats, rock, and a message. But success for Linkin Park—Charles Bennington, Mike Shinoda, Dave "Phoenix" Farrell, Brad Delson, Rob Bourdon, and Joseph Hahn—came only after years of struggle and reinvention. Bennington relates that it took them nearly 40 label showcases before a record company would sign them. "It's like a cycle, too," Bourdon added. "The more showcases you do, the more you get rejected. It's like, if you're the 21st person to see us, you know the band has been rejected 20 times. It got worse and worse." The fans always knew what the labels refused to hear, and for almost five years the band engineered their sound, refining, reconfiguring, reinventing, and building a national fan base.

Bourdon and Delson first came together in seventh grade at Lindero Canyon Middle

School in the San Fernando Valley, a Los Angeles suburb. As kids, they formed their first band and named it Relative Degree. By all accounts, the group made an inauspicious debut—after writing and rehearsing for a year, they performed one show at The Roxy in West Hollywood—and promptly broke up.

Mike Shinoda's first instrument was the piano, for which he spent a decade studying both classical and jazz techniques. During this formative period he also added the guitar—and rapping—to his repertoire. Shinoda, born to a Japanese father and a Russian mother, was raised in the middle-class San Fernando bastion of Agoura Hills, also home to band members from Hoobastank and Incubus. Shinoda was a classmate of the Bourdon and Delson. His interests were in crafting hip-hop beats for local DJs, so when he joined their musical venture merging two conflicting styles—metal and urban music—it was a strained formula at first. The three persevered, however, and built up a catalog of songs.

Higher Education

After high school, Shinoda studied illustration at the Art Center College of Design in Pasadena, CA, and says that his songwriting is influenced by his visual style. "I went to school for illustration and we would carry sketchbooks with us all the time and were constantly sketching. You'd be on the phone, you'd be sketching. Eat lunch, sketching. Every once in a while you'd sketch something and say, 'I want to develop this idea more.' And so you'd put it on canvas, you'd paint it, you'd work on it some more. That's kind of how working in music works for me. I like to come up with a lot of ideas with the guys and pick ones that are really good." Dave "Phoenix" Farrell and Joseph Hahn, college classmates of Delson and Shinoda respectively, were drafted as additional band members, and the now-complete group adopted the name Xero.

Day Gigs

At the time, Delson was interning at Zomba Music in Los Angeles, working for Jeff Blue. Blue was pursuing publishing deals for Matchbox Twenty and Macy Gray. "I've always had interns working for me," Blue recalls. "When I was at Zomba Music Publishing, I had an intern from UCLA named Brad Delson. He saw me signing Macy Gray and Limp Bizkit. He was a very talkative kid, very self-assured. He told me that he was starting a band and that it was going to be bigger than any of my other bands. He was like a kid brother to me. He gave me some early songs, and I gave him a hard time about them. I went to see his band anyway, the first show they ever did, was really impressed, and offered them a publishing/development deal on the spot. We ended up doing the deal, but I couldn't get the band signed. I went through two bass players and one singer."

Blue takes credit for introducing the band to Chester Bennington. "I was at a music conference and a friend told me about this singer from Phoenix. I was so desperate, I called him up when I was in Texas and told him, 'I'm sending you the music and the original songs and I want you to sing over them.' It was his birthday, and he said he couldn't do it, so I promised him that this band was going to be huge and asked him if he could please do this for me. He actually left his birthday party, went into a local studio at night, sang the tracks and sent them back to me the next day. When I received them at my house, I listened to them, thought they were really good, and told the band that I had found their singer. It took a while. They auditioned a lot of people, but eventually Chester managed to get into the band. I was adamant about Chester being in the band. I was totally convinced, so I flew him out on my own dime. I just knew this was the kid. Obviously, he is one of the most talented vocalists in the music business. He combined with Mike, Brad, Phoenix, Joe, and Rob are just pure talent." (Already a recording veteran, when Bennington was 16, he played in a band called Grey Daze that recorded two albums, *No Sun Today* and *Wake Me*.)

Grey Daze hired an L.A.-based attorney to help send their demos to the major labels, but never succeeded in gaining much interest from the record companies. Chester Bennington's young career was nearly derailed by a severe interest in drugs, but by the time he was in his early 20s he was married and had turned much of his life around. Although they were by no means well-off, he and his wife owned two homes in Arizona and were working in a local real estate market. To learn more about the business world, he sneaked into classes at Arizona State University without paying the required tuition fees. (Unlike the rest of Linkin Park, Bennington doesn't have a college diploma.) And although Grey Daze was but a fading memory, Bennington stayed in touch with his attorney in California. At 23, Bennington later had the opportunity of a lifetime when he heard about the young L.A. band named Xero, who desperately needed a singer.

The band was still testing their commitment to each other, still testing the music. Phoenix left to tour with another band. With college graduation looming for the other group members, the musical future was uncertain. Meanwhile, Bennington left his new wife and new home in Arizona to relocate to Los Angeles. "I had to say, 'Honey, you stay here. Pay all the bills with half the income that we had before and wait for me to tell you when it's cool.' That was really hard, but I knew deep down inside that if we put in the right amount of work and we focused on the music that it was going to work," he recalls.

A new band name, Hybrid Theory, was adopted to explain the band's fusion of metal and hip-hop, and Bennington and Shinoda began writing lyrics together. To showcase the new material, the band played an initial show at the Whiskey A Go-Go nightclub. With the funds advanced to the band from Zomba, Hybrid Theory purchased enough equipment to record an EP worthy of shopping to record labels and selling at shows. After selling only a handful of records, the band invented a more effective outlet for the EPs: they began shipping copies for free to fans they found on the Internet. This following grew into a street team, which they continued to nurture with stickers, samplers, and other handouts. Says Shinoda, "Our street teams and fan base was born and raised on the Internet. It has been a very important part of our evolution."

It was this aggressive approach, coupled with their Zomba affiliation, that impressed Warner Bros. Records. Having passed on the band on three previous occasions, the company finally made an offer to Hybrid Theory in the spring of 2000. "They were like, 'Wow, these guys are doing so many different things that are proactive. They are excited and hungry about playing music and are willing to work at it,'" Phoenix said. "We would actually go down to Warner Bros., five or six of us at a time, and go in and sit in the boardroom at the big table with all the different departments and just talk to everybody about what we were doing and our plans. We would actually bring in letters from our street team of kids that said, 'I like this song so much.'"

They posted MP3 files of their early songs on the site and asked for feedback, Bennington recalls. "We'd invite people from other websites and chat rooms to come check out our stuff, and every once in a while those people would say, 'Hey, when are you guys going to play?' And we'd go to a state close to us like Arizona and play."

"I would assign everyone in the band to go on the Internet and recruit five or six people a day," says the business-minded drummer Bourdon. "We'd go into a Korn chat room and say, 'There this new cool band. Go check out their MP3,' pretending like we weren't in the band." When interested kids emailed asking for more music, the group sent mountains of tapes and instructions to pass them out to anyone with ears. By the time Linkin Park signed with Warner Bros. in November 1999, the group had fans in Scotland, Japan, and Australia and a worldwide 1,000-person unpaid street team. "We had these pockets of fans all over the place. They were small, but they were so dedicated," Shinoda says.

But a name change was in order. An electronica band using the title Hybrid was making waves, so to avoid confusion the group lifted the name of a park in Santa Monica, CA, and changed the name from "Lincoln" to "Linkin," another variation on a theme. It was Bennington's suggestion for the band to take the name of America's most common park, misspell it, and use it as an Internet domain name. "We changed from Hybrid Theory to Linkin Park because of some simple legal issues. We didn't want to get into a big battle over it, so we changed the name. Our Lincoln Park is in Santa Monica, CA. But when we started national touring, everyone thought we were a local band wherever we went, because there are so many Lincoln Parks everywhere. It was basically our band joke: we were local everywhere we went," says Shinoda. But in homage to their original title, they named their label debut, with a cover designed by Mike Shinoda, *Hybrid Theory*. The entire band's outside creative endeavors added power to their vision, and band member Joseph Hahn directed their video to their massive hit single, "In the End." *Hybrid Theory* received three GRAMMY® nominations for Best Rock Album and Best New Artist. A month later, Linkin Park walked away with an award for Best Hard Rock Performance for "Crawling." Eventually, the album was certified eight times platinum.

RECAP: Road to the Dotted Line

LINKIN PARK

- Formed their initial alliance in their early teens
- Grew up in a music capital, Los Angeles
- Had band members interning for major record/publishing labels
- Showcased nearly 40 times for labels
- Enlisted a street team to amplify grassroots support
- Used the Internet to win fans worldwide

LOS LOBOS

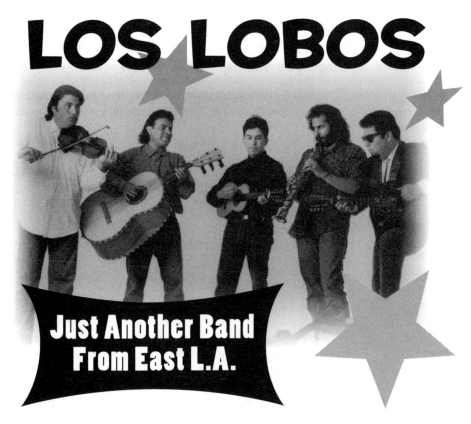

Just Another Band From East L.A.

The terms "longevity" and "rock bands" are rarely found in the same sentence. Sure, The Rolling Stones and Sir Paul continue their age-defying roles, but classic bands usually reunite only for special events or lucrative summer "rake in the bucks" shed tours. Not so for Los Lobos—Louie Pérez, Conrad Lozano, David Hidalgo, Cesar Rosas, and Steve Berlin. For over 30 years, the self-proclaimed "Just Another Band from East L.A." has continued making their cross-cultural music. Melding elements of the classic Brown-Eyed Soul—invented in their neighborhood by Thee Midnighters, Little Willie G, and Tierra— with classic Mexican folk songs, spiced with heavy shots of classic R&B, Los Lobos, despite the prevailing winds of changing tastes, styles, and trends, have continued rocking the house with their rhythmic roots revelations.

"It doesn't seem like 30 years, really," remarks Louis Pérez. "I think a lot of it has to do with

"What it comes down to is friendship. We make music because that's what we were put on this earth to do. It's what we're good at."
—Louie Pérez

the fact that we were friends before we ever put the band together. We more or less grew up together. David and Cesar have known each other since junior high. I've known Conrad since high school. That had a lot to do with it, but there's some mysterious thing that keeps us together. From the very beginning, there was a chemistry that felt right. Whatever that thing is, what we felt from the very beginning, it was something we wanted to hold on to." Eighth-grade plastic shop at Stevenson Junior High, on East L.A.'s main thoroughfare Whittier Boulevard, is where Hidalgo first encountered Rosas. Pérez and Lozano lived a block from each other, but didn't meet until they both attended Garfield High School. Rosas played in a Tower of Power–style horn band. Lozano was in the Chicano Eastside outfit Tierra. The four friends jammed as Los Lobos del Este de Los Angeles (The Wolves of East L.A.), a name derived from the norteño band Los Lobos del Norte. When Lozano began spending more time with Los Lobos, Tierra gave him an ultimatum.

Shared Roots

Los Lobos began to play the Mexican folk music they heard around their parents' homes: corridos, rancheras, norteños. They performed everywhere: restaurants, backyard parties, and quinceañeras. With a repertoire of some 150 traditional songs, they became proficient on the acoustic instruments—bajo sexto, guitarron, jaran requinto, and button accordion. For almost ten years, the band played an informal circuit of weddings and parties around East L.A. The band members attended college in the mid-Seventies at Cal State L.A. and at East L.A. College. It was an era of rising Latino consciousness, so hip young professors used the band to re-introduce Mexican folk music to their peers and to the students. Los Lobos's folkloric outreach was so impressive that PBS taped a special on the group in 1975. Los Lobos recorded their first album in 1978, the independent release *Just Another Band from East L.A.*, which contains classic folk songs such as the Mexican bolero "Sabor a Mí." Mark Guerrero, whose father, Lalo Guerrero is known as the Father of Chicano Music, recalls hearing the band at a house party in the early Eighties. "I remember them playing inside the house while most of the people were outside talking, not realizing that in a short time they would become a famous band."

Punk Power

After a decade of acoustic playing, the band turned to some of their other musical influences, such as Curtis Mayfield, B.B. King, and Jimi Hendrix. At one ongoing gig at an Orange County restaurant, they brought their electric instruments along and shook up the house with a mix of rockers, R&B tunes, and blues covers.

"Our own culture had a hard time with us," Pérez says. "The first time we crossed the L.A. River to play punk-rock clubs, our people didn't know what was going on. We had to get beyond that, because for us the music was liberating." Two momentous events would change the destiny of the local band. In 1980, a group called the .45s canceled their opening slot for John Lydon's Public Image Ltd., the English band fronted by the Sex Pistols' former lead singer, at the Olympic Auditorium in downtown L.A. A friend from another band on the bill, Tito Larriva of the Plugz, recommended Los Lobos for the gig. The punks hated them and they were pelted with everything that wasn't tied down. Pérez recalls, "We were scared shitless. But at the same time there was this rush. We had to do more. We decided to become a mirror of our culture, saying, 'This is who I am.'"

Still, they got their name out there. And at least one audience member was highly intrigued by the abbreviated set: Steve Berlin, a Philadelphia-born saxophonist who would soon be performing with the Downey-based roots-punk band The Blasters, fronted by two brothers, Dave and Phil Alvin from Downey, CA. "Up to that point, aside from John Doe [of seminal L.A. punk band X] and Phil Alvin [from the Blasters], there weren't any great singers in the scene," Berlin explains. "And here's a band with two great singers. The musicality was really the difference. There wasn't anything close to what these guys were doing."

"You couldn't really say there was an 'L.A. Sound' back then, like you could with the Eagles in the Seventies," Berlin says. "I think what it was is that we carried the ethos of that time, the revelation of '79 when it was X and the Blasters and all these other bands coming to fruition. Los Lobos showed up right in the middle of all that. In that era, there was a lot of experimenting going on. You had bands like Wall of Voodoo ("Mexican Radio") that were way ahead of the game doing electronic stuff. A lot of people were taking extreme liberties with everything they could think of musically."

One night at the Country Club, they met Phil Alvin of the Blasters and gave him a five-song tape of music they had recorded in Lozano's garage. "We're from East L.A.," Hidalgo told Alvin. "What part of East L.A.?" Alvin inquired. Then he recognized them from the PBS special. A month later, he called them and asked, "Hey, you wanna open up for us?"

The Blasters were the hottest band in L.A. at the time, doing five nights a week at the revered Whisky A Go-Go nightclub. On January 22, 1982, Los Lobos blew away the packed punk crowd. The guys from the other side of the river were now part of the Hollywood punk scene, where they would share bills with the Germs, X, and the Circle Jerks, even opening for The Clash. Their early champion, Steve Berlin, joined the band as a full-fledged member. He helped Los Lobos secure opening slots at such punk strongholds as the Cathay de Grande, Club Lingerie, Club 88, and the Music Machine.

Slash Stronghold

At the time, L.A.-based Slash Records was the preeminent Los Angeles punk label. As the publisher of the punk magazine *Slash* from 1977 to 1980, Bob Biggs was exposed to a lot of music that wasn't getting the attention he thought it deserved. This led to the founding of Slash Records in 1978. The label began signing the cream of the L.A. scene, which soon enough attracted the attention of Warner Records, beginning a mutually profitable distribution deal that left Biggs in control of his label. It also allowed Warner Records to pick up acts they thought needed the clout of a national label, beginning with the Blasters self-titled first album in 1981. Meanwhile, a Slash subsidiary, Ruby Records, released the debut albums by the Misfits, the Dream Syndicate, and the Gun Club, along with albums by Lydia Lunch, Green on Red, and the Flesh Eaters. Operating under the slogan "small enough to know the score, big enough to settle it," Slash expanded its horizons far beyond L.A., releasing debut albums by the Del Fuegos (from Boston) and the BoDeans (from Wisconsin), along with one-offs by Australia's Hunters & Collectors, English psyched-electrician Robyn Hitchcock, and reggae legend Burning Spear.

Steve Berlin recalls, "Slash signed Los Lobos and a band called Green on Red on the same day. Bob Biggs [president of Slash at the time] said he was more excited about signing Green on Red. He thought Green on Red would be big stars." An EP, *...And a Time to Dance*, was released in 1983. The record ranged from such original rockers as "Let's Say Goodnight" and "How Much Can I Do?" to a prophetic cover of Ritchie Valens's "Come On, Let's Go" and the traditional two-step "Anselma." The latter song put Los Lobos on the national map and in 1984 it received the GRAMMY Award® in the newly-instituted category of Best Mexican/American performance.

Through the mid-Eighties, Los Lobos was recognized as one of L.A.'s most prominent bands. Their Slash albums *How Will the Wolf Survive?* (1984) and *By the Light of the Moon* (1987) chronicle the group melding their traditional and roots-rock influences on original songs such as "Don't Worry Baby," "A Matter of Time," "Will the Wolf Survive?," "One Time One Night," and "River of Fools." Both albums reached the national Top 50 and topped critics' year-end lists. They toured nationally and abroad, and their concerts at L.A.'s Greek Theatre became an annual summertime event that found pierced punkers and tattooed homeboys dancing in the aisles side-by-side.

In 1987, Los Lobos broke through to unprecedented commercial success when director Luis Valdez, founder of the Latino theater troupe El Teatro Campesino and author of the breakthrough East L.A. historical drama *Zoot Suit*, asked the band to supply the soundtrack for *La Bamba*. His feature about the life and tragic death of Ritchie

Valens, the first Chicano rock 'n' roll star, became a box-office smash. The soundtrack album was even huger, selling two million copies. Los Lobos's version of the title track (which Valens himself had adapted from a traditional Mexican *huapango*) reached #1 on the Billboard Hot 100 Singles chart, exceeding Valens's original, which went only as high as #22 in 1958.

Los Lobos believed that their chart-topping status could become an artistic backwater. In 1988, the band returned to the foundations of their music with *La Pistola y el Corazón*, an album of acoustic traditional music. It won the group a second GRAMMY Award®.

Los Lobos has extended the tradition of helping other East L.A. acts such as Quetzal and Ozomatli, offering them opening slots on shows. "That's what it's about, giving opportunities, to help and give a hand," says David Hidalgo. So some 30 years after they started—when most groups are broken-up, broken down, or humping it out and prostituting themselves on the oldies circuit—Los Lobos continues making vital music because, Louie Pérez says, "What it comes down to is friendship. We make music because that's what we were put on this earth to do. It's what we're good at."

RECAP: Road to the Dotted Line

LOS LOBOS

- Met and began performing while still teenagers
- Shared common musical roots
- Made alliances outside their local community
- Opened a show for a major touring artist
- Were signed to a label with a specific demographic

MAROON5

COLORS OF SUCCESS

"You could just sit in a bar and play music for the rest of your life, if that's what you want to do. But by choosing to go into the commercial realm, you have to know and expect a lot of things that come along with it, and be able to choose your battles as far as what things you're willing to fight to the end for and what things aren't that important in the grand scheme of things."

—Ryan Dusick

With their GRAMMY®-nominated debut, Maroon5 ushered their soulful pop and R&B synthesis into whopping airplay and acceptance. *Songs about Jane* was an auspicious entry, but it was a long road for the band, stretching from their high school debut through a failed record deal, a name change, transatlantic relocation, a regrouping, and finally... success.

The mid-Nineties in Los Angeles was an era of post-grunge and eager garage bands. As always, there was a steady stream of aspiring rock stars out in full force any given night of the week, shuffling their gear into the city's bastions of blast-up on the fabled Sunset Strip. Though still in their teens, the members of Kara's Flowers were veterans of the L.A. rock scene who had played their first gig together at the Brentwood Junior High School dance under the name Edible Nuns. In September 1995, the renamed band from West Los Angeles, students at

Brentwood High School, made their West Hollywood debut as Kara's Flowers at the venerable Whiskey A Go-Go with Adam Levine (vocals/guitar), Jesse Carmichael (guitar), Mickey Madden (bass), and Ryan Dusick (drums). By this time, the band was playing entirely original songs. Hundreds of high school kids gathered to see them.

Kara's Flowers recorded a three-song demo at Room 222 Studio in Hollywood. The same night they recorded the demo—which featured the songs "Loving the Small Time," "Future Kid," and "Pantry Queen"—they played a beach party in Malibu. It was that same evening, while jogging on the beach, that independent producer Tommy Allen heard the band playing "Loving the Small Time." Gravitating toward the music, he was captivated by the power and polish of the young band. Tommy and his partner, John Denicola, offered Kara's Flowers the opportunity to record an 11-song debut album. Both producers were industry-connected, so once the songs were mixed and mastered, a strategy was developed to shop the band to the major labels.

Through a continual string of industry showcases in Los Angeles, Kara's Flowers began courting label interest. Management came next, and Atlas Third Rail manager Pat Magnarella signed on to shepherd the band. With this prominent company attached to the band, the ante was raised. Next in was producer/A&R executive Rob Cavallo, who heard the band at a high school gymnasium show and offered to sign them to Reprise Records with Cavallo behind the board. By now, Ryan Dusick had finished high school, but Adam, Jesse, and Mickey were still in their senior year when the band entered the studio. With the band still living a high school life and Cavallo's wife expecting a baby, production of the album was sporadic and eventually took a year to complete. Finally, by the summer of 1997, Kara's Flowers had completed *The Fourth World*. The band and everyone involved was optimistic, Levine recalls. "Especially like when you're 17, you're in high school, you're cocky, and you have people telling you you're going to be huge and giving you a bunch of money and all that. You're like, 'Sweet. Cool. We're going to be famous. Our problems are going to be solved.' By Christmas we were going to be famous. What happened was, by Christmas, the record was in the garbage can."

Flowers of Fortune

Adam, Jesse, and Mickey graduated high school in June 1997 and the band hit the road to support their debut. Despite their well-reviewed shows, their single didn't take off on radio or MTV. Rob Cavallo exited Reprise records, and Kara's Flowers was orphaned at the label. Mickey Madden recalls this period: "We were discouraged because we had tremendously high hopes and we were very young and we thought we were on top of the world. Then when everything fell through, it was an extremely important learning experience for us. It helped us a lot in terms of how we behaved in the future. I think the biggest lesson that we learned from that was to be as personally involved as possible on every level, because if you leave things out of your control completely, it's much harder to keep your foot in. It's important to know everyone at your label who's distributing your record in whatever capacity you can, and just to be active and take things into your own hands and collaborate."

Reprise released them from their contract, and their management company had other priorities. Dusick says, "The music business is different than any other business because when you sign a record contract, it's a negotiation that is one-sided. The money is all on one side and the product is on the other side, which is the art. In most negotiations there's some kind of middle ground, so the balance is a little off in that context. So it's definitely something that—over the years, from the beginning of the recording industry—the artist has had to deal with, being, at times, an unfair balance."

It looked like the end of the band. Levine and Carmichael departed Los Angeles to attend college in New York. For the duo, the East Coast was an invigorating change to their musical approach. The pair wound up at a small college on Long Island, where they soaked up the music and cultural influences of their predominantly African-American neighbors. "It was culture shock in a lot of ways," Levine explained, "but every single morning when you walked down the hall, there was gospel playing, R&B that we'd never even heard before. There was underground stuff. It was when Jay-Z was just getting into the mainstream and we were hearing him for the first time. We were just so sick of being a typical rock 'n' roll band and doing the things a typical rock 'n' roll band does. So, we started to latch on to that, and we wanted to be that. I think there was a lot of audacity about that, just because of the way that we look. And what kind of turned us on was, we thought, 'Maybe we're doing something new.' I was born and raised listening to Simon & Garfunkel and The Beatles and stuff, which was really good for songwriting. But I felt like I needed to look elsewhere for some vocal inspiration." Inspiration came through the sounds of Missy Elliott, Timbaland, the stuttering beats of Rodney Jerkins, and The Neptunes. The two returned to Los Angeles and reunited with Madden and Dusick. They added guitarist James Valentine to flush out the sound.

Renamed and Rocking

Without a label but wiser, the band returned to the local circuit. At a show at the Viper Room, James Diener and Ben Berkman, veterans of the major label circus, offered to sign the band. Three months earlier, they had formed their own label, Octone. It took 18 months to refine the sound and to incorporate the neo-Soul influences into their rock idiom. Madden recalls, "In particular, I think the breakthrough came from embracing hip-hop and R&B, Stevie Wonder and Herbie Hancock, and The Police, and Prince... things like this that were all hugely important influences for us, when we started working in that sphere and aspiring to see what we could learn from those artists." To signify the fresh start, the name Kara's Flowers was abandoned. Says Dusick, "It was very difficult, whenever people asked us the name of our band, for us to say clearly 'Kara's Flowers' and have them understand what we were saying. People would say 'Cars and Flowers,' 'Carlos Flowers,' or 'Carson Flowers.'"

Songs about Jane, the band's debut under their new moniker, was tracked at Rumbo Recorders in Los Angeles with producer Matt Wallace, who had also produced for Train, Blues Traveler, Kyle Riabko, and Third Eye Blind. Most of the material that wound up on Maroon5's debut album was directly inspired by Levine's tumultuous relationship with his ex-girlfriend, Jane. "We were breaking up as the band entered the studio," he explains. "After compiling a song list, we decided to name the album *Songs about Jane* because it felt like the most honest statement we could make with the title."

The band, in their new incarnation, was now being guided by manager Jordan Feldstein of W.F. Leopold Management and the more nurturing environment of a smaller enterprise, Octone Records. "I think the strategy has always been that their record label—Octone Records, who originally signed them in a joint venture with J Records—planned from the beginning to grassroots the band, to sell them on the basis of their live shows, before going to radio," Feldstein told *Pollstar.* "In order to do that, you need to get in front of a certain number of people. That's why they did the Jeep tour [with Sheryl Crow], O.A.R., John Mayer, etc. But the goal was always to bring it back to their live shows, so for every tour they go and do in support, we always attempt to get them back into the clubs to play their own gigs as well. Phase one was almost no radio, so we had to figure out ways to expose them to a wider audience without depending on radio or TV or even press, for that matter. Getting on festivals and packages and supporting, really, was the way we did it."

Looking back on a tumultuous history, Dusick concludes, "Somebody once told us that nobody is ever going to love, or work as hard, or support our band as much as we are. Do you know what I mean? No one's going to love what you do and stand behind you until the end as much as you are. So really, I think the struggle as far as finding people who are going to represent you in any way—whether it's management, a record label, or booking agent—is to find the people that really support you the most of all the options out there, the people who really feel like the project is their project almost as much as it is yours.

Obviously, it will never be as much theirs, but if you can feel like they're invested in it to a very high degree, then that's how much they're going to work for you. I think the thing to remember, though, as any artist trying to get, or getting, a record deal is that you're choosing to put yourself in that context. You could just sit in a bar and play music for the rest of your life, if that's what you want to do. But by choosing to go into the commercial realm, you have to know and expect a lot of things that come along with it, and be able to choose your battles as far as what things you're willing to fight to the end for and what things aren't that important in the grand scheme of things."

The group won the GRAMMY Award® for Best New Artist in 2005, and *Songs about Jane* has gone gold, platinum, and triple platinum.

RECAP: Road to the Dotted Line

MAROON5

- Began performing in high school
- Lived near a major music capital, Los Angeles
- Endured the breakdown of their first label deal
- Reinvented themselves with new musical reference points
- Hooked up with a fledgling record label

Matchbox Twenty

Southern Fire

Wirth a savvy blend of arena-rock and post-grunge attitude, the band Matchbox Twenty slipped into consciousness of the record-buying public as they slipped under the radar of critics and tastemakers. By 1998, one year after its release, the band's debut, *Yourself or Someone Like You*, had sold an astonishing number of copies without ever dominating the charts. Both classic and modern, Matchbox Twenty became one of the most successful bands of its era.

The images of rock bands generally mirror the images of their lead singer. In the case of Rob Thomas, this is undeniably true. An Army brat born on a military base in Germany, Thomas spent most of his child-hood traveling between his mother's house in Florida (his parents had divorced) and his grandmother's place in South Carolina. By all accounts, the stress of movement and general rootlessness spilled over into his schoolwork. He dropped out of high school

"We knew they had great songs, but it was the radio that did it. I would say they were one of the bands that did not have a huge following before they were signed."

—*John Nardichone*

at age 17. Music was the only constant in his life. Settling in Orlando, FL, he fronted a series of local rock bands.

Tabitha's Secret, formed in March 1993, was originally comprised of Rob Thomas (vocals), John Goff (guitar), Jay Stanley (guitar), Brian Yale (bass), and Chris Smith (drums). Six months later, in September, Paul Doucette joined the band as a second percussionist, only to replace Chris Smith a year later, making him the lead percussionist.

Latin Heat

Meanwhile, in Florida, songwriter/producer Matt Serletic was studying music at the University of Miami, playing trombone in various salsa and merengue bands, and acting as a *de facto* producer when the bands ventured into the studio to record. "We would go make these recordings in one or two days. We would take the whole band in there to record five, six, maybe a whole albums' worth of material. Nobody really knew the studio as much as I did by that time, because I spent days and days and days in there. So I ended up producing these records. Some of my first professional productions were salsa/merengue bands in Miami. They would get on the radio in Miami and be hits—and apparently in South America as well, at times. So from that point on, I just loved being in the studio, wanted to be a producer, started to have an idea of what a producer did."

While in college, Matt continued to work with Ed Rollins in the band Collective Soul, going home to Atlanta in the summer to play. This back-and-forth continued right up to the time Matt had his masters' thesis defense. That same day, Atlantic Records offered them a deal and the next day Collective Soul was out on the road. "All throughout college I was coming back and doing the summers. We would play out here in Atlanta and just try and get signed. We had so many close calls. 'We love it. Send four more songs.' So we'd go back in the studio and put out four more songs and we'd send it and they'd say 'We love it. Send four more songs,' never quite getting a deal. We went through that process for years. That went on, Ed was doing it full-time and I was coming back and working with him full-time in the summer, then going to school. We were talking a lot on the phone and half working, but he kept going when I was in Miami. That literally went up to the day of my defense for my masters' thesis. Up to that day we were saying 'Maybe we'll get something happening.' Atlantic Records showed up and offered us a deal and we went out on the road. The day after my masters' defense, I got on the tour bus with Collective Soul and we were off touring."

After six months, Serletic returned to make a second Collective Soul record. He attained Los Angeles management, left the band as a player, and redefined his role as a record producer. Matt's brother,

Dean Serletic, was also in the music business. He was establishing a production company and was impressed with the local band, Tabitha's Secret. He shared this enthusiasm with his brother. Rob Thomas recalls, "We got a call from him and he was like, 'Hey, this is Matt Serletic. I did the Collective Soul records.' We were like, 'Yeah, whatever. Everybody knows somebody.' Then he flew to Orlando and sat down and had a meeting with us—this was with the old band—and then we broke up and we thought we were fucked 'cause we had all of these labels looking at us and it seems like you don't get that far twice. We thought it was over, but luckily it wasn't."

Tabitha's Secret was in realignment. Thomas, Yale, and Doucette parted ways with the other players and added guitarists Adam Gaynor and Kyle Cook. Gaynor had worked at the legendary Criteria Sound in Miami; Cook had been a student at the Atlanta Institute of Music. With Serletic, a knowledgeable song-driven producer and songwriter in his own right, the band recorded a series of demos.

Radio Waves

Radio dialed in. John Nardichone, a radio promo man from Atlantic Records, relates that it was local exposure on the airwaves that led directly to Matchbox Twenty's signing. "Kim Stevens, who does A&R out of Atlanta, signed these guys. He basically listened to their demo and just heard hit after hit after hit. Even though they were green at the time, you want to take a band that writes hits and bring them on board. That was just an instance where a band had been gigging around. To be honest with you, they hadn't been Matchbox Twenty for a long time, and we just took a chance on them. They were a very green band. They had been getting some radio play in the Tampa and Orlando areas."

It was local shows on commercial radio, not *über*-hip college radio, that exposed the band to new audiences. Nardichone says the cumulative effect of having multiple stations made an impact on the record labels. "When you have a guy who works in the South like Kim does—he networks with all the radio programmers that are down there—when you have three major market program directors telling you, 'Hey, this band Matchbox Twenty, we're playing their demo tape and kids are requesting it,' that's how Matchbox Twenty got signed. We knew they had great songs, but it was the radio that did it." Contrary to popular opinion, the band's live following was not a substantial factor. "I would say they were one of the bands that did not have a huge following before they were signed."

Their album was released in October 1996 to little attention, but Matchbox Twenty continued to tour America, cultivating a fan base. They eventually landed their single, "Long Day," on several influential radio stations, which paved the way for their breakthrough hit, "Push." In the spring of 1997, "Push" began climbing to the top of the modern rock charts, thanks to heavy airplay from radio and MTV. By the summer, the single was in the modern rock Top 10, and *Yourself or Someone Like You* had reached the album Top 40 and gone gold.

As it turns out, "Push" was only the beginning of a success story. During the fall of 1997, the record picked up momentum, as "3 a.m." became a bigger hit than "Push," propelling *Yourself or Someone Like You* to multi-platinum status. Early in 1998, the group was named Best New Band by *Rolling Stone*'s annual reader's poll, proof that, even if Matchbox Twenty weren't winning critics, they were winning over a wide, mainstream audience. The band's debut album continued to sell at a steady pace throughout the year as the singles "Real World" and "Back 2 Good" joined "Push" and "3 a.m." as radio favorites. Through it all, Matchbox Twenty stayed on the road, at home and abroad. They did well in foreign territories, including Canada, but they truly connected with Australia, where they went platinum eight times. In neighboring New Zealand, the band went quintuple platinum.

Matchbox Twenty reserved 1999 as the year to record their second album, but they didn't disappear from the spotlight, due to the unexpected success of "Smooth," a Santana song co-written and sung by Rob Thomas. "Smooth" was one of many songs sung by guests on Santana's cameo-studded comeback album *Supernatural*, but it was the one chosen as the lead single. A collaboration with songwriter Itaal Shur, Thomas was connected to the song by his publisher, Even Lamberg at EMI.

Shur was in Brazil when he heard through his manager, Suzanne Hilleary, that Santana was looking for material. "I brought in a whole song with a different lyrics and hook. Pete Ganbarg [Sr. Director A&R at Arista] said, 'I love the track, but the song's a little too sexual,' He hooked me up with Rob Thomas, who actually lived four blocks away from me in Soho. Rob heard the track and came up with the verse, but he didn't have a chorus. In the meantime, I came up with 'Give me the ocean/Give me the moon' which eventually, over six rewrites with Rob, turned into 'Just like the ocean/Under the moon.' We got along famously and we just worked really easily. The first line went through a number of rewrites, all preposition changes. We didn't know who was going to sing it. They thought maybe George Michael, but Rob ended up recording the vocal on the tune."

After some fine-tuning, the demo was created and sent to Clive Davis, who was producing the project. He asked Santana to record it with producer Matt Serletic behind the board. At first, it was only the adult alternative radio stations who started playing it, but very soon the song was everywhere, ultimately becoming the biggest song of the year and *Billboard* magazine's #1 song of the entire rock era. It drove *Supernatural* to multi-platinum sales and several industry awards. Throughout the second half of 1999, "Smooth" was inescapable and its chart-topping position delivered still more attention to Matchbox Twenty. *Yourself or Someone Like You* sold more than ten million copies, which now qualified it for the RIAA's Diamond Award, bestowed on records that have moved over ten million units. Thomas was named BMI's 1999 Pop Songwriter of the Year, for "Smooth" and for his contributions to Matchbox Twenty. Early in 2000, Thomas won three GRAMMYs® for "Smooth"—Song of the Year, Record of the Year, and Best Pop Collaboration with Vocals.

RECAP: Road to the Dotted Line

MATCHBOX TWENTY

- Enlisted a strong lead singer with a powerful image
- Hooked up with a rising producer
- Garnered local radio support
- Developed a fan base through touring only after an album release
- Received more attention after Rob Thomas guested on a GRAMMY®-winning album

THE MATRIX

POP'S POWER PRODUCTION TRIO

"Producers working with artists need to pick that amazing song out of the repertoire, and not just something with a thrashy guitar, because the public wants to hear something that moves them and is emotional."

—Lauren Christy

Lauren Christy, Graham Edwards, and Scott Spock have rocketed into the stratosphere of modern pop. Nominated for a pair of GRAMMY Awards®, including Producers of the Year, their studio wizardry and hook-heavy songs have powered the multi-platinum success of Avril Lavigne ("Complicated," "Sk8R Boy"), the mainstream pop of Hilary Duff ("So Yesterday"), and the artful wordplay of Jason Mraz ("The Remedy").

London-born Lauren Christy is the child of parents who had ties to the entertainment industry. Performing poorly in school, she switched to the Bush Davies Ballet School when she was 11 years old. She remained there until she was 17, when she trained her attention on music rather than dance. She pulled together a band, Pink Ash, and remade herself into Susie Reptile, the leader of the band of seven in which she was the only female. Over the course of a year, she holed up in her room to write and record, using a four-track and some keyboards. She emerged with 15 new compositions and dreamed of a publishing deal. Before the year was over, Christy signed a contract with publisher EMI and was set to begin recording for Polygram Records. She settled in Los Angeles and in 1993 put out her eponymous debut, an effort that is largely auto-biographical. She garnered some success as a songwriter, with credits including the feature films *Batman* and *Great Expectations.*

Graham Edwards, from Aberdeen, Scotland, was a seasoned bass player with a resumé that listed Go West and Mick Jagger. "Through the Eighties and till the early Nineties, I toured with Go West, made their albums, and I used to get calls for sessions," he confirms. "I got fed up with going on the road, being the bass player, being the side guy, so I started writing and did a publishing deal with Virgin."

The Beast with Three Heads

Scott Spock, born in St. Louis, was an accomplished trumpeter turned programmer and remixer who had worked with Diana Ross, Nick Carter (Backstreet Boys), and Chaka Khan. Christy and Edwards, now a couple in real life, had joined artistic forces on previous projects. Spock met Edwards when he remixed tracks from Edwards's group, Dollshead. Spock and Christy had also recorded together. When manager Sandy Roberton suggested that the three co-write and produce one song, it was a radical circle. "We can't believe we've gotten to where we are," marvels Lauren Christy. "It seems like only yesterday Sandy Roberton said, 'I'm going to make you the biggest producers in the world,' and we were like 'Yeah,' and kept our heads down and worked." The Matrix actually came out of a project that didn't succeed, a girl group for whom they wrote songs. "Nothing came of the group," explains Christy. "Then people were saying, 'but the production sounds great,' which was the real lynchpin. We went, 'Let's try something.'"

"Sandy Roberton suggested we come up with a name, because it was hard to constantly describe the three of us," explained Christy. "So we came up with the name The Matrix. The matrix is a name for the womb, or the rock, which everything comes from. Our name wasn't inspired by the movie *The Matrix* [which came out later]."

The Matrix began procuring cuts and projects. One of their first projects was writing and producing a song for Christina Aguilera's Christmas album. They wrote and produced songs for Irish artist Ronan Keating. But their big break was when Roberton hooked them up to collaborate with a new, then-unknown Canadian artist named Avril Lavigne, who had been signed to Arista Records by A&R exec Josh Sarubin. With Lavigne, the trio created mega-hits "Complicated,"

"Sk8R Boy," and "I'm With You." (See more on this collaboration in the profile of Avril Lavigne in this book.)

"Avril was an artist that Sandy had brought to us," said Christy." "We began collaborating in L.A. in June 2001, and the first song we came up with was 'Complicated.' Avril loved it, and Josh Sarubin immediately thought it was a hit. Arista President L.A. Reid freaked out when he heard our first two songs with Avril. We ended up working the whole summer with her. With Avril, we would come up with the initial ideas, and play her the melody and concept," explained Christy. "She would then come up with great melody and lyric ideas. Five of the songs we wrote together made the album, and we finished the album on October 27, 2001, which was Avril's birthday."

The trio has the advantage of being able to create complete tracks. As Edwards notes, "We really don't have to go outside of our team. We like the flavor of certain musicians, but we are self-contained." Christy adds, "Our manager will call and say they need a song at the last minute for a movie, and we'll throw something together in maybe three hours. Sometimes that's what ends up on the radio or in the movie, all of us playing the stuff, doing backing vocals, programming, everything." The Matrix do not make demos since the initial DNA of the production remains in the final mix. Immediacy continues in collaboration: "The Remedy" was written and produced start to finish with Jason Mraz in only six hours.

All three members of The Matrix are in awe of the commitment and vision of their manager, Sandy Roberton. "You can send Sandy an email at three in the morning," says Edwards, "wake up at six, and have a reply." Christy disagrees about the time. "It will be earlier," she avows, "because he goes to the gym at 5:30 a.m. And you'll see him at the Viper Room at 1:00 a.m., checking out acts. From day one, he's had the same enthusiasm he has today, and you can't help but catch it. Whether it's a brand new artist or Ricky Martin, he calls later in the day, 'How did it go? When can I hear it?' It's hard to find someone who will put their name on the line, go in when no one has ever heard of you and say, 'These guys are the shit. You've got to use them.' When we had nothing, he made us feel totally special and successful. I'll always be grateful. Coming from being an artist, doing a record deal, I was going, 'What am I going to do?' He said, 'This is what you're going to do with your career and you'll be brilliant at it. The three of you are going to conquer the world.'"

Scott Spock adds, "The reason we work so well is that all three of us come from different backgrounds. When you have three people in the room who do the same thing or think the same way, by the end of the hour they're already butting heads. We do think a lot alike in certain terms, but our backgrounds are so different that our ideas come from different angles. We constantly inspire each other."

Label Deals

Christy confirms that The Matrix, having been through the artist mill themselves, understand "the record company thing. We know if they're having a bad day, someone saying, 'This is the single.' That can happen. Sometimes we'll spend an hour bitching with the artist about how tough it is. I remember the problems in the system, when people at the label you're attached to are fired."

"I still go out and hear bands at coffee shops," Edwards asserts. "It's amazing the talent that's out there that hasn't had the break." Providing that break is one advantage of their trio's now-potent track record. "Sometimes it's really nice, as producers, not to have things brought to you by the record label," says Lauren Christy. "Then you can find something you believe in and watch it blossom." Keaton Simons, a recent addition to The Matrix production stable, made their acquaintance at a barbecue. "He ran out to his car when he found out what we did and he said, 'Check this stuff.'" Edwards continues, "We took him into Danny Strick at Maverick and had him sing live. They signed him on the spot." Christy acknowledges that Simons has the necessary qualifications for the pop arena: "He's unique, and he looks amazing."

Lauren believes an effective producer has to understand the absolute value of a song. "Strictly as producers, you can make a silk purse out of a sow's ear, but it helps if the foundation is a brilliant song. So producers working with artists need to pick that amazing song out of the repertoire, and not just something with a thrashy guitar, because the public wants to hear something that moves them and is emotional." Edwards relates that setting the creative mood is also a key factor. "We make a connection with the artist. We understand where they're coming from and what they're going through. We have a bond. That's a part of production, too, making someone comfortable in the environment.

Band Aid

With the success of The Matrix, there was a well-publicized announcement that they were planning to record their own project. For two years, The Matrix were holed up in a studio grafting beats for their debut LP, but once the production trio realized that the demands of being a band provided little time to actually make music, they quickly pulled the plug. "There was going to be a Matrix record until we found ourselves standing outside our own studio doing interviews all day and not being able to actually work on anything," Lauren Christy said. "So we decided it would be far more beneficial for us to be behind the scenes and not have to go to radio stations all around the country promoting our album. We were like, 'We're too old for this. Forget it.'"

The Matrix have since returned to production with Britney Spears, Shakira, Ricky Martin, and the band Korn.

RECAP: Road to the Dotted Line

THE MATRIX

- All three first entered the business as performers and writers
- Created a group name to spotlight their identity
- Hooked up with major management
- Brought three diverse sets of influences to the collaboration
- Continue playing and singing, although behind the scenes

JOHN MAYER

Welcome to His Real World

In 2005, John Mayer's song "Daughters" won two GRAMMY Awards®—for Best Song and Best Male Pop Vocal Performance—for the singer/songwriter. His formidable guitar chops notwithstanding, it has been Mayer's attention to songcraft and lyrical detail that has been an overriding factor in his astounding success. Like many young artists, there is a significant backstory to John Mayer. His signing to Aware/Columbia was reward for years of intensive labor.

He seemed to materialize from nowhere, but suddenly he was everywhere—being touted as a favorite new artist by Sir Elton John, joshing with Jay on *The Tonight Show*, posing for a fashion spread in *Rolling Stone*, and selling upwards of 500,000 copies of his Aware/Columbia debut, *Room for Squares*. "I like that kind of entrance," explains Mayer, "There's a certain kind of machismo

"We're artists. We know the effect we want to have."

in 'Who the hell is this?' It's like the moment in the movie when the guy realizes he has super powers."

Schools of Thought

Originally from Connecticut, John Mayer was a kid who fell asleep at night cradling his Stratocaster. He drew inspiration from a deep well of blues—Buddy Guy, Robert Cray, and, most significantly, Stevie Ray Vaughn. By age 15, he was already tearing it up in local blues clubs. As a first year student at Boston's Berklee School of Music, he encountered academic theories of music with decidedly mixed results, most pointedly with regard to songwriting. "I took a lyric-writing class. I got a lot out of it, but I thought a lot of it was bullshit," he says. Mayer feels that if the art of songwriting is subject to rigid rules of gravity and logic, the emotions are destroyed. "I turned in lyrics to songs that I have on my record and there's so much red pen on them you don't know what to do," he states. "Once you learn the protocol for something, it's very difficult to remove it. Then, you start getting into rhyming schemes." He imitates a snooty academician as he mimics, "'I'm sorry John, but your first verse is an AABB and your second verse is an ABAB.'"

Mayer figures that Berklee might have been designed for another type of artist, probably not one who makes records, as he explains, "proprietary to themselves at their own time, their own pace, in their own way. Berklee is for people who are more on the utilitarian side of music, forced to write love songs over lunch." Exactly who is he referring to? "I'm talking about songwriters who sit around with yellow legal pads and say, 'I've got an idea for a song called "If That's Love Calling, Take a Message." What can we do with that?'"

First Takes

Prior to *Room for Squares*, Mayer recorded *Inside Wants Out* which, depending on perspective, was either a demo or an indie release. Mayer's still not sure. "It was a demo that I think was confused with an indie record because it was on a CD and had packaging. You know what? It was an indie record. I always approached it like a demo." Whatever the definition, it was a solo acoustic album with several tracks featuring a full band. It was a vibrant calling card. Soon, Mayer was a regular at a steady string of clubs in his adopted hometown of Atlanta.

He claims that he moved to Atlanta only because he had one really close friend who convinced him to do so. It was a good choice. Although the city has a population of roughly 425,000, it boasts a vibrant club scene, an influx of record labels and studios, and supportive local radio. Recording artists such as Lil Jon, Black Crows, Collective Soul, Indigo Girls, OutKast, and TLC all hail from Atlanta. Producers Dallas Austin, Jermaine Dupri, and Kenneth "Babyface"

Edmonds have homes there, as do transplants Elton John, Sinéad O'Connor, and Public Enemy's Chuck D. Clearly, Atlanta is the New South's emerging music capital.

Acoustic-based Atlanta artist Shawn Mullins was an early John Mayer champion. "Sean was just about putting on his seat belt for his rocket ride when I first moved down to Atlanta. I moved down on a Saturday. On Sunday there was a local music show, and they played 'Lullaby.' I said 'Oh my god, if this is the local talent in Atlanta, I'm getting out of here,'" laughs Mayer.

Mullins is also a label owner with his Atlanta-based imprint, SMG Records. "His label was interested in me and even when we decided that wasn't the best place, he was championing me to Columbia Records. He was really selfless. You'd think a guy who was trying to maintain his ground wouldn't do it for anyone else. He's a rare guy who can. Just the way he handled his success and the way he relates to people. When fans say they like the show and he looks them in the eye, I took a lot from that."

Mayer is a powerful live presence, too. It was his exuberant live performances that sealed the deal. In 2000, Mayer performed at SXSW, the annual music event in Austin, and the labels came courting. Sterling songwriting and musical integrity aside, the 24-year-old Mayer's handsome boy-next-door looks made him instantly identifiable in the video age. Moreover, Mayer is a work horse of a touring artist. Since the release of *Room for Squares*, upwards of 300 shows annually have burned his imprint on a growing live audience.

Constant touring extracts a physical toll. Mayer relates these rigors: "To wake up at six in the morning after doing a show the night before and sing on a morning TV show, you've got to rehearse each song three times. If you're singing two songs, now you've got six songs— actually eight songs—in the morning, including the performance. After that, you go and do radio—another five songs. For every song you sing, there's some jackass who didn't set the levels right. You're into the bridge and you get the international arms waving stop sign. 'Sorry, John, the level's messed up. Let me hear it from the beginning.' It turns your voice to chopped liver." Still, the final time in the day that he sings a song is invariably his favorite, because he shares it with a live audience. "I can play my songs a million times as long as it's in front of a crowd that wants to hear them," he proclaims, "instead of a dented microphone that some guy insists is picking up both the vocals and the guitar."

Finding a Voice
Mayer's confiding vocals are his distinctive trademark, but he explains that finding this voice has been an ongoing process. "At the time of

recording the vocals for *Room for Squares*, I hadn't totally figured out my style," he says. "I finally figured out what makes me sound like me." He concludes that now he thinks his vocals on his debut sound too much like spoken-word. "I was figuring out the nuances. I think I have a lot more projection and I'm a lot more passionate."

He believes that this may be indicative of many first artists' records. "On the first Counting Crows record, the vocals are very placid—like a guy who hadn't gotten onstage yet and felt the energy of six thousand people pulsing at him. The second record is the response of a guy getting off the road, going in front of the microphone and now, instead of the microphone being this thing he's singing into, it's just a thing in the room like a person in the room with a great memory who's going to recite it to everyone."

Adapting his stage techniques to the studio, particularly with regard to the microphone, has been a challenge for Mayer. "Onstage you have an SM58 that you could sing into underwater. You have it up to your lips and it becomes a wind instrument. Then you go into the studio and you have this mega-million-dollar microphone about eight inches away from you with a pop stopper and a little green light—its own power supply—and everyone is saying it's the greatest mic in the world, but you can't get up on it. You have to totally readjust your dynamics. It's like weightlessness."

The solution for Mayer was to sing into another mic placed in close proximity to his lips, one that was not even plugged in. "It took me forever to figure that out," he laughs. "I was nailing vocal takes as soon as we did that, with the dummy mic." But recording vocals is still a chore. "I'm a nut," he claims. "Guitar tracks, I'm a pro, no question. I can pick up the guitar in my sleep. But if I did a vocal today and I went home, I'd still come back tomorrow and go, 'I can do it better.' It's the bane of the vocalist's existence."

In addition to his vocal and six-string contributions in the studio, he also plays keyboard parts—simple, repetitive figures that weave into the sound to create monophonic sub-hooks. "It's become a style on the record, counterpoint melody," Mayer says. But he doesn't consider himself a good musician, let alone a dexterous keyboard player. "I couldn't play on people's records," he confesses, "so I'd stay on these note patterns. Because I was playing on singer/songwriter stuff, most of the music would stay in the same relative key. I could play the same couple of notes and it would work. That's not genius, that's slack. I promise you."

The Song is the Thing
One of the Berklee songwriting theories that Mayer most disagrees with is that if you have two great ideas you shouldn't put both in the

same song. "'Why Georgia' was lifted from a song I did at Berklee. The song was OK, but the chorus was stronger than the verse. I wrote the opening riff and they both plugged together and it was magic," he recalls. Again, it's a process he feels may be indicative of artists in the early stages of their careers. "They have so much time. I listen to artists who take half of a good song and half of another song and put them together. It's time-consuming. I think that's the essence of people saying, 'You have your whole life to write your first record.' I don't think it's about having your whole life, it's about whittling it down."

What Mayer envisions as his main hook may be, in the final draft, only a single line. "That makes the song better," he states. 'My Stupid Mouth' could have been called 'Captain Backfire,' 'Social Casualty,' a whole bunch of things that just exist in the verses. 'Why Georgia' was going to be called 'Quarter Life Crisis.'"

Mayer refers to his technique as composting ideas. "Your best idea becomes a supporting idea. When you have a song full of lyrics and anyone of them could have been the hook idea, that's when you have an interesting song—when your verse isn't just Styrofoam peanuts to package your chorus, because you're so fragile about it."

Mayer's songs reveal themselves only through time, sweat, and polish. "It's really that illusion of sitting down and going 'Here's what I've got to say.' It's not like my fans are in the bathroom watching me do that. It's just native to me. I don't sit down with a pen and paper and spill. And I don't trust people who say, 'I just get so fucking mad and sit down with pen and paper and tell it like it is and when I'm done I have my record.' I think that is so postured it's not even funny," Mayer says passionately. "We're artists. We know the effect we want to have."

RECAP: Road to the Dotted Line

JOHN MAYER

- Began performing live in his early teens
- Realized formal academic music studies weren't for him
- Developed a style in tune with the times and with his own life's development
- Relocated to a city with a vibrant music scene
- Recorded an indie release
- Built an undeniable regional buzz
- Showcased at SXSW

BRIAN McKnight

Soul Sensations

"People say, 'What about voice lessons?' I say, 'Man, I had the best education in the world. I grew up singing in front of people in a church situation and they're very difficult to fool. If it's not coming from your heart, they'll know.'"

Brian McKnight's brilliantly-crafted songs have something for everyone—power, soul, drama, and classic melodies. In a musical era dominated by hip-hop, the continuing, unqualified success of this multi-talented melodic songwriter, vocalist, arranger, and producer is a stunning confirmation of the enduring power of quality pop music.

"With my first two records, I was trying to find out where I fit in—between satisfying the musician in me and really learning how to be a songwriter and then being a singer," says McKnight. "It's tough wearing all those hats all of the time. At the end of the day, if you want to be successful in this business, it's about those things, trying to find the right combination—how I can be satisfied musically, how I can melodically be okay and from a production side, compete against everything else and to write a hit. It's all those things I'm thinking. I finally figured out what the audience wanted from me and what I could do to be satisfied with what I was doing."

Brian McKnight grew up in a family where music came naturally. He was a member of the church choir and his grandfather was the choir director. "The church," he explains, "was Emanuel Temple in Buffalo, where I grew up. I'm the fifth generation of Seventh Day Adventists and the youngest of four brothers. When I was still very small, we formed a gospel quartet. Our models were the great gospel groups, the Swan Silvertones and Mighty Clouds of Joy. The McKnight Brothers were serious singers. The reputation went out, these boys could shout. My big brothers—Claude, Freddie, and Michael—man, they were my heroes. Each was a leader in his own right."

McKnight credits the sacred sounds with teaching him how to sing the truth. "People say, 'What about voice lessons?' I say, 'Man, I had the best education in the world. I grew up singing in front of people in a church situation and they're very difficult to fool. If it's not coming from your heart, they'll know.'"

Outside of the sanctum, they listened to jazz. "Church music thrilled me, but jazz stimulated my mind," says McKnight. He absorbed everything else around him in what's he's described as a "childhood of Platters, Nat Cole, Woody Herman, and Gino Vannelli." He explains, "My brothers loved sophisticated multi-leveled music—they loved Steely Dan, for example—and I inherited that appreciation from the get-go. They'd come home with albums by The Four Freshman and The Hi-Lo's. We'd hear those gorgeous close harmonies and rip them right off the records. I sat down at the piano and taught myself by ear." It wasn't all music, because McKnight was a self-described "sports freak" who had two dreams—playing professional sports and performing professional music.

When McKnight was eight, the family relocated. "We moved from the snow to the sun, from Buffalo to Orlando. The Florida 'burbs were a little rednecky at first, but I was programmed to excel," he recalls. "Obstacles were there to overcome." McKnight continued with his self-taught piano exercises, teaching himself to play jazz piano. With an uncanny ear, he could absorb complex chord changes and improvise. On his own and with his brothers, he discovered the masters, Art Tatum and Oscar Peterson. He was still a jock, running track and playing football and basketball. The accomplished young pianist kept his singing to himself, not yet ready to step out as a vocalist, until he discovered the music of Stevie Wonder. "For me, Stevie is the Michael Jordan of music, a category of his own. *His Original Musicquarium* changed my life. He drew me deep into the tracks. His vocals are almost athletic. I call him a 'hard singer,' someone who can sing gently but has the power and range to do whatever he wants. That's what I wanted, the sound I heard in Michael McDonald, Kenny Loggins, James Ingram, Michael Sembello, Bobby Caldwell—guys with power and the ability to compose pop songs based on superbad jazz chords. I loved that combination."

Higher Powers

Brian followed his older brother Claude to Oakwood, a Christian college in Huntsville, AL. Oakwood is a historically black, liberal arts, four-year co-educational Seventh Day Adventist institution. Founded in 1896, it is recognized nationwide as one of America's premier colleges in the preparation of African-Americans for medical school and health science careers. It has as its fundamental purpose a quality Christian education.

"Claude had formed Take 6," says McKnight, referring to the celebrated gospel group whose trademark harmonies have had a strong impact on contemporary music. "Just when I arrived at school, Claude was heading for Nashville. Take 6 had finally gotten a deal and was about to make their first record. It was 1987." In 1989, during his second year at Oakwood, Brian's college career screeched to a sudden halt when he was caught with a girl in his room. He was dismissed for the infraction. "Mom said, 'Come home now,' but I said, `I'll come home in June... if I don't have a record deal.' So I went to work at Sound Cell, worked day and night, turned out three tunes a day. By the time summer came 'round, I had 65 songs. I couldn't be stopped. I had to convince some record exec that I had the goods."

Studio Chops

Take 6 had been developed at Sound Cell Recording, a local Huntsville studio that represented McKnight's first foray into recording. Doug Smith, the founder of Sound Cell, began signing and developing talent in 1983 and founded Smith Music Group in 1991. At the same time, he began an affiliation as a talent scout for PolyGram Music with the directive and singing power to develop new artists.

Sound Cell was also the home of Brandon Barnes, a gifted staff writer for the company's music publishing division, who became Brian's primary mentor and partner. The two were in the writer's room every day. "The turning point came when I started writing with Brandon Barnes," says McKnight. "He was the man who taught me everything I know about song structure and songwriting. We met when I was at a local mall to pick up a check for a jingle I had done. He happened to be in the writer's room, so I guess it was serendipity that brought us together. Brandon came from a funk-soul background, I was more into jazz. The idea was to send out a demo that would be a springboard to get songs placed. We weren't aiming for a record deal."

By the time Kenny Ortiz from Capitol Records showed the first interest in one of Brian's early demos, the Sound Cell team of writers and musicians was contributing to Brian's career at full speed. The studio walls still display rejection letters on Brian. Once the tape landed on the desks of executives in Los Angeles, Brian was asked to do a couple of live showcases. "They liked that I was self-contained, that I wrote, sang, played. They wanted to do 'development' deals with me, and then Sam Sapp, who worked with Ed Eckstein heard my tape."

Taking Flight with Wing

Ed Eckstein, the son of legendary bandleader Billy Eckstein, signed McKnight to Wing Records (a division of Polygram) in a deal orchestrated by Doug Smith. The process of making his all-important first album took almost three years. "I credit Ed for having the foresight and sticking with me, but at the beginning, it was very frustrating. I wanted a record out! Around the same time I got my deal I got married, so it was difficult because advances from record companies only last so long. When I signed the deal," says McKnight, "I was 19 and arrogant. You couldn't tell me anything, couldn't tell me how to sing or what to write. Man, I knew it all. I had a lot of growing up to do, as a person and artist. Fortunately, Ed was patient."

Until *Brian McKnight*, the debut album that wasn't released until 1992, the record company raised awareness of McKnight within the music business by having him showcase with only voice and piano at key industry events. It worked. The album, a critical and commercial triumph, yielded the smash single "One Last Cry." Brian's production work with Vanessa Williams on her *Comfort Zone* sessions was widely praised. The McKnight/Williams duet, "Love Is," from the soundtrack to *Beverly Hills 90210*, became a Top 5 hit.

Since his debut, Brian McKnight has become emblematic of the smooth, modern-day soul man. His songs have crossed over from R&B to pop and even to country. He believes there is a distinct separation between Brian McKnight the songwriter and Brian McKnight the person. "The hard thing to do is live up to the songs because women think, 'Oh, this is the perfect man. He's so this.' Really, I'm like all the jerks and idiots you know, I just happen to write songs. I think people think I'm sitting around brooding all the time, like I'm just 'Mr. Love Song.' I'm silly. I love to have fun and I really only spend three or four hours a day writing music and being musical. The rest of the day, I'm just living my life, having fun doing my thing."

RECAP: Road to the Dotted Line

BRIAN McKNIGHT

- Had an older brother established in the business
- Dropped out of college to focus on his songwriting craft
- Connected with other writer/producers at a recording facility
- Endured rounds of rejection before garnering label interest
- Incorporated old-school soul and applied a new veneer

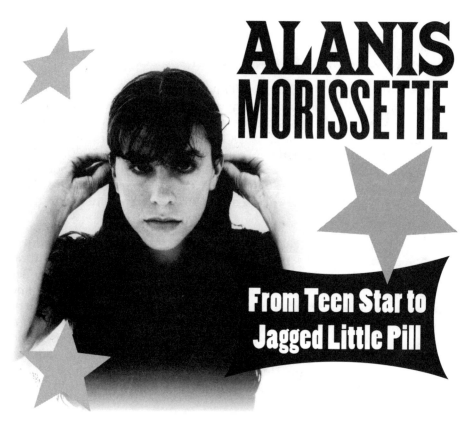

ALANIS MORISSETTE

From Teen Star to Jagged Little Pill

With her incendiary lyrics and raw, explosive voice, Alanis Morissette was an instant sensation when she first exploded onto the international music scene in 1995. Or so it seemed. Only those north of the border were aware that Morissette was a seasoned show business veteran, a former child star on a hit television show. She had recorded a best-selling dance album and had even lost a round in competition on the Eighties U.S. television show *Star Search*, hosted by Ed McMahon.

Such is the anonymity of many of the musicians who are stars in Canada. Artists such as Ian Tyson, Jann Arden, and Barenaked Ladies perform in sold-out shows in Toronto, Montreal, and Calgary, but play small clubs and concert venues—if they perform at all—in the States. This "living next to a giant" mentality has given birth to a growing crop of Canadian artists, intent on overcoming their second-class scenarios. Particulary in Los

"I heard her voice and it seemed to be rich and powerful and full of potential. I predicated everything on that voice, on that incredible instrument."

—Glen Ballard

Angeles, there is a powerful behind-the-scenes network of Canadian musicians, songwriters, and producers.

Born on June 1, 1974, in Ottawa, Ontario to schoolteachers Alan and Georgia Morissette, the young Alanis displayed her precocious love for singing and songwriting at an early age. She auditioned and became a regular on the Canadian children's television show *You Can't Do That on Television*. The program was an on-air staple until 1990. At nine years old, when most kids were navigating the grade school playground, she was writing her first song. With the money saved from her stint on the show, she recorded a debut single, the prophetically-titled "Fate Stay with Me."

Her first step toward a real recording career came in 1987, when local impresario Stephan Klovan visisted the Morissette home to audition the 12-year-old for Ottawa's annual Tulip Festival. Struck with her maturity, strong voice, and sharp creative instincts, he realized she was a potential superstar. Klovan subsequently became her manager, booking her in showcases that included the ill-fated trip to *Star Search*. He paired her with Leslie Howe, an Ottawa pop composer and recording technician whose own band, One to One, had enjoyed Canadian chart success. Howe supplied most of the music, while Alanis added plenty of vocal gusto. They had a hit partnership.

Publisher's Persistence

Morissette had a powerful ally in fellow Canadian John Alexander. It was this relationship that was to be the key to her success. Alexander first met Morissette in 1988, when she was 14, and expressed interest in working with her. Alexander was head of A&R for MCA Records Canada and head of MCA Publishing Canada. A demo tape of the nine-year-old Alanis, sent to him by a disc jockey friend from Ottawa, initially piqued his interest. Although he believed the tape was very promising, marked as it was with Morissette's strong voice and original songs, his first thought from an A&R standpoint was "What am I going to do with a nine-year-old?" So he ended up passing.

Alexander next heard about Morissette five years later, this time through a video sent to him by a producer. He now felt she was ready. Initially, Alexander didn't get the full support that he needed from MCA Records Canada to sign Morissette, so he spoke to Leeds Levy, president of MCA Publishing for North America. He asked if MCA Publishing would sign Morissette to a publishing deal and also help finance her record deal. (This was possible because MCA Publishing had set up an independent label called Hot Mustard Records, distributed by MCA to fund and develop promising new artists.) Levy, too, was a believer in Morissette's talent, and he personally approved and fully supported her signing. As a result, Morissette's album was recorded as a production venture financed by MCA Publishing (via Hot Mustard) and distributed by MCA Records Canada.

Morissette's debut album, *Alanis*, was subsequently released in Canada, and featured the #1 chart single "Too Hot." The album eventually sold 150,000 units. She used only one name at this time to avoid possible confusion with fellow Canadian singer, Alannah Myles. In 1992, Morissette was nominated for three Juno Awards, the Canadian equivalent to the GRAMMY®: Single of the Year, Best Dance Record, and Most Promising Female Vocalist (which she won). In the same year, she released *Now Is the Time*, her follow-up. The album attempted to move Morissette away from her debut album's dance-pop sound, and featured the single "An Emotion Away." It was a futile cause, however, because audiences identified her with bouncy dance tracks. Subsequently, *Now Is the Time* sold less than half the number of copies of her debut album. With her two-album deal with MCA Canada completed, Morissette was without a major-label recording contract. In 1993, she departed her hometown of Ottawa for Toronto, the Canadian musical capital. Living alone for the first time in her life, Morissette met with a bevy of songwriters, but the results frustrated her. A move to Nashville a few months later also proved unfruitful.

In 1991, Alexander was named Vice President of Talent Acquisition, East Coast, for MCA Publishing. He moved to New York and started working with U.S. writers, artists, and producers. A year later, Alexander was promoted to the position of Senior Vice President of A&R, North America. Alanis, following the failure of her second album, began reevaluating her musical and artistic direction. It was also during this period that she was seeking a manager to propel her career upward. Based on a referral by MCA Creative Manager Sherry Orson, Alexander met with Scott Welch. After hearing Morissette's two albums and seeing her videos, Welch told Alexander that he was intrigued by the possibility of working with her. Soon after, Alexander introduced Welch to Alanis and the management link was secured.

Hollywood Dreams

Alanis initiated several new writing collaborations in New York, Toronto, and Vancouver, with Alexander assisting her in this process. Morissette informed Alexander that she planned to come to Los Angeles to write. Enter Glen Ballard, also signed as a songwriter to MCA. Ballard was already established as a top writer/producer in Los Angeles, having produced and co-written hits for Wilson Phillips, Curtis Stigers, and Jack Wagner. He had co-written the classic "Man in the Mirror" for Michael Jackson. Ballard has enjoyed an enduring stint—over two-and-a-half decades—with the Universal Music Publishing Group. "They're the best publishers," he proclaims. "They're responsible for me meeting Alanis Morissette, among many other things throughout my life. There are a handful of the big publishers who perform remarkable services, sustaining creative people, artists waiting to get record deals. I love the fact that Universal steps in an A&R capacity. I'm always interested in what publishers have to say. They're so song-oriented anyway; you rarely get something that doesn't work on a song level."

"When she hooked up with Glen, the songwriting process became very prolific," says Alexander. "Their inspiration and chemistry led to writing many songs and recording them as demos, the better part of which became *Jagged Little Pill*." Morissette recalls, "It was a real collaboration, the ultimate collaboration, the connection that Glen and I had. From a production end of it, he was much more well-versed in so many more things than I was at the time. I think there were elements of who I am as a person, as well as an artist, that really stretched him and we both felt really stretched and propelled forward, so that was a really good connection." Ballard is keenly attuned to vocals, he says. "The connection is always to me to someone's voice first, and through that instrument I'm able hopefully to nourish and enhance their real artistic self. I'm a good listener. When I hear someone's voice, it's a source of great inspiration to me, just the pure voice. Whether it's Michael Jackson or Alanis Morissette, the first step is to listen, and to listen sensitively."

And Glen Ballard listened intently to the sound of Alanis Morissette. "I heard her voice and it seemed to be rich and powerful and full of potential. I predicated everything on that voice, on that incredible instrument, and it didn't take long. We had a cup of tea when we first met, and I knew that she had a lot on her mind and a lot she wanted to express. I just instinctively felt there was some way we could collaborate, to give her the platform to say what she wanted to say. And I certainly tried to encourage the honesty everyone is familiar with now. But for a 19-year-old woman coming to Los Angeles from Canada, the kind of fearlessness with which she was able to express herself was, given that context, even more remarkable. We take it for granted now, her outspoken and fearless explorations of her own life and soul and relationships, but that's hard for a 19-year old in the circumstances in which I've described. So if I did anything well, it was create a sanctuary in which she felt safe in saying what she wanted to say and to help her with the musical and define the musical landscape she felt comfortable to run through."

Ballard—who has since worked with No Doubt, The Dave Matthews Band, and Christina Aguilera—concludes, "I've been lucky enough to fall into it in other instances, but that one taught me just to go with what felt right. When you have someone whose only interest is just to express, not 'Is this a hit or not?' it's liberating, because I'm going to try and make it a hit anyway. I'm always trying to make sure people get it. I choose to be able to communicate rather than something being obscure. If you have to explain a song, you're in trouble, you know?"

The recording of *Jagged Little Pill* was accomplished in 13 days, a testament to the creative chemistry which also involved a third, less high-profile team member, engineer Christopher Fogel. Credited with mixing the majority of the *Jagged Little Pill* album, Fogel was undoubtedly an essential figure in the whole process. As the 28-year-old graduate of Fullsail, the Centre for Recording Arts in Orlando, awkwardly puts it, "The person that was there the next most was me."

"I was brought in piecemeal at the beginning," admits Fogel. "Glen and Alanis wrote everything between them and they'd help each other. It was a very good partnership. Sometimes Alanis would get a lyric at two or three in the morning and they'd lay the track down real quick—just the basics: a loop, a couple of passes of guitar, a vocal—and then I would come in and add any embellishments on top of that. We'd re-do some guitars on occasion, but rarely, because most were done in a single pass and Alanis had grown attached to them. We added real drums to five of the songs, and did organ on all of them. I'd say that on three-quarters of the songs I cut the vocals myself; the other quarter Glen did at the demo stage." To add to the record's authenticity, Flea and Dave Navarro of Red Hot Chili Peppers were drafted into studio action.

One of Morissette's lawyers, Ken Hertz, gave the Morissette and Ballard music to Guy Oseary, a young A&R executive at Maverick Records, a label owned by Madonna. Soon, Oseary and Freddy DeMann, the label president and Madonna's manager, visited Ballard's San Fernando Valley studio to meet with Alanis and hear her sing live. DeMann immediately wanted to sign her. The deal complete, Morissette and Ballard completed recording *Jagged Little Pill.* Everyone involved was quietly confident that the album would be successful, although certainly no one could predict the magnitude of the album's eventual impact. *Jagged Little Pill* ultimately became *Billboard* magazine's Album of the Decade and has now sold nearly 30 million units worldwide.

In 2005, Morissette revisited *Jagged Little Pill,* re-recording an acoustic version of the record with Glen Ballard. Having emerged as one of music's enduring artists, she continues to redefine her artistry as her music influences successive generations of strong female singer/songwriters.

RECAP: Road to the Dotted Line

ALANIS MORISSETTE

- Was a child star in her native Canada
- Used her own earnings to finance her recordings
- Reinvented herself as a dance diva and the preeminent female singer/songwriter
- Moved from her hometown to Toronto, a recording capital, then to Los Angeles
- Made an early ally with a powerful music publisher

Jason MRAZ

Words of Wisdom from Mr. A-Z

"I'm sure every story has been told again and again, but as long as it's told from one person's perspective it will always be unique," begins Jason Mraz. Sure, we've heard it before, but we've never heard it as it sounds when it comes from Jason Mraz. As his song craft blossoms, exuberance and innocence belie a sly lyricism and a sophisticated musicality.

In addition to his skills in spinning tongue-twisting lyrics into best-selling records, Mraz is a commanding, crowd-pleasing performer whose rowdy onstage charm has elevated him from the coffeehouses of San Diego into major concert venues. "Every day is a high point," says Mraz. "I'm amazed I get to do what I do for a living, you know? I definitely practice gratitude."

Remarkably, Mraz has been performing music for less than nine years. Given this short-term musical experience, he is much more comfortable with his vocals than his

"There are certain rules you can follow and certain protocols for the business, but as far as the creative side and just being yourself onstage, everyone is just doing their own thing. There is no right or wrong way to do it."

still-developing instrumental abilities. "When I go into any recording situation, I'm always nervous about my guitar. What I'm confident about doing, and what I've been doing since birth, is talking. And what I've been doing since I began talking was singing. The voice has always been my favorite instrument. It was through my voice and singing that I began giving a shit about writing and reading."

Born and raised in Mechanicsville, VA, Mraz moved to New York City in the mid-Nineties to study at the American Music and Dramatic Academy. "When I graduated from high school, I had this idea that I'd do musical theater. Then I saw how competitive that was. In addition to singing, you had to have a body for the stage and know how to act. When I got out of high school, my only skill was singing. The only way I'd be happy in the world was if I could find a job doing that."

But it was making this musical commitment, Mraz avows, that forced him to focus. "I think coming into songwriting so late in life, the best thing that prepared me for it was my willingness to stay involved and participate everyday in every step of the way. Every day for the past nine years now, I was always playing out in the coffee shops and playing with the other songwriters. I always do well and do my best after working with others. I think it's just an eagerness to stay active."

He says that Mechanicsville is, in many ways, a typical small town. "It's a great place to grow up, and I think because it's such a small town you become quite bored with your surroundings, you're forced to entertain yourself. I was very creative with my video camera, and we had a piano, so I'd always be making up songs there. In Mechanicsville we have a special kind of stew, Brunswick stew, every vegetable and meat. Now, I feel like that's what my music has become, a stew that takes. I still have a special place in my heart for Mechanicsville."

Mraz has described his high school days when he was "that annoying guy" who took part in all the choir and drama productions, befriended his teachers, and spent his Friday nights partying at Skate America. Upping his geek factor considerably, he even attended a local cheerleading camp that, given the female-to-male ratio, was a romantic haven for a young teen with raging hormones.

All Roads Lead West

"With my move to the West Coast I was looking for inspiration and adventure, having lived my whole life on the East Coast. I felt my songs were ready to be performed, but I still wanted to write more songs. What I found in San Diego were a lot of coffee shops and the same audience supporting every artist and artists supporting other artists. It was a real working environment. It was a place I could instantly participate. I bounced around from coffee shop to coffee shop until I eventually made my home in one of them, Java Joe's, sleeping in a booth before I would drive home to L.A. It's a great scene—people who can't play clubs, young people, people who prefer not to join huge audiences and a lot of acoustic musicians. It's pretty fascinating."

During a visit to Las Vegas in 1999, he sang in a hotel room for friends and strangers, among them San Diego's powerful promoter and manager Bill Silva.

What instantly set Jason Mraz apart from most acoustic performers was his willingness to connect with a live audience, to make them a part of his show. "I try to get the crowd involved as much as I can. Sometimes it's just making eye contact or taking a few moments to breathe with them. Sometimes it's taking questions, requests, if I don't know what to play. We do a good amount of getting people singing along. Anything goes. We bring people from the audience and have them make up a song or perform freestyle."

While still a coffeehouse act, Mraz documented his performances with live recordings that he could sell at subsequent gigs, including *Live & Acoustic at Java Joe's*. "I made those as practice because I knew I'd be making an album with Elektra. I thought, 'I can't sign on with a major label and make albums that I expect people to buy,' so I recorded those little albums at Java Joe's. Then I'd go home and fool with the set list, whip up the artwork and have them printed. It was practice for making the real record."

But he wasn't content simply to entertain the folks in San Diego. "My early days of touring were in my little car, my Mazda, and we'd drive till we'd run out of gas. The first major tour was with three of us in a pickup truck driving from San Diego to Seattle so we could play in a parking lot before a Dave Matthews show. We played for free, and still had to hire our own P.A. It cost a lot of money, but it was well worth it. Eventually he invited us to open for him. These were the humble beginnings."

Hard Drives
He built a coast-to-coast legion of loyal fans that followed his comings-and-goings via the Internet. "My online journal became a way to write home, but as I continued, I realized I was writing to more people. Now it's turning into writing to God. When I first got into the coffeehouse scene—back in those days you know everyone who's coming to your shows, and they become your "friend base;" they're not your fans, they're your friends—I would try to get everyone to sign up on my email list and then I'd let them know when my next show was. I'd always add something goofy to it. Then as the years went on, the list got bigger and eventually I couldn't email about every show, so I started to put up my website journal entries. The whole thing was to try and keep in touch with everyone that came to the shows, 'cause they're more friends than anything. But I didn't realize what an impact it was having until our

last tour. We finally were going to cities that we had never been to— Lawrence, KS; never been there in my life—and to have 500 kids show up, all singing the songs that aren't even on the record, old songs, I realized that had been online. They had been communicating. They had been reading about what we had been doing."

The record company Elektra signed Mraz on the strength of his live performance and the power of his draw. Dane Venable, the label's vice president of marketing and artist development, recalls the company's first showcase for Mraz at New York's Mercury Lounge. "We thought there'd be 50 to 75 company people, and that would be it," he said. "When we got to the club, the entire front of the stage was filled with college-age fans who knew every single word to every single song. Where were they from? How did they find out? They were San Diego and Los Angeles college kids who'd seen Jason in California and were back home in New York for the summer. A simple email blast had alerted them to the show and completely shocked us at how loyal his fan base was. From that point, word-of-mouth on Jason's live shows led the way."

"We were never quite eager to get a record deal and do the record-making thing," says Mraz. "I wasn't ready. We figured we would let them come to us and let things happen naturally, and let it feel like a natural evolution. We started talking with labels a good year before we started making decisions on how we were going to make the record. It was a very calm, slow process—very easy for me, 'cause I didn't have to change my life in any way. And I didn't have to cram for any tests. I could take my time learning and accepting these new challenges, so it wasn't one experience that led me to it. It was a gradual process. Careers can disappear just as quickly as they're made, so I'm in no hurry. I just want to do my thing, and whoever wants to get aboard, we'll do it."

Doing more than is expected follows a through-line from concept to completion in many phases of Jason's artistry. "It's not a mantra, but I like to think it's in me somewhere, because of all the drama and musical theater and the great coaches through high school, the people who taught me those things. Also, my dad always encouraged me to be prepared. I think my writing of songs too long, because I can trim them down, is being prepared."

He's described his hometown as a normal middle-American locale, and Mraz seems at peace with both his background and his family. He recently returned to Mechanicsville on career day and spoke to the choir and drama classes at his alma mater. "It was pretty crazy. For the first 20 minutes I was stuttering, then I got into a flow. 'Just be yourself, moron, and tell them how it is.' I don't know if I could see myself teaching down the road. I have this philosophy that everyone out there is making it up as they go. There are certain rules you can follow and certain protocols for the business, but as far as the creative side and just being yourself onstage, everyone is just doing their own thing. There is no right or wrong way to do it."

"What I've found is what makes individuals in the arts is just people being themselves. You're born an individual. Your parents tell you growing up, 'You are you, there's no one like you in the whole world.' Well, then you should carry that through the rest of your life. I see so many acts trying to get started, giving me their demo CDs and telling me what their bands are. Most people tend to think they need to be something that's already out there. 'Sing like this band, sound like this band.' It's just a copy. Just be you. Keep your own name. If you're naturally goofy or you stutter, maybe that's what you're supposed to do."

RECAP: Road to the Dotted Line

JASON MRAZ

- Moved to a city with a built-in college audience
- Built up his crowd through regular coffeehouse performances
- Traveled to perform for free in parking lots at Dave Matthews Band shows
- Made indie CDs and never pursued the major deal
- Built a strong national following via the Internet

THE NEPTUNES

A Tide of Hits

"When we work with an artist, we're like tailors. We try to make the right clothes to fit that person."

—Chad Hugo

In this modern pop universe, powerhouse songwriter/producers have emerged from the shadows of the studios to attain superstar status. One duo that best epitomizes this trend is Pharrell Williams and Chad Hugo, the writing and production team known as The Neptunes. Their hits include Britney Spears's "I'm a Slave 4 U," Nelly's "Hot in Herre," "Frontin" with Jay-Z, Snoop Dogg's and Justin Timberlake's "Signs," Kelis's "Caught Out There," and Toni Braxton's "Hit The Freeway." They were producers for Gwen Stefani's "Hollaback Girl," half of Justin Timberlake's solo debut, and Mariah Carey's return to the top of the charts. The duo recently launched its own label, StarTrak, and has signed and produced Snoop Dogg. Willams performed with the influential rapper on selected tracks.

"When we work with an artist, we're like tailors," says Chad Hugo. "We try to make the right clothes to fit that person. The songwriting dimension in that case is where they're coming from in as far as what they write in their songs and how they want to be perceived by the public. We're like tailors, and at the same time we're like psychologists and psychiatrists. You've got to know where an artist is coming from. You can't just push a sound or your own thoughts on somebody. Once you do that, you can start playing some chords and start vibing. Before you know it, you have a session. Everyone is bouncing off each other. It's like a game of ping-pong that takes place in the studio."

On the Beach

Pharrell Williams and Chad Hugo are based in their hometown of Virginia Beach, VA, a town with a mix of luxury hotels, a glamorous beachfront, Section 8 housing, and grinding poverty all within walking distance. "It's like the backwoods of suburbia, where we grew up," says Hugo. A Filipino-American, his father is a retired Navy officer and his mother a medical technician. He thinks that there is an advantage to growing up in an environment that was not star conscious or a media center. "I think it helped us create our own world in the studio and made us come up with our own shit. If you're stuck in a scene, bands have a certain sound and you could get influenced a lot by what's around you." Pharrell Williams grew up with what he calls "a big melting pot of influences," not listening to any one song style.

Young Chad Hugo saw something on TV that forever changed his life— Stevie Wonder demonstrated a Synclavier on *The Cosby Show*, manipulating the kids' voices with a keyboard. Soon, Hugo was the proud owner of a Casio SK-1, an early sampling keyboard. He relentlessly manipulated the cheap little piece of gear. His eighth-grade science project was to turn two boom boxes into a multitrack recorder. "I'd record into the boom box, put the first track on, and then I'd play it back on my big stereo, put another tape in my boom box and record the big stereo along with me playing along with that," he says. "I was doing 2-track recording when I was 13. That's how I learned how to minimize the sound—have the least number of instruments, but have them do the most that they can. That's kind of what we do now."

The duo first met at a school summer-camp program. Neither was a musical slouch—Hugo held the honor of first-chair saxophone for all-state jazz and Williams played percussion in his high school band. As the two connected, they studied the acts that they considered musical greats—Led Zeppelin; Rush; Earth, Wind & Fire; Parliament; Herbie Hancock; The Beatles. They studied more than the music, examining album covers and photo images. "I was making music for the hell of it, no lyrics or anything, just samples and beats and stuff," remembers Hugo. "When I hooked up with Pharrell, he was actually making songs. He had hooks and rhymes." Williams was also performing. One notable combo was a hip-hop outfit with the catchy moniker Surrounded by Idiots, wherein Williams played behind DJ Timmy Tim, who would eventually be renamed Timbaland.

Fishing with The Neptunes

Hugo and Williams formed their own band, The Neptunes, with Sheldon Haley (aka Shay) and another friend, Mike Etheridge. They entered a talent show where they were discovered by producer Teddy Riley, who had, in Hugo's words, "set up camp across from Pharrell's high school." Riley's Future Recordings and Lil' Man Records were literally a stone's throw away from Princess Anne High School.

In the early Nineties, no producer was hotter than Teddy Riley. He had relocated his recording base to Virginia Beach after considerable gold and platinum success with Guy, various albums with the Jacksons, Bobby Brown, Keith Sweat, and the Winans, all laying the foundations for a style of production dubbed "New Jack Swing." Guy included Riley and brothers Aaron Hall and Damion Hall. In the early Nineties, Guy disbanded and Riley formed Blackstreet with Chauncey Hannibal, Dave Hollister, and Levi Little. The self-titled debut album went platinum. Their second album, *Another Level*, followed suit and spawned the million-seller "No Diggity." Riley heard Pharrell Williams and Chad Hugo in a classic battle-of-the-bands competition. He immediately signed them to a development deal and they began recording. It led the two in another direction completely, to writing and producing.

"At first, we were signed to Teddy Riley as band," says Hugo. "Back then, we would just see what Teddy was doing in the studio, while working on the songs for our band. But one day, Teddy came to us and asked if we had any songs to offer him. That's when Pharrell and I started working together as a production team."

Through Riley, the duo helped out with the first Blackstreet album (Hugo even contributed some saxophone), while Williams also helped write the Wreckx-N-Effect hit "Rump Shaker." From there, the duo started racking up production gigs with SWV, Maxi Priest, MC Lyte, and Noreaga, all eventually leading to Janet Jackson and Mary J. Blige. The Neptunes were on their way.

In 2001, The Neptunes reteamed with Shay as a side project, N.E.R.D. (Nothing Ever Really Dies). Unlike many production projects, this one had legs, spawning hit singles and glowing reviews. (In March 2005, due to difficulties with Virgin Records, the band called it quits, although The Neptunes continue full force.) Pharrell Williams, a guest on the latest Snoop Dogg tracks—dueting and featured in the video of "Drop It Like It's Hot"—is expected to continue as a solo artist.

"If you're really serious, you're going to find different ways out, different avenues," relates Chad Hugo. "That's what we're about. We try to write different types of music for different genres. If you're trying to take that one road, you'll be upsetting yourself. The road to success in the music business isn't all ups. It's ups and downs. You've got to experiment and find the right chemistry—with labels, other song-writers."

In addition to their record label, the duo has launched a line of clothing, Billionaire Boys Club.

RECAP: Road to the Dotted Line

THE NEPTUNES

- Joined forces in their early teens
- Created their own rock entity
- Moved into writing and production under the tutelage of a mentor
- Derived their own sound in tune with modern hip-hop
- Although behind the scenes, created a strong visual identity

NICKELBACK

Canadian Coin

Hanna, Alberta sits in the center of what is described as "Canadian Goose Country." More recently, the town has distinguished itself as the home of the hugely popular hard rockers, Nickelback. Like many bands, Nickelback began as a cover band, Village Idiot, performing locally and regionally. Although the region was great for waterfowl, it held less appeal to the progressive rockers. Chad Kroeger and his brother Mike were both aspiring rock stars, but they didn't play together. As Chad explains, "This has been our first band. When we were growing up, we never jammed together. He would be in his bedroom across the hall jamming on his shit, and I would be in my bedroom jamming on mine. I'd be learning this Metallica song, he'd be learning that Megadeth song. I'd be practicing my scale, he'd be practicing his. But we never really got together because we weren't writing stuff at that time, we were just honing our chops."

Vancouver Movers

Singer/guitarist Chad Kroeger eventually began penning his own songs. With his burgeoning repertoire, he borrowed $4,000 from his stepfather and traveled to Vancouver to record them in a friend's studio. Based on the results, Kroeger's guitarist brother Mike and pal bassist Ryan Vikedal relocated to Vancouver in 1996. "When we got to Vancouver and recorded our first demo, we slept on the engineer's floor for two months. In that situation, you eat a lot of Kraft dinners and try to stay alive. You work any job you can, try not to sell drugs, and just make a go of it," recalls Kroeger.

Kroeger, to support himself and advance his musical career, landed a job where his verbal skills could be honed to a fine edge—selling advertising for a soccer magazine. It was perfect training for what was to come. "I didn't want to work a job for the rest of my life that I was going to hate. So I got this one! Also, I just hate to lose. I view life, and every single time we play a show, as a personal battle, and I want to win them all." But it was tough times at first. "I had to do anything I could to get by," recalls Kroeger. "I walked into a Taco Bell one time and ate half a burrito that was sitting on a table. I was pretty desperate."

Phone Sales Savvy

Nickelback recorded and released their inaugural EP, *Hesher*, and followed with a full-length release, *Curb*. They had not yet signed with a label, but they embarked from Vancouver on bare-bones van tours. Kroeger hammered the phones on his band's behalf and asked his friends to fax and phone radio stations to request Nickelback's single. Vancouver rock station CFOX provided radio support and the group cultivated a grassroots fan base in Vancouver. *The State* sold 10,000 copies without a record label or management. Nickelback embraced the DIY ethic, and kept track of the radio exposure they were getting in each city they traveled through. They often used Kroeger's sales chops to pitch their wares to various record shop owners and to the DJs themselves. The strategy worked, and their music was played often enough for Nickelback to pick up fans on their own. Nickelback eventually tried working with management, but in late 1998 the band decided their managers were unable to bring them to the next level and started managing themselves. "These managers were getting us gigs, but they were charging for ridiculous things—posters that never got made, G.S.T. [goods & service tax in Canada], which they wouldn't submit to the government. It was 20 percent off the top before expenses. We were completely getting screwed around," said Kroeger.

Taking charge, Mike Kroeger handled all the distribution, brother Chad handled all the radio tracking, and Ryan Vikedal handled all the bookings. The group had also invested $30,000 into a new album. *The State* was released independently in January 2000 during a slow rock period when Canadian content requirements were increased and local rock radio began desperately seeking out homegrown product. Cancon is the Canadian law that requires a certain percentage of music played on Canadian radio to be from Canadian bands. It was a tremendous advantage for Nickelback's single, "Leader of Men."

Running the Road

When Ralph James, from Toronto-based The Agency Group, started booking Nickelback, everything finally started falling into place, Kroeger said. "It was Nickelback and Ralph James together that really built Nickelback, because he had the best way to break bands." James put the band on bills with his biggest clients—like Big Sugar, Headstones, 54.40, and Wide Mouth Mason—until Nickelback became a headliner. "The main thing is: the band was willing to do whatever it took. They never complained," recalled James, who was tipped to the band by CFOX's Rob Robson.

Nickelback's breakthrough came in late 1999, when they signed a deal with Roadrunner Records. "I was mailing out our CD, and I did a mailing to a gentleman named Jan Seedman from Los Angeles, who worked for a music publishing company," Peake recalls. Seedman has worked at various companies, including EMI Music Publishing, where he brought Stone Temple Pilots and Filter to the company. He was working as an independent A&R contact for Roadrunner Records. Seedman also has extensive experience in song-plugging, especially to film and television projects, pitching selected catalog from, among others, BMG Music.

"He couldn't do anything for a record deal specifically, but he sent our music to his buddy Ron Burman at Roadrunner, who came out and saw us play," says Peake. It was the song "How You Remind Me" that impressed Burman. "When Chad sent me the demo, I was like, 'What a huge smash!'" remembers Burman. "I actually got chills when I first heard it. It's just such a catchy and memorable tune. Roadrunner had never previously had a commercial crossover song like this before, so we didn't quite grasp the worldwide scope of it. It really sunk in when I looked at the *Billboard* International Chart and saw us in the Top 10 in eight different countries."

Continuing to tour the rest of 1999 in Canada, where the record was immediately re-released with new artwork, the band released the album in the U.S. at the beginning of 2000 and started over from scratch. By then, Nickelback had signed on with Union Entertainment's Bryan Coleman—"one of the most trustworthy people on the planet," according to Kroeger—for management and Steve Kaul at The Agency Group (U.S.).

"Essentially, what we did with Nickelback here in the U.S. was as soon as the first single came out, we had them on the road supporting as many different bands as possible," Kaul explained. "In between each of these tours with Sevendust and 3 Doors Down, we had them do headline shows in markets where they were getting some radio airplay, trying to keep them working."

Although Roadrunner is a label with international distribution, they had nowhere near the clout of the major conglomerates. But Chad Kroeger thinks that if the band had inked a deal with a major label, they probably would have been swept under the carpet. "In our first week of sales, we probably sold 1,000 copies of *The State*," says Kroeger. "In the first eight weeks on a major, if you're not selling upward of 15,000 records a week, you're going to get dropped. Roadrunner just kept plugging away and putting money into us."

Roadrunner re-released *The State*, and the band's fortunes advanced dramatically. It eventually sold an impressive 500,000 copies. Nickelback became the first Canadian group since The Guess Who to have a #1 single—Kroeger's "How You Remind Me"—in Canada and America at the same time.

Although Vancouver remains the band's creative center, Chad Kroeger, who has stated that his band's music is defiantly blue-collar, relates that he is not that tuned in to the city's artsy mien. "I don't know what the creative culture is like in Vancouver, I only know what it's like when we're recording. The mornings are filled with Bailey's-and-coffees, the afternoons are filled with sushi and Coronas, and the evenings are filled with bong hits and loud guitars and away we go."

Kroeger confesses that the band knew they'd conquered the States when they appeared live on *The American Music Awards*. "These are your peers, those people in the audience. Those are the hardest critics everywhere, the same people who do the same thing every single night. We brought the explosions and pyro, and when we got finished playing, with all the explosions and the fireworks, everyone stood up and gave us a standing ovation. I just could not believe it. Rappers, country artists, rock artists, everyone was there and everyone got out of their seat and was giving this massive applause to Nickelback. You literally could not kick the grin off of my face."

RECAP: Road to the Dotted Line

NICKELBACK

- Moved to a Vancouver, a recording capital
- Used phone sales to promote themselves
- Used the DIY approach to touring and recording
- Signed to an indie, not to a major

NO DOUBT

Pizza to Platinum

"It would take an act of God for this band to get on the radio."

—KROQ program director

Television viewers can marvel at the weekly exploits of a well-to-do tribe of affluent teens who cavort under the golden sun, on pristine beaches, beneath verdant palm trees, and populate the hit show *The O.C.* It's a glorified scene of California's promised land, Orange County, a region so named for the abundant fruit that once one grew in opulent groves and offered a free taste of sweetness and promise to all who came. No more. The orange groves are mostly gone now, bulldozed to make way for miles of tract homes, sprawling industrial parks, monolithic office buildings, and a faceless, anonymous suburbia. Once a bastion of California's extreme right—and white—wing, Orange County is an increasingly multi-ethnic pantheon, from the Latino town of Santa Ana to the Vietnamese enclave of Westminster.

The progeny of the white middle class are vast hordes of teens, disaffected children who rebel with skateboards, misogynistic t-shirts, shining surfboards, loaded bongs. There is a fertile breeding ground for music to mirror this resolute disaffection—violent, ear-searing punk and a soundtrack for endless partying, Ska. No Doubt is a perfect musical product of this environment, a high-profile chart-topping band led by a glamorous, platinum-blonde goddess of a vocalist, Gwen Stefani. Her lustrous demeanor masks stories of suicide, a broken romance between two band members, and an almost-15-year history of struggle.

Family Focus

As a young teenager, Gwen Stefani, whose musical tastes were mainly attuned to *The Sound of Music*, agreed to sing lead vocals on her older brother Eric Stefani's first song, "Stick It in the Hole," written about a pencil sharpener. No Doubt's future bassist, Tony Kanal, born and raised in England, relocated to Southern California at age 11 and joined his high-school jazz band as the bass player in tenth grade. In the ninth grade, drummer Adrian Young attempted to drum to "Bend Over" by O.C. band Doggy Style at a school talent contest; his parents bought him a kit when he was 18. Just down the 405 freeway from Anaheim, in Irvine, young Tom Dumont dreamed of being a rock star and spent endless hours practicing guitar.

In the Stefani family, Eric was the guide, and Gwen the hesitant follower. Eric was particularly enthralled by the high-energy antics of Madness, the English Ska band, in the early Eighties. This group became Gwen's favorite as well. When Eric began writing and playing music influenced by the genre, Gwen became a performer, too. "He used to force me to sing stuff," she recalled. "He'd beg me, 'Please sing this.'" In 1987, the Stefanis formed the band No Doubt, with Gwen trading vocals with John Spence, a classmate from Loara High School in Anaheim and a co-worker of the Stefani siblings at the local Dairy Queen. More a barker than a singer, he brought a gymnastic energy to the shows and gave the band its name—"No Doubt," his pet phrase.

After several raucous party performances, No Doubt played its first official gig at Fender's Ballroom in Long Beach, California. The band was second on a bill of 14, with The Untouchables headlining. Tony Kanal, a high-school junior, was one of several hundred people watching. Shortly thereafter, he auditioned for the band. By the summer, Tony, an organized perfectionist, became not only their bass player, but also the band's unofficial manager.

"Gwen Stefani worshipped Madness in high school," says Kanal. "She was a full-on nutty girl. Her brother Eric was big on soundtracks. Adrian Young grew up on Seventies rock like Hendrix, Journey, Steely Dan. Tom Dumont was a big KISS fan who then got into Black Sabbath, Judas Priest, and all those heavy metal and Brit rock outfits. For me,

Prince was the first major musical thing. So I guess when you take all that, we're bound to produce an open-ended sound. None of us would want it any other way. You know, just one sound would be so limiting and boring. But for a long time, it didn't work in our favor. While record companies were running around signing up everybody that could play a note in Orange County, we were totally overlooked. Even the press overlooked us. It got frustrating. We'd be sitting there reading these articles about the Orange County scene and there'd be all these bands and no No Doubt. No matter how well we were doing, how big the vibe was on us, how many shows we played, we were just overlooked."

Then, Spence killed himself just before Christmas 1987, apparently overwhelmed by family problems. The band carried on, but Gwen had qualms about being out front on her own. "We were scared we would lose the hard edge without a male foil," she recalled, so one of the horn players moved into Spence's slot. When he left in 1989, Gwen was ready to fly solo as a vocalist, and drummer Adrian Young and guitarist Tom Dumont were drafted into the band.

The band's musical diversity was both a selling point and a distraction, says Kanal. "For so many years you have these record companies telling you 'You've gotta focus, you've gotta focus.' You've gotta have all the songs sounding the same and then you overcome that shit and people are running round telling you how good it is that you have such a broad range of sounds and that the songs are so different. And we've always been that."

Without a manager, a record company, or even a self-financed release, No Doubt somehow managed to lay the foundation for a lasting career as part of a thriving Ska scene that included Fishbone and The Untouchables. The band cultivated a following at area colleges. Promoters at Goldenvoice and Avalon Attractions liked the members' positive attitude and work ethic. They offered No Doubt opening-act slots at such major venues as Irvine Meadows and Anaheim's Celebrity Theatre. While opening shows for the Red Hot Chili Peppers, Ziggy Marley, and Mano Negra, their fan base broadened to the college crowd. Pizza mailing list parties become the modus operandi as the band's fan list, which they started in 1987, grew to include thousands of names, eventually reaching a database of 7,000 names in 1993.

Buoyed by their huge fan base and increasing visibility, No Doubt attracted the attention of Interscope Records and signed a minimal deal. Although Interscope head honcho Jimmy Iovine predicted Gwen would be a star in five years, the label was characteristically miserly, offering a minimal outlay of money as an advance, and certainly not enough for the band to live on. They continued driving around O.C. in their same old cars and working day jobs—Gwen and Tony as department store salespeople, Adrian as a steakhouse waiter, and Tom running a small music equipment rental business. They also pursued higher education, with Gwen studying art at a local college.

Recorded for only $13,000, their eponymous debut appeared at the height of grunge, sold a measly 30,000 copies, and couldn't get the band played on local radio. Adrian remembers the program director for L.A. powerhouse KROQ saying, "It would take an act of God for this band to get on the radio." In support of No Doubt, the band embarked on its first two-week, 13-show, Western-state headlining tour in two vans (five members, a three-piece horn section, a roadie, tour manager/soundman and equipment). A video for the single "Trapped in the Box" was created for a mere $5,000, but MTV never played it. Relentlessly, No Doubt once again made a two-week Western run. Finally, in the fall of 1992, they undertook a two-and-a-half month national tour, albeit still in vans. Although predominantly headlining small clubs, they also increased their fan base by opening shows for Public Enemy, Pato Banton, and The Special Beat.

Still, it felt as if the band was treading water. As No Doubt's primary songwriter, the bulk of indifference and rejection fell on Eric Stefani. His involvement ebbed as Gwen, Dumont, and Kanal filled in, writing much of No Doubt's catchiest stuff. Gwen's lyrics focused on another casualty of band life, her long-standing romance with Kanal. Eric, already thrown by the changing band dynamic, knew he had to quit when he awoke from a terrible nightmare, looked out his window and saw five crows on a telephone wire, four together, the other apart. "I looked back and one had flown," he recalled. "That was a sign from God. It was telling me something about what I had to do to survive in this life." He had other creative outlets, including his job as an animator for the hit Fox television show, *The Simpsons*. Since local fans were craving new music, No Doubt self-released the ten-song *Beacon Street Collection*, named after the house on Beacon Street in Anaheim that housed several band members and the garage studio where most of the tracks were recorded. They sold the first thousand CDs within two weeks. Laying the groundwork for *Tragic Kingdom*, No Doubt played the main stage on the first Warped Tour. A few months later, executives at Trauma Records, an Interscope affiliate, heard No Doubt's nearly-completed album and loved it.

Ironically, *Tragic Kingdom* was crafted with very personal songs, lyrics penned by Gwen about her romance and subsequent break-up with bandmate Tony Kanal. "I think there were times when it was really painful for us. When Tony and I split up and I wrote the lyrics of that record, *Tragic Kingdom*, that record wasn't going to be heard by anyone. It took three years to make that record. Sixty songs later—we were on a different label at a certain point—who would think that album would come out, let alone sell 16 million copies about our life?

It was crazy that it happened. We were really open about it, because we didn't know any better. We really used our sense of humor to get through it, but it really was painful. I think we have a few regrets about being very touchable about our relationship, and we learned about that. But I think that also it is a weird situation where you got, like, two-and-a-half-years' touring with that album and two-and-a-half-years of sitting in a room and people picking at our wounds."

In December 1996, *Tragic Kingdom* reached #1 on the *Billboard* Pop Album chart, a peak no other Orange County act had attained. It stayed there for nine of the next ten weeks. U.S. sales eventually passed seven million. No Doubt has achieved whopping success, and Gwen Stefani, a pop icon, has delivered her first solo record.

RECAP: Road to the Dotted Line

NO DOUBT

- Opened shows for major artists
- Developed their own mailing list and promotional plan
- Toured regionally to develop a fan base
- Were together almost 15 years before achieving a breakthrough

OutKast

The Player and the Poet

With the GRAMMY®-winning success of the Atlanta-based duo OutKast, modern pop audiences have marveled at the flamboyant style and edgy musical eclecticism that seemed to explode out of nowhere. Guess again. As fans of hip-hop were well aware, the phenomenon that is OutKast was well over a decade in the making and, tellingly, the duo's success mirrors the rise of Atlanta, GA as the new capital of Southern music.

There is a syndrome in pop music that virtually everything of value comes from a specific "scene," like London, Liverpool, and San Francisco in the Sixties, New York in the Seventies. Successful recording artists have to either go where it is—New York, Nashville, Los Angeles—or make it happen where they are. And with the decentralization of the might of major record labels, unlikely capitals have sprung up—from Seattle, WA to Asheville, NC.

"Once you start getting preachy, that's when you start being like an overbearing parent. We're just giving you everyday life, how we see it."

—Antwan Patton (Big Boi)

Andre Benjamin (Andre 3000) and Antwan Patton (Big Boi) point to a friendship goes back to the early Ninties, where both attended a school for Tri-Cities School for the Performing Arts in the East Point area. A single child, Benjamin lived with his mother for most of his early life, eventually moving in with his father at 15. In contrast, Antwan Patton lived with several brothers and sisters in Savannah before moving to Atlanta as a teenager. The two quickly connected around a shared sense of art and fashion. As Benjamin says, "The name OutKast started out just because being from Atlanta, there's more bass music and I guess what they would call Gangsta Bounce music, and we were doing hip-hop. When we were in high school, the people we looked up to were De La Soul and NWA, which was Gangsta music, but I loved the music that Dr. Dre was doing. We were into more and more hip-hop, but a lot of people from our school and our neighborhood didn't listen to A Tribe Called Quest, De La Soul, or Das EFX or anything like that. So we became outcasts from there. But as we got into it, we really started living up to the name. The music started being different, the look started being different, so it just sort of became a natural progression."

Pundits in the Projects
Benjamin dropped out of high school during the tenth grade. While Patton received his diploma, they continued to rap together. Dre recalls, "At the school we went to—it was the school right up the street from the projects—peoples' tastes in music really weren't that wide. They only listened to local acts and booty-shake music. We were kind of the in-crowd, in that we knew good music. So what Big Boi and I would do was go to the Five Points Flea Market and buy Ron G tapes. Ron G was a famous DJ in New York and he would make mix tapes, so it was a thing for us to go and buy these tapes to know what the new beats were."

"We were listening to Tribe Called Quest, Poor Righteous Teachers, KMD, Leaders of the New School," echoes Big Boi. "We were like some preps, dressing in a style that really wasn't going on in Atlanta, wearing all the stuff Grand Puba talked about in his raps. One day we were sitting at my auntie's house, and I knew Dre had some rhymes, and I had some, so we just started picking up where the other ended, every four or six bars. After a while what would happen is we'd just walk around the kitchen table, rhyming our rhymes, practicing to go to the club."

The Duo Hits the Stage
Originally called 2 Shades Deep, Big Boi and Dre decided to change their name because of an R&B group coming up called Four Shades Deep. Had it not been for Glenn Danzig and company, Big Boi and Dre may have ended up Misfits, because they were searching for a word that reflected the fact that their styles deviated wildly from the norm. They made their public debut at Club Fritz, in Atlanta's West End.

"We'd hitch a ride with one of our homeboys, hope they had an open-mic night so we could get it on," Big Boi recalls. "At Club Fritz they had only one Korg mic, with a short-ass cord, so we'd pass it back and forth, trying to catch the other's word and pass the mic."

It was that uninterrupted flow that first gained OutKast attention. To "audition" for Rico Wade of production collective Organized Noize, Big Boi and Dre put the instrumental of A Tribe Called Quest's "Scenario" in the Isuzu Trooper of Goodie Mob member Big Gipp, who they had just met. They rhymed back-and-forth for seven minutes straight in the street outside Lamonte's Beauty Supply, unaware of hip-hop conventions such as hooks and choruses.

Wade later invited the duo back to The Dungeon, the studio in the unfinished basement beneath his house, where Organized Noize—Wade, Ray Murray, and Patrick "Sleepy" Brown—developed the beats that became OutKast's first album. *Southernplayalisticadillacmuzik* (1994) introduced the sound that set 'Kast apart from the coasts.

"Ray from Organized Noize taught me how to rap," Big Boi admits. "I was a writer and he just showed me things about being an MC. It was more mental than it was showing me specific things. We call him the Yoda." Jermaine Dupri, a young songwriter/producer who discovered the duo Kriss Kross rapping at the local mall and turned them into superstars, exemplifies the entrepreneurial spirit of Atlanta. Organized Noize similarly made a name for itself after producing TLC's mammoth hit song "Waterfalls" in 1994. They later worked on several rap and R&B hits—including Curtis Mayfield's comeback LP, *New World Order*, TLC's *Crazysexycool*, and Goodie Mob's debut, *Soul Food*—as well as their own side project, Society of Soul's *Brainchild*. The close relationship led many to believe that OutKast's success was due to Organized Noize's production genius, a misconception the former would soon dispel.

Along with Organized Noize and the Goodie Mob, the Dungeon Family grew to include like-minded artists such as Witchdocktor (*A S.W.A.T. Healing Ritual*), and Cool Breeze (*East Point's Greatest Hit*). The duo also contributed to several soundtracks, notably "In Due Time" for *Soul Food* and "Benz or Beamer" for *New Jersey Drive*.

A list of recording artists over the years have called Georgia home—Ray Charles, Johnny Mercer, Otis Redding, Ray Stevens, James Brown, and Gladys Knight, to name just a few. Elton John and John Mayer are two more recent additions to the city's roster of hit makers. LaFace Records—the result of an agreement that Clive Davis, then-president of Arista Records, signed with Antonio "L.A." Reid and Kenneth "Babyface" Edmonds in 1989—marked the arrival of a major label in town. It sparked a growth of support businesses—photographers, production companies, artist managers, promoters—that sprang up in the shadow of LaFace. When the record company left Georgia in early 2000, most of the offshoots stayed. So So Def Recordings, Hitco Music Publishing, Dallas Austin Recording Projects, Silent Partner Productions, and Sony Music ATV also established home offices in Atlanta during the Nineties.

Organized Noise had a direct connection with LaFace Records. The duo invited OutKast to add a track to *A LaFace Family Christmas*, released in November 1993. In retrospect, the song they included, "Player's Ball," was a strange choice for a seasonal release, leaning on references to hustling and dope dealing, themes far-removed from OutKast's later GRAMMY®-winning themes.

Southernplayalisticadillacmuzik spawned two hit singles, the title track and "Get Up and Get Out." It went platinum later that year. The contrast between "Player's Ball" and the motivational anthem "Get Up and Get Out" became a hallmark for OutKast. Ever since, the group has tried to strike a careful balance between positive messages and street-oriented stories. As Big Boi explained to *Vibe*, "Once you start getting preachy, that's when you start being like an overbearing parent. We're just giving you everyday life, how we see it."

"We did some 30-odd songs," Andre says of the recording process. "We cut it down to a tight 13 or 14 cuts, some of our tightest rhymes and beats. We got Goodie Mob on the album. I mean, it's just a whole collaboration between Organized Noize, OutKast, and the whole family." Outkast's second album, *ATLiens*, did even better than the first, selling 1.5 million copies and launching another gold single, "Elevators (Me and You)." In 1998, Outkast released its third opus, the double-platinum *Aquemini*, which became its most successful album yet. Debuting at #2 on the *Billboard* charts, it received acclaim from music critics and fans alike, satiating the alternative audience who bought *ATLiens* as well as the hardcore fans who first discovered them. Finally, with *Speakerboxx: The Love Below*, they broke through to mainstream success.

RECAP: Road to the Dotted Line

OUTKAST

- Met and began performing together in high school
- Had access to a music scene that was both local and national
- Hooked up with local producers
- Landed one song on a holiday compilation
- Satisfied an initial, loyal audience while moving toward the mainstream

Ozomatli

SHARP HORNS

Far from the city's glittering, trendy Westside, there is another Los Angeles. It stretches across low hills and past squat stucco shops with hand-lettered signs—taco stands, tire repair and car upholstery shops, beauty parlors, nail salons, and fortune-telling dens. This is Ozomatli territory. Named for the Aztec God of dance, Ozomatli is a ferocious, politicized fusion of salsa, reggae, jazz, rap, and funk. First coming to national prominence on the Warped Tour, the group came to international attention while opening for Carlos Santana on his triumphant comeback tour. Their *Street Signs* album won the band a GRAMMY Award®.

Ozomatli was originally created to perform exclusively at social-action benefits, says vocalist Wil-Dog Abers. "Ozomatli started April Fool's Day 1995, basically to raise money for a community center that we started in Los Angeles called The Peace and Justice Center. The center was dedicated to

"It doesn't matter how much you practice at home, because playing at the gig and playing at home are two completely different things."

—Asdru Sierra

creating awareness around arts with inner-city youths. There are no places in inner city Los Angeles for kids to go after school and on weekends, so we were trying to provide that. Every weekend we had a party or a benefit and that's where the band got together. We just called each other and said, "Come down and jam for this center to raise money for art supplies." We bought wood for skateboard ramps, spray paint for graffiti art—we spray painted the whole building— musician instruments, and that's how we came together. We played there every week for about six months." Word spread and soon kids were appearing on the Los Angeles streets with Ozo tattoos. "We represent all the ghettos of L.A." became the band's motto.

Ozo was part of a thriving scene that included other bands—Aztlán Underground, Blues Experiment, Lysa Flores, Ollin, Quetzal, Quinto Sol, Slowrider, and Yeska—along with visual artists, activists, and of course, audiences. The band members raised their visibility playing for free for fundraisers for various non-profit groups. This popularity resulted in steady paid gigs at two popular Hollywood nightclubs, Opium Den and Dragonfly. The success of Ozomatli's live shows brought about their first self-produced recording, which sold over 14,000 copies in the L.A. area.

Their incendiary live shows turned into sold-out block parties and Almo Sounds, founded by Herb Alpert and Jerry Moss, signed the band. A&R exec Andy Olyphant recalls that the band was signed on the strength of their live show. Their self-titled debut sold upwards of 100,000 copies on the basis of fervent press, relentless touring, and word-of-mouth, with virtually no radio airplay. (Almo was folded into Interscope Records, and Ozomatli now records for the venerable jazz label Concord Records.)

First Course: Salsa

Asdru Sierra, a founding member of the band, plays trumpet. "I was trying to get away from singing. My dad was really hard on me. I was one of the little kids who used to sing and my dad would say 'Oh, he's a prodigy?' I'd say 'Oh, no. Leave me alone.' I went to seventh grade at Irving Junior High School and a teacher there encouraged me to play trumpet. I wanted to play trombone because it was big and I always listened to all of those Willie Colon records and that's trombone right there."

"For a time I was a used-car salesman, but it was hard paying the bills. Then there was a time when I was doing good, gigging, but then the phone stopped ringing. It happens to everybody. I played the salsa circuit in L.A. Salsa became hip in the clubs, but then people just started hiring DJs."

"When I was 16, I played in a *cumbaia* and we had after-show gigs from 8 p.m. until 4:30 a.m. I had a pretty big mouthpiece, but I had to get a shallow one. If you're going to play seven 45-minute sets and you're playing salsa and you're the only trumpet player *and* you're playing lead all night, that's when you find that plateau."

Class in Pasadena

Education has been key to the band's musical development. Sierra explains, "One of the main influences on the band is a professor, Bobby Bradford, at Pasadena City College. Even though he's a cornet player, he was one of the biggest influences on all of us. We all, in one way or another, floated through PCC and Bobby has such a rich musical background it was like finding a jewel, real jazz history. He was there. He played with Ornette Coleman. He was definitely the one who gave me a real concept of what improvisation was. It was like 'Study this! Listen to this!' He really focused on us and gave us a lot of love. We were hyped on learning. I would follow him around and ask him questions and he got off on us loving the tradition, loving the heritage, loving where it came from, listening to the old records that no one listens to anymore and only he has."

"Bobby would tell us, 'Most of you are fresh out from high school and I want you to wake up and know you don't know shit.' Some of us were 'Hey, I won all these awards in high school,' and he's like, 'But you don't know shit.' And that's the attitude he needed to convey, otherwise we weren't going to learn anything."

"They were all very talented," recalls Bradford. "Espinoza was really a live wire, full of energy and curiosity. What they hadn't had before was someone in my age group who had grown up playing in high school, and was then playing bebop with Charlie Parker and Dizzy Gillespie and the Count Basie thing, then went into college, military bands, then New York in the early Sixties with Quincy Jones, Ornette Colemen, and Charles Mingus. This was the first time they could have a hands-on relationship with somebody with my experience. A lot of times, the teachers in high school just went to college and were good musicians, but had no real professional experience. I did have a varied background in performance. And they had access to records that I had made, and videos, and it made them feel like they had an inside track on something that was really important."

What about the statement, "Most of you don't know shit"? "Which is true," laughs Bradford. "And so those guys said 'We just figured out, brother, we don't know shit and we wanna learn something.'"

Ozomatli credits Bradford with teaching them improvisation. "We offer classes here in beginning, intermediate, and advanced improvisation," he clarifies. "They could all kind of noodle around, especially Espinoza. He had a lot of talent for just noodling around, but he had to learn how to specifically hook up with true improvisation based on chord progressions like Miles and Coltrane, Sonny Rollins, Dexter Gordon, all those people. What I introduced them to was a formal approach to improvisation so they could study and get inside of it and get better at it. A lot of kids come here from high school who can kind of noodle around, play their horn along with the radio or play along with a record and make noise, but can't be specific with a song like 'Days of Wine and Roses'—play the melody, then start to improvise based on the song. They'd be in a little trouble then, but that's what they learn how to do here. We have classes here that meet two days a week. You've got an hour-and-a-half each time to practice the craft of improvising over the chord pattern of a given song.

Bradford's thoughts on the band Ozomatli? "I like it a lot. I have their last record. I like the mix of salsa and jazz and pop and Ska. It's a sign of coming together of all these musical cultures."

"A little bit after us it was getting toward the end of generations of horn players," muses Bella, "and they started cutting arts and music. That's why there are all these 'Rescue the arts' movements. It's not like classical clarinet was hip but there were people who were into it and wanted to study it. But now these opportunities are fading, especially for people who don't have any money."

The Zen of Gigology

Given that the band is educated, what are some fundamentals they didn't learn in school? "I guess one thing is how to keep a gig," responds Sierra, "How to find a gig, and don't quit your gig until you find another gig. High school and college never taught us or pushed us to hit the streets and go play for people. If you can live with your parents, do it. Otherwise you've got to save your money, because it isn't a steady life. Be tight, don't spend money on stupid shit, just your horn and some clean underwear. If you're going to school to learn about music, what better way than hands-on? When you mess up is when you learn. You also learn so much more from playing gigs. It doesn't matter how much you practice at home, because playing at the gig and playing at home are two completely different things. When that red light goes on, you've got to be on same as when you're in front of thousands of people. If you're not, you'll get some guy who'll fire you. I've had gigs where they were nice to me even though they fired me. I couldn't hang, but when you get burned or fired or someone plays better, it humbles you."

The band has enjoyed a long management relationship with Amy B. (Amy Blackman), who began her career as an intern for Jon Sidel (V2 Records). As an artist ally, she has built a thriving independent company by representing bands, producers, and engineers. She has recently joined forces with Tsunami Entertainment, a Los Angeles-based firm.

"Since we started, our perspectives have changed as our lives have changed," concludes Bella. "We just trust each other more now. Everyone gives everyone the space we all need. This band did not start, at all, to get a record deal. It started out of love for the music we made, and that's exactly where we still are."

RECAP: Road to the Dotted Line

OZOMATLI

- Shared community roots
- Organized around social-action issues
- Turned shows into events
- Developed a formidable live show
- Formed with a common love of music, not recording aspirations

Pink

Rebel Colors

Pink

"I decided that I was going to be me to the fullest extent, that my songs were going to reflect relationships I've had, things I've been through, and even the stuff I'm embarrassed about."

If rock is a game of edge, then Pink is a mistress of the game. Outspoken, controversial, given to outrageous press statements and uncompromising political stances, her image and antics enhance, rather than outshine, her music.

Although her name is invented—its origin has been explained by her in two different versions, one quite explicit—there is nothing artificial about the artist now known as Pink. She began life as Alecia (sometimes spelled "Alicia") Moore, born in the Philadelphia suburb of Doylestown, PA, the daughter of a Vietnam vet and a nurse. Her parents split up when she was seven, a traumatic milestone she commemorates on "Family Portrait," a track from her album *M!ssundaztood*. She identified strongly with her father's music, specifically the songwriters of the Sixties and Seventies. "Ever since I can remember," Pink recalls, "I think before I could talk, I sang. I just ran around the house making up my own fantasy world."

School was problematic Pink says. "I knew a lot of girls with eating disorders, drug problems, any form of escape. There's a lot of pressure on girls, and it makes you nuts after a while, especially when you're in school and you just want to belong." Although she didn't find acceptance in the classroom, it was there for her in the clubs. "I met this guy named Skratch, who was the best dancer in Philly," she says of her 13th year. "I started dancing with him and eventually I was singing hooks in the background for his rap group, Schools of Thought. I wrote some of my own stuff, about the way it was growing up in Philly. We would just get up on the stage at clubs and hang out in studios hoping to get some songs down on tape. At the time, making music was medicine." The same year, a local DJ at Club Fever began allowing her onstage to sing one song every Friday. "My little five minutes on Friday night was all I wanted out of life. I loved the thrill of being onstage. It was the only place that I felt like, okay, I'm cool now."

When Pink was 15, her mother, Judith, threw her out of the house. "We were constantly butting heads. 'Get out of the house. Fuck you. You're just like your father.' She couldn't take it anymore." Pink moved in with her father. A job at the local fast food joint didn't garner Pink a nomination as employee of the month. "I worked there for an hour-and-a-half. I'd have my friends drive through and I'd hang out the window: 'Want free cheeseburgers?' They were about to fire me, and I quit. I just hate taking orders." Her paycheck for the day: $4.23, "which I came back for." Pink estimates she has ten arrests on her record. She was busted for trespassing on school property at night with beer in her car, for running away from home, for disorderly conduct. And there was one botched theft of a *Showgirls* video from the nation's largest video retailer.

Despite her ever-shifting image, from club kid to skater chick and far beyond, Pink's sense of song was imbedded in personal experience. "I decided at 15 that I didn't want to be one of those artists that gets up and sings love songs they don't mean," Pink says. "I decided that I was going to be me to the fullest extent, that my songs were going to reflect relationships I've had, things I've been through, and even the stuff I'm embarrassed about."

She's had some help. Her cousin is Bernie Resnick, a local entertainment lawyer who signed her to her first management deal. "She's been singing in public for so long, stage fright isn't part of the equation," says Resnick. "Don't think that because her first gig in Philly is at a sold-out *NSYNC show that she's not ready for it." Later, her father Jim also assumed early management duties. "Nothing's better and wilder than seeing *her* do this. She said she was going to do it as a kid, and she meant it," he avowed.

Club Nights in Philly

Pink had her first brush with the record business at Club Fever. A local rep from MCA Records came down to the club and spotted the young singer as a possible replacement for a local R&B group called Basic Instinct. Although the project was short-lived, Pink had her first taste of the big time. Next, another group invited Pink as one of three female leads. The trio, named Choice, made a demo and was immediately signed to LaFace. Although the group didn't last—reportedly, one member wanted to sing Broadway tunes, the other wanted to make alternative records, and Pink wanted to do it all—Pink's place in the LaFace stable was solidified. LaFace was hot. From the late Eighties to the mid-Nineties, no single artist owned the R&B and pop charts with a tighter or more fluid grip than co-founder Babyface and his partners L.A. Reid and Darryl Simmons. Reid, a Cincinnati native, started out as a drummer in a soul band in the Eighties. He and bandmate Kenneth (Babyface) Edmonds later became a successful songwriting team, penning R&B hits (33 #1 singles). They launched LaFace Records in 1989, a joint venture with Arista. By 2000, their stars included TLC, Toni Braxton, OutKast, and Usher.

During studio time with Choice in Atlanta, Pink reignited her songwriting and hooked up Simmons. "He asked me to write the bridge for 'Just to Be Loving You.' I thought that was so cool, because no one had even asked me if I wrote. So I just closed my eyes and out it came. I wrote that, and it was the beginning of my career."

The Singer Writes the Songs

Pink also found her voice as a solo singer, utilizing the top end of her sound. Pink began writing songs to display this sound and to combine it with her love of the pop side of R&B. She wrote compulsively, which impressed L.A. Reid. "I kept playing him my songs and going, 'What about this one? What about these?' And he was like, 'Yeah, I like that one. Yeah, that's a single.' He looked at me as a self-contained unit, which he thought was interesting. It's always been really cool with him." Reid signed Pink as a solo artist and hooked her up with various writing partners, from She'kspeare to Babyface and 112. She started composing at a frenetic pace. Within months, Pink had not only written more than half the songs that would comprise her debut CD, she had also signed a lucrative publishing deal with EMI.

(Giant conglomerate BMG bought out Reid and Edmonds, and dumped the legendary Clive Davis at Arista for L.A. Reid. There, he signed a new talent named Avril Lavigne and brought Pink to the label.)

With Reid and Edmonds credited as executive producers, Pink's full-length debut, *Can't Take Me Home*, was released in April 2000. It earned double-platinum status for sales and produced the Top 10 hits

"Most Girls" and "You Make Me Sick." She earned an MTV Video Award nomination for Best New Artist. Paving the way for the CD's appearance was "There You Go," a Top 10 single which had already sold half-a-million copies by the time *Can't Take Me Home* hit record stores. Though reviews tended to be lukewarm—*Rolling Stone* snidely remarked that Pink "makes a pretty good Monica, but we already have one of those"—fans were taken with the feisty spirit that defined many of Pink's songs. Indeed, in its June issue, *Teen People* named Pink one of the 25 Hottest Stars Under 25, and by September, *Can't Take Me Home* had been certified platinum.

The debut was a hit, but it was her sophomore album, *M!ssundaztood*, created with producer Linda Perry, that catapulted her into superstardom. The tough girl from Philly explained her search for a personal truth in these lines: "L.A. told me/You'll be a pop star/All you have to change is everything you are/tired of being compared to damn Britney Spears/she's so pretty/that just ain't me."

In truth, despite the lyrics and the corresponding video, she says Reid was always a staunch supporter. "L.A. pushed me to be myself, always," says Pink. "He was hip on me, not what anyone else wanted me to be. I brought everything to the table. He left the music and lyrics to me and set me up with the best producers possible to bring out my sound. He's my biggest cheerleader."

"I rebel against anyone who tries to classify me," Pink avows. "I refuse to be tagged and have always fought against people trying to control and make decisions for me. I've never wanted to be anybody's puppet. I'm me and nobody knows who I am and what I do, apart from me. People ask if I have a stylist, hair adviser, the lot. No, this is me. What you see is me and nothing has been manufactured. I hate it when people aren't sincere. Not many people can handle the truth. Everyone in the music business is diplomatic and polite, but I'm not. I just tell it as it is. Some people probably think I'm a smart ass, but that's just me." Emphasizing the importance of being honest she adds, "I'm not perfect and I'm not the safest person to look up to, but my main quality is that I don't lie. Everything I do is honest."

RECAP: Road to the Dotted Line

PINK

- Hails from a music center, Philadelphia
- Joined two bands prior to a breakthrough as a solo act
- Created an undeniable persona based on a single name
- Changed direction from pop to rock

Queen Latifah
Royal Rhymes

"I was taught from a young age that many people would treat me as a second-class citizen because I was African-American and because I was female. I thought, 'What the hell is that?' It was a challenge. It meant I'm going to have to be twice as good and work twice as hard."

There is the concept of an artist and an artist in their time. The rise of Queen Latifah is significant for any number of reasons. Although not the first female rapper, she is certainly the most successful. Since her debut in the early Nineties, Queen Latifah has become a multi-disciplinary achiever of the first order—as a talk show host, an Academy Award-nominated actress, and a vocalist. In firm control of her destiny, she is also a motivated entrepreneur with her hand in a multitude of creative projects.

It may seem a leap for an urban hip-hop artist to become a mainstream success, but it is the nature of American media to embrace edgy and controversial art forms, rub off their rough edges through familiarity, and then introduce them into the rarefied stratosphere of film and television. Ice Cube, whose incendiary raps with NWA inflamed law enforcement supporters in the Nineties, has been handily defanged as a jovial star of family-fare motion pictures, while the frigidly similar Ice-T stars on a network television series.

Jersey Girl

In the Eighties, however, hip-hop was outlaw music and Queen Latifah was a regal presence. Her debut album, *All Hail the Queen*, earned a GRAMMY® nomination. It was the culmination of years of backstory. From Newark, NJ, Latifah was born Dana Owens to an art teacher mother and a police officer father. The intellectually-gifted Latifah first began singing in the choir at Shiloh Baptist Church in Bloomfield, NJ. She added pop music, especially rap, to her repertoire around the time she entered Irvington High School, where she also played power forward on her school's championship basketball team. Athletic, outgoing, and popular, Owens balanced her extracurricular activities as a school basketball star with an interest in music and theater, performing in a local production of *The Wiz*. She became "Latifah" at the suggestion of a Muslim relative. (The name means "delicate" and "sensitive" in Arabic.) Latifah's love of rap inspired her to form a group called Ladies Fresh along with two of her friends, Tangy B and Landy D. The trio sang in talent shows and made other local appearances.

From the onset, Latifah balanced street smarts with intellect. "That's part of the example to set. It's all about showing versatility. I've been fighting to show that rappers are articulate. We can speak. Will is another person who's had to break that wall down. LL Cool J is another. You realize that to get into other rooms, you have to move in different ways. My mother wouldn't allow me to speak slang when I was growing up, but when I got outside, around my friends, it was 'Yo' and 'That's the joint' and 'Yo, what's up?' So I had my game for my friends and my game for my mom. It doesn't make you a sellout or a chump," she added. "It doesn't make you corny. If anything, it makes you intelligent, and opens up your world to more things."

Meanwhile, the seminal sounds of rap and hip-hop were being invented by inspired teams of innovators. Three of these individuals directly affected the future of Queen Latifah. DJ Mark the 45 King was, like Owens, a New Jersey native. DJ'ing locally in the mid-Eighties, his ability to make beats from obscure 45-rpm records was the basis for his nickname as "The 45 King." Mark gained notoriety with his breakbeat track "The 900 Number" in 1987. Looping a tenor sax solo from Marva Whitney's "Unwind Yourself," Mark made an anthem that would rock many parties from that year on. The 45 King was signed to Tuff City Records that year and given a production deal.

Cramped Quarters

In the course of two tumultuous decades in popular music, Tommy Boy founder and CEO Tom Silverman has created a striking success story for himself and his company. In 1981, Tommy Boy was a one-man, singles-only label, riding the first wave of hip-hop and operating from the spare bedroom of Silverman's Manhattan apartment. In 1978, Tom and two college friends began publishing *Disco News*, a newsletter aimed at the DJ community. Silverman wrote the reviews, created the layout, and sold the ads. It was no way to make a living— "I was earning about 23 cents per hour," Tom recalls—but it put him in the epicenter of the burgeoning hip-hop and dance music movements. *Disco News* soon mutated into *Dance Music Report*, a bi-weekly tip sheet that many considered the bible of the dance music scene. With no formal business education or background, Tom learned every aspect of the music industry from hands-on experience. "For articles in Dance Music Report, I would interview people in the business and ask them why this record didn't happen or that one did," he explains. "I learned about record distribution by cold-calling distributors on behalf of a dance label called Importe 12. I actually volunteered five hours a week just to learn that aspect of the business."

With an investment of $5,000 from his parents, Tom Silverman released the first Tommy Boy 12-inch single, "Having Fun" by Cotton Candy, in the spring of 1981. It sold well enough to finance a second Tommy Boy 12-inch, "Jazzy Sensation," recorded in two versions by both Afrika Bambaataa & the Jazzy 5 and The Kryptic Krew. "Jazzy Sensation" sold 35,000 12-inch copies and paved the way for Tommy Boy's breakthrough hit, "Planet Rock," by Afrika Bambaataa & Soul Sonic Force. Its eye-opening sales of 620,000 proved what Tom Silverman had always believed—the new music born in the playgrounds and clubs of the Bronx was the sound of a prosperous future.

Afrika Bambaataa doesn't consider himself old school. The pioneering New York DJ who soundtracked the mid-Seventies birth of hip-hop, alongside Kool Herc and Grandmaster Flash, prefers to think of that era as true-school. When Bambaataa was still known as Kevin Donovan, he was a persuasive leader in the Black Spades gang, a notorious group of street toughs who, along with other gang members, later reformed in 1973 as the Zulu Nation, a grassroots activist organization. When Zulu Nation formed, its DJs, MCs, writers and break dancers were the cultural ground-troops helping their founder guide hip-hop toward the mainstream. Bambaataa held early b-boy battles, encouraging conflict resolution through dancing. He spun records in downtown rock clubs. He organized hip-hop's first Eurotour with the Rock Steady Crew, Grandmaster DST, and Fab 5 Freddy. He even collaborated with James Brown, George Clinton, and John Lydon of the Sex Pistols.

Using his newfound clout, the 45 King was able to "put on" members of his crew, dubbed The Flavor Unit. The first album came in 1988 with Lakim Shabazz's "Pure Righteousness," but Tuff City's small budget and limited distribution kept the album from blowing up. Queen Latifah and Ladies Fresh attracted the interest of Mark James, and they became a part of a loose aggregation called Flavor Unit. Venturing into New York, she fell in Afrika Bambaataa's Afrocentric Native Tongues collective. Soon, her DJ 45-produced demos were being played on local underground hip-hop shows in the New York metropolitan area.

Latifah recalls, "I lived and breathed hip-hop. I remember when I was 15 being in this club, Latin Quarter, and I was one of the few people from Jersey there. It was a place where, when they screamed, 'Is Brooklyn in the house?' the whole club would erupt. You didn't want to say your ass was from Jersey or you'd get your ass robbed! But right in front of my eyes, the new era of hip-hop was being born— Grandmaster Flash, Salt-N-Pepa, Beastie Boys. I watched them grow, and they inspired me."

Although women in hip-hop were a novelty, Latifah wasn't intimidated. "If anything, I had a lot of people coming up to me saying 'I like you,' Ice-T, Doug E. Fresh, and Biz Markie, and just like a lot of the rappers that were out at the time and had platinum records, they gave me respect when I came in the game. A problem came with the labels, with marketing and promotion money. There was still this stigma of a girl not being able to sell records. Salt-N-Pepa were the exception to the rule because they came out on an underground tip, but then they went pop with 'Push It.' They just blew up, so their record companies put money behind them. But there were a lot of females that came out and didn't sell at all. I think it was more about the kind of records they were making than it was the fact that they were females. A few of us had to fight to get our record companies to kick up the money that we needed to go to where we needed to go."

"I got my break because Fab 5 Freddy of *Yo! MTV Raps* heard my demo and played it for someone at Tommy Boy records," Latifah explains. The program, which ran from 1988 to 1995 on MTV, was the first showcase of hip-hop music on the network, and was hosted by Dr. Dre, Ed Lover, and Fab 5 Freddy. In addition to videos, the show featured interviews with rap stars, Friday live studio performances, and comedy. At first, it aired only once a week, but expanded to six days a week after its popularity grew. Its ratings and status dipped after pulling Public Enemy's video "Arizona" in 1991, claiming it was too violent.

In 1988, Tommy Boy Records released Latifah's first single, "Wrath of My Madness," with the lines, "You gotta let 'em know/you ain't a bitch or a 'ho." The record was a smash. By the time Latifah graduated Irvington High School and entered Borough of Manhattan Community College, her first two single releases already had sold 40,000 copies.

Since her musical breakthrough, Queen Latifah has become an actress and a no-nonsense businesswoman with multiple platforms, from makeup to fashion. "I was taught from a young age that many people would treat me as a second-class citizen because I was African-American and because I was female," Queen Latifah said. "That's the most hurtful thing for a kid to hear, that somebody's not going to like you because of your skin color or not give you an opportunity because you're a woman. I thought, 'What the hell is that?' It was a challenge. It meant I'm going to have to be twice as good and work twice as hard."

She notes that the knowledge of the economics of the business have expanded dramatically. "It used to be, 'Oh, I just want to get signed. I just want to hear my record on the radio. I just want to perform.' But your music is making somebody a lot of money. You hear enough horror stories and you go broke enough times and you decide, "I need to control my destiny a little more." We were one of the first production deals around. That wasn't a common thing. This was 1990 and not a lot of people were doing this, but we did it. I didn't own all my publishing when I first got signed. I gave up some of my publishing and I really did not understand the significance of that. When I left Tommy Boy to go to Motown, there was no way I was giving up my publishing because it was really about a steady stream of income."

And despite her success as an actress, she hasn't forgotten about music. Fifteen years after her hard-hitting hip-hop debut, *All Hail the Queen*, she has a new CD, *The Dana Owens Album*, a collection of jazz, soul, and pop standards covering artists as diverse as Dinah Washington, Al Green, and Billy Strayhorn.

RECAP: Road to the Dotted Line

QUEEN LATIFAH

- Was raised across the river from a major music capital
- Hooked up with a local scene
- Was signed to a small indie label
- Exemplified a new positive direction in rap

REM

Song of the New South

From San Francisco in the Sixties to Seattle in Nineties, significant music has always sprung up from distinctive locals and specific "scenes." The geographies shift dramatically, but what unites them is the presence of young, passionate audiences—generally of college age—and input from other complementary creative mediums: visual art, fashion and cinema. In the Eighties, no scene was hotter than Athens, GA.

With lyrics alternately anthemic and obscure, ringing guitars and admirable pop craftsmanship, the band REM is credited for ushering in the transition from hardcore punk to alternative rock. The band formed in Athens in 1980, but Mike Mills and Bill Berry were the only native Southerners in the group. The duo had attended high school together in Macon, playing in a number of bands during their teens. Michael Stipe was a typical military brat, moving throughout the country during his

"With the exception of U2, there's no one who has stayed together and stayed relevant for as long as we have. As long as people are excited about our work, we're going to expend the energy to do it."

—Michael Stipe

childhood. By his teens, he had discovered punk rock through Patti Smith, television, and *Wire*, and began playing in cover bands in St. Louis. He enrolled in the University of Georgia in Athens as an art major in 1978 and began frequenting the Wuxtry record store where he met a clerk and fanatic record collector named Peter Buck. Buck had dropped out of Emory University, but with an interest in everything from classic rock to punk and free jazz, he was just beginning to learn how to play guitar. Discovering they had similar tastes, Buck and Stipe began working together, eventually meeting Berry and Mills through a mutual friend, Kathleen O'Brien.

"As we started the band, I was 19," Stipe recalls. "I had bad skin, a terrible haircut, couldn't deal with my sexuality, and was pathologically shy. I think life meant it well with me since those years, although my skin hasn't become any better and actually I'm still shy. But my job doesn't allow me to be shy. That's why the man you see onstage is a different one. It's not like Dr. Jekyll and Mr. Hyde, but what you see is a giant show version of my personality."

Vintage Vespers
In April 1980, the band formed to play a party for O'Brien, rehearsing a number of garage, psychedelic, bubblegum, and punk covers in a converted house of worship, St. Mary's Episcopal church. At the time, the group played under the name The Twisted Kites. By the summer, the band had changed its name to REM. (Origins of the name remain shrouded in myth, with Michael Stipe alternately claiming the band flipped through a dictionary or rolled around naked in an ecstatic state writing possible band names on walls. In either case, it was the perfect moniker for the emerging group.) At the birthday party, a local promoter, Mike Hubbs, witnessed the band's performance and offered to book them into Tyrone's O.C., a local venue.

Bill Berry, in particular, knew how the booking business worked. He previously had been employed by the Paragon booking agency in an entry-level position. Touring other college markets was a natural move, and the Athens, GA to Chapel Hill, NC pipeline was a popular route for bands—one college town to another, each with a strong music underground and college-radio support. On the band's first out-of-state show in North Carolina, they met another ambitious record clerk, Jefferson Holt, who was employed at a local store, Schoolkids. Duly impressed by REM's performance, he signed on as their tour manager and moved to Athens to direct their increasingly busy affairs, ultimately becoming their manager. To supplement his income, Holt took a position as a doorman at Tyrone's.

Tracks to the Drive-In

Meanwhile, down in Dixie, a young producer, Mitch Easter, had appropriated his parents' garage in Winson-Salem, NC, knocked holes in the walls to run wires, and created Drive-In Studios. Easter's friend Peter Holsapple knew Jefferson Holt, who was searching for an appropriate venue to record REM. Easter recalls, "I had seen a poster for them at The Pier in Raleigh. I had the idea they were this electro-band like old Depeche Mode. When they showed up, I guess I was still thinking that. They got to the house the night before the session and we sat around and talked. It was very apparent they were a rock-and-roll band in every sense of the word. They really seemed like a Sixties band to me. They had the Fab Four feel. These guys looked good together as a band. There was something reassuring and classic about the four guys up there. I had a great time talking to them. We liked the same stuff."

Mitch Easter knew Athens well. "The thing that was so cool about Athens back then was that it lived up to its reputation. There would always be 25 parties going on every time I was there. If you went to one, you were likely to see 10 or 15 people you knew, or who were figures in all this. A band would play, and people were on their feet and bouncing off the ceiling. That support for a local band was something you always wanted but never had. I thought it was Utopia."

The group came in with three possible songs: "Radio Free Europe," "Sitting Still," and "White Tornado." Mitch Easter was impressed. "I thought these were songs that other people would like. Even by then I was bothered by the fact that you'd record people even while thinking, 'Nobody really wants to hear this.' With them, it seemed to leap out of the speakers. This is a record people would buy. I wasn't one of these guys who think in terms of sales, but it just seemed that way. It was so clear. They had everything. Michael was the mysterious but very star-like singer. Mike and Bill were sort of bemused and doing that good job back there. Pete Buck was the rock-and-roll zealot. I used to think back then it was Venus appearing fully formed. The whole deal was there."

DIY

From punk rock, the band had appropriated a strong DIY (Do-It-Yourself) ethic. "You have to remember," said Peter Buck, "growing up at the time I did, there wasn't anyone who made records like us. Rock-and-roll was full of super-rich guys that had mustaches and were ten years older than me." A tiny local label, Hib-Tone Records, released the group's first records. "Radio Free Europe" evoked huge excitement. With the market still in the clutches of the increasingly unwieldy major labels, independent record labels had not yet reached their zenith of power. The single's reach, without major promotional muscle, was even more remarkable, and revitalized the dreams of the independent recording scene. Due to strong word-of-mouth, the single became a hit on college radio and topped the *Village Voice*'s year-end poll of Best Independent Singles.

Still, to take the band to the next level, Jefferson Holt realized that he'd need the clout of a bigger label. He approached IRS. Records, the company invented by Miles Copeland, whose brother Stewart was the drummer for The Police. Copeland's other sibling, Ian, ran a booking business; drummer Bill Berry knew Ian from the time Bill worked at the Paragon booking agency. Executive Jay Boberg came down to hear the band in a New Orleans club, The Beat Exchange. It was a less-than-full house—REM played to an audience of five, including a soundman who left during the third song to shoot up in the bathroom. It didn't matter. Two songs into the set, Boberg wanted to sign the band. After the set, Boberg went backstage and introduced himself to Stipe, who replied, "I was afraid you were Jay Boberg. We were pretty ordinary." The next day, over shrimp and oyster loaves at the Bright Star Café, a deal was initiated that would lead REM to seven albums and as many years with the label that became famous for breaking ground as a true indie.

Bill Berry recalled, "Signing to IRS was what we wanted. We had recording offers from major companies, but that would have meant subscribing to their idea of what we should be. We didn't want to do that. We knew, or at least thought we knew, that it was very short-lived thing. It was like, 'Hey, this is fun. We're no great band. We're pretty good, we want to make records, but we want to do it on our own terms.' That's why we were so interested in signing with IRS, because we knew that it was their thing. It was like low budget, small advance. They would give us tour support, but they would generally leave us alone as far as making the records. That was what we wanted."

IRS wanted Steven Hague to produce the band. By all accounts, the sessions were disastrous, with Hague's perfectionist approach at odds with the band's organic mission. The label ultimately allowed REM to track with Mitch Easter and his accomplice, Don Dixon, at a larger studio, Reflection, in Charlotte, NC. An extended-play single, "Chronic Town," paved the way for the band's full-length release.

Bertis Downs first saw REM perform at the 11.11 Koffee Klub in Athens, GA in 1980. A long-time confidant of the band, he assumed the title of manager after Jefferson Holt left in 1996. He'd first seen them play during his second year of law school at the University of Georgia in Athens, where he still teaches today. Upon graduating, he started helping them out on a voluntary basis, assisting with contracts, trademark issues, etc., and it turned into a real job. "Since the earliest days, if we were sitting about, wondering whether we going to take time off, were going to tour, where we were going to play, what promoters we should use, what the ticket prices should be, whether we should take sponsorship or not, they've always looked to me for advice for that stuff—the direction of the business. It used to be the six of us talking around a table, and then it became the five of us. After Bill [Berry, former drummer, now a farmer] left, it became the four of us," says Downs.

With the release of the resulting major-label debut, titled *Murmur*, REM was catapulted into the stratosphere of major artists awarded Record of the Year in *Rolling Stone*. The magazine proclaimed that the band had ascended to "mainstream popularity without caving in to record-industry dictums or betraying its original college-radio constituency." In 1988, the band left IRS for Warner Bros. In 2006, the band will be eligible for nomination into the Rock and Roll Hall of Fame.

"With the exception of U2, there's no one who has stayed together and stayed relevant for as long as we have," says Michael Stipe. "We can't possibly compete with Limp Bizkit and Britney Spears, and I have no real desire to. But as long as people are excited about our work, we're going to expend the energy to do it." Stipe later adds, for good measure, "I'm only two years older than Tom Cruise and three years older than Brad Pitt."

RECAP: Road to the Dotted Line

REM

- Were part of a larger scene in a college town
- Played other college towns to build a buzz
- Recorded an indie CD
- Were joined by-low level but high-energy management
- Retained their indie production contacts for their major release

Jill SCOTT

Philadelphia Freedom

"I wanted folks to have an opportunity to listen to the words, think about the words, place them somewhere in their bodies— whether it was their head or their heart or their soul, over their feet when they're walking down the street, snapping their fingers."

Who is Jill Scott? (Words and Sounds, Vol. 1) was much more than just the title of a 2001 GRAMMY®-nominated release. It was a challenge, an invitation, and an invocation to word-driven, intellectually-charged R&B. It is also a question that Jill Scott admitted she did not yet know the answer to, but she was working on it.

In person, Scott projects a pronounced radiance. She is not shy. Her conversation flows like her lyrics, a rhythmic, cerebral narrative with unexpected word choices and bright flashes of genuine epiphany. With the kudos for her GRAMMY®-nominated album, comparisons to her predecessors—Macy Gray, Erikah Badu, and Lauren Hill—are perhaps inevitable. But Jill Scott is first and foremost a poet and, as such, she owes an equal artistic debt to the literature of Nikki Giovanni and Gwendolyn Brooks.

Who Is Jill Scott? was released in mid-2000. Within 14 weeks it had sold over 500,000 copies. How did Scott and her label, Hidden Beach Recordings, keep the heat turned up? "When we decided to put the album out, I really wanted it to be something that grew on people," says Scott. "I didn't want it to be a big campaign with billboards and every magazine and 'Up next.' I didn't want the word 'hot' to be a part of my presentation. I wanted the album to be more of an offering and less of something to sell."

Asking the Question

Asking a certain question was the key to an alternative marketing plan. "I thought that by naming it *Who is Jill Scott?*, it would be a question that would be passed on to the next person and the next person, and just in case somebody didn't know, someone else could easily say, 'Do you know who Jill Scott is? You have to get this album.' I wanted it to be very much a word-of-mouth effort. I think when people talk about something, whether it's a doctor or a car dealer, it's a lot more genuine rather than if you see a commercial or a billboard. I put a lot of myself into this, so I wanted it to be genuine. Hidden Beach just followed. I can't thank them enough for that."

Scott's singing voice is a supple, expressive instrument that segues effortlessly from spoken to sung words. The spoken words came first. In North Philadelphia, Scott hung out with the local poetry crowd, went to Temple University, and studied English. But she heard the legendary soul sounds—Gamble & Huff, Thom Bell, the Spinners, The Ojays, Harold Melvin & the Blue Notes, and latter-day local heroes like D.J. Jazzy Jeff and The Fresh Prince—all around her. Growing up in a city with deep soul roots was bound to influence the musical upbringing of an emerging artist.

"The thing was, it was *in* Philly," Scott affirms. "It wasn't so much that I was influenced by it, I couldn't help but know it, I couldn't help but smell it. It was there. It's always been there. As a child, I went to the Robin Hood Dell East to hear jazz and R&B. At eight or nine years old I went to see The Temptations. My mother took me to see Jazz on the Waterfront. It wasn't anything new or different for me. It was something to do on a Saturday for my mom and me. I liked it."

Given the slightest chance, Scott will wax lyrical about her hometown. "To me, Philly is block parties, penny candy, riding my bike round the block, children to play with, older people to talk to, loud music. Porches are a big part of Philly, so in the summer people are out sitting on them. But more than anything, Philly is my mother. She took me to the museum, ballet. She enrolled me in this school, Greenfields, where mayor's kids, congressmen's kids went. She's just a beautiful person."

But singing was something Scott did only for herself. "I was between me and God," she says. "I always sang, but I didn't let anybody hear it. I didn't know anybody had heard it until I was older and my mother said, 'You were in your room and you had that towel under your door. You don't even know, me and grandma were sitting on the floor with our ears to the door listening.' I had no idea. I guess that's the same way as me with my grandmother. She would sing in the tub and my mother and I would listen to her."

"So I never intended to sing in front of people. But getting in front of people, being onstage, reading the words, just opening myself through poetry, I opened a lock and so much of me just came out. I got up to read poetry one day and instead I just sang. I didn't think about it, I hadn't planned it, but I did it and it was great. I haven't stopped since."

Roots in the Philly Firmament

Meanwhile in Philly, Jazzy Jeff and Fresh Prince rocked Central High School parties and The Roots were street performers, Jill was reading poetry at places like October Gallery and the "Black Lily" at The Five Spot. Every Tuesday night, this popular Old City club hosted a talent showcase that featured amateurs as well as popular neo-soul and hip-hop artists. In addition to Scott, other performers—Musiq Soulchild (now known as "Musiq"), Kindred, Floetry, and India.Arie—honed their skills. Word of "Black Lily" spread beyond Philly. Stories appeared in the national press, including *The Source* and *Vibe*, so a New York location was opened at The Wetlands as well. If you were in Philly on a Tuesday night, The Five Spot was the place to be. In keeping with the feminist perspective, the door charge was $5 for women and $10 for men.

Scott remembers, "The first time I went to Lily, I performed some freestyle songs and some written stuff, too. I actually did my first Lily show at the New York venue, which was a big deal to me at the time. Along with myself, that night showcased the Jazzies, Flo Brown, and Jaguar. It's extremely important to have a place for female artists to cultivate their craft. All kinds of women hit the stage—no particular size or style. All kinds. People seemed to notice the talent, or lack of, before anything else. So we all came at the same level—hungry artists. In the beginning, every night was magic. We didn't even know if anyone would show. We had no idea what the reaction would be. It was thrilling. The last time I went, it was different. The vibe felt created, not organic the way I remember. So many big-name artists and producers had come through. It appeared that people were there to get on or to see who was walking through the door. I'm not saying we didn't go and perform, 'cause we did. But the biggest reason to be at the Lily was to be a better artist. We tried new styles. There was a real sense of family. It was a black women's renaissance." The club closed in 2005.

The crowds were growing and Jill was starting to hear things. "Sounds," she says, "sounds in the words. Eventually some parts would be spoken, some sung." Roots drummer Amir caught Jill's performance at Black Lily and told producer and band member Scott Storch. The band invited Jill into the studio one night. She came and wrote what would be the lyrics to "You Got Me" in five minutes. Amir called Jill the next day to say the song would be The Roots' first single. Sung by Erykah Badu, the track went on to garner The Roots a 1999 GRAMMY Award® for Best Rap Performance (Duo or Group). Meanwhile, Scott toured with the Canadian cast of *Rent*, continued collaborations with The Roots, worked with Eric Benet and eventually with Will Smith, contributing to the *Wild Wild West* soundtrack.

In time, Jill Scott joined forces with another Philadelphian, "Jazzy" Jeff Townes, the Fresh Prince's cohort and the producer of her debut album. Townes invented a hip, urban pastiche with street-wise kick drums and insinuating bass lines, cushioning Scott's vocals between fat Rhodes sounds, flutes, and choruses of backing vocals. On her debut, her spoken/sung narratives sit front-and-center in the mix, with plenty of space around them.

"I didn't want it to be weighed down by anything," says Scott. "I wanted folks to have an opportunity to listen to the words, think about the words, place them somewhere in their bodies—whether it was their head or their heart or their soul, over their feet when they're walking down the street, snapping their fingers. I wanted it to be open enough that people could own it, sing along. I didn't want it to be so convoluted that there wasn't a place for them to find themselves in it as well." And, she concludes, "Here we are."

Catching a Wave with Hidden Beach

Jill says she signed with Hidden Beach Recordings because she was impressed with the fact that CEO Steve McKeever ("the keeper, the young visionary, the Chicago Brother") was interested in her music, her heart, and where her music comes from. Other industry executives, says Scott, only wanted to know, right up front, how she looked. Previously an entertainment lawyer, McKeever joined Motown Records as senior vice president of artists and repertoire in 1991. He expanded the label's line-up with people like Queen Latifah, while at the same time managing blockbuster acts like Boyz II Men and Stevie Wonder. The following year, he started MoJAZZ Records, a subsidiary of Motown, where he launched a number of new artists. In 1993, McKeever played an instrumental role in the sale of Motown to PolyGram Records. He left Motown in 1995 to work on his own projects, founding Hidden Beach Recordings (HBR) in 1998.

"Jill's the ideal artist to usher in Hidden Beach," says McKeever. "She's both a throwback to the days of 'real music' and compelling artists, and a representative of the emerging cadre of new, relevant performers who will set the tempo for the next generations."

One of Hidden Beach's guiding philosophies is to give artists the creative freedom to try new genres and musical styles. That obviously is what caught Scott's attention. "Steve has a passion for and sincerity in music and about music," she says. "I also knew I'd be able to run my own show. There would he nobody telling me what I could and could not do, from the artwork to the presentation, not only the music."

Jill Scott considers herself an artist, not an entertainer. "I can entertain," she clarifies, "but I'm an artist entertaining. I'm not an entertainer. I think typically entertainers are folks, especially right now—I'm not going to say always, because there have been great entertainers; Michael Jackson and Fred Astaire are great entertainers—that the industry has mass-produced, kids who can dance and sing and they call them artists. They are not. They haven't created anything. What they've done is mimicked and followed and studied and rehearsed and they've made something out of that. I don't think that's an artist. I think with an artist, from the time they're born, there's a plan. Artists have their own voices."

RECAP: Road to the Dotted Line

JILL SCOTT

- Came from a secondary music capital, Philadelphia
- Channeled the music around her into a hybrid music/poetry format
- Was part of an art scene with extensive visibility
- Hooked up with a top local band, The Roots
- Choose to affiliate with a new (although well-funded) record label
- Channeled a strikingly-original form of expression

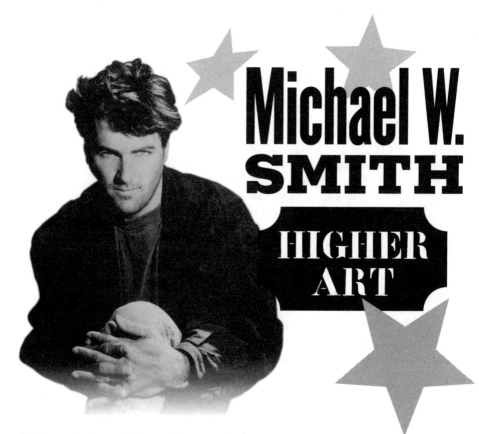

Michael W. SMITH

HIGHER ART

He has performed for millions with his patriotic "There She Stands," sung before President George W. Bush's speech at the 2004 Republic National Convention. He jammed with U2 during a studio visit in Ireland and most recently developed his acting abilities by accepting the lead role in the indie film *The Second Chance*. Fourteen albums, 25 #1 songs, a mantle full of GRAMMYs® and Dove Awards bear witness that Michael W. Smith's music has resonated for millions of devoted listeners. Smith is an artist whose career path has been mapped by faith and lit with a burning creative intensity. "I don't want to sit here dreaming up parameters," he asserts. "I think the best thing for me is to wipe the slate clean and forget everything I've done."

Born in Kenova, WV, Smith grew up with a father who was an oil refinery worker and a mom who was a caterer. His father had played minor leagues baseball, so both

"My prayer every night is, 'God, I want to be the perfect conduit. I just want to be the perfect vessel and I want to stay out of the way. So you come and you do your thing and if I need to say anything, then Lord, you say it!'"

music and sports appealed to Smith. But music was a place of security as Smith played piano and sang with the Baptist youth choir. He became a devout Christian at age ten and spent his teens hanging around with a solid support group of fellow believers who frequently gathered to play and make music.

When he enrolled in college at Marshall University in West Virginia, music triumphed over athletics after his first semester. Encouraged by positive feedback from a friend, Shane Keister, a session player in Nashville who told him, "If music's really in your blood, you should probably move to Nashville," he left for Tennessee.

Music City Moves

He settled in Music City, but it was a struggle to connect to the industry. Through his friendship with Keister, he expanded his circle of music biz contacts and, to pay the bills, was employed in a landscaping job with Shane's brother, Beau. He also co-wrote a few songs with Shane's wife, Alice, a songwriter who had a staff deal at a music publishing company, Paragon. Days were spent landscaping, trying to make ends meet. Spare moments were spent trying to write songs,

As a proficient keyboard player, Smith had other opportunities available to him, mainly backing up singers in clubs. He asked his parents if they would sign a promissory note so he could purchase his first synthesizer. But music still wasn't paying the bills, so Smith moved from job to job, waiting tables, selling clothing, bottling Coca-Cola. He soon owed the bank $1,400, but still had no real income. Meanwhile, there were other tribulations; Smith has spoken extensively, on record, about his struggle with drugs and alcohol during this period.

His first break came when he joined the band Higher Ground, a praise-based group. "My experience with Higher Ground was a time of healing for me," Smith remembered. "I was with the band for eight months, singing in churches and just spending time with those guys. Some of those churches we went to were just phenomenal. We met some genuine people."

Song Sense

But touring was only a sideline, and Smith felt that songwriting, not performing, was his calling. Back in Nashville, Paragon signed him to a one-year songwriting contract. During that year he penned over 100 songs, although he confides that most of them were negligible. "But I had to go through that, you know. Just write them out. I grew a lot that year." In the months that followed, Michael collaborated with the Gaithers and others.

Meanwhile, praise-based music was undergoing radical changes in Nashville and across the country. The rise of a young star, Amy Grant, exemplified the changing parameters of the genre. Contemporary Christian Music (or CCM) is a somewhat archaic term originally used in the Seventies to describe a new form of pop/rock music whose lyrics were based in the Christian faith. This music had its roots in "Jesus Music," which sprang from the hippie Jesus Movement of the early Seventies. Artists such as 2nd Chapter of Acts, Love Song, Barry McGuire, and Larry Norman were making folksy pop music about their faith in Jesus Christ.

Due partly to a separatist attitude, and also the economic fact that finding mainstream radio play would be quite difficult, an entire Christian music industry sprang up to promote Christian-only artists, record labels, radio stations, and record stores. By the Eighties, CCM was a very large and lucrative music industry. Over time, however, many Christian artists opposed the idea of a separate Christian music "ghetto" and began working outside the confines of the Nashville-based CCM industry.

Rev. Jimmy Swaggart, a famous televangelist and CCM oppositionist—and, not coincidentally, the cousin of rock pioneer Jerry Lee Lewis—was clearly referring to Amy Grant when he said that "So-called Christian rock is a diabolical force undermining Christianity from within. I turn on my television set. I see a young lady who goes under the guise of being a Christian, known all over the nation, dressed in skin-tight leather pants, shaking and wiggling her hips to the beat and rhythm of the music as the strobe lights beat their patterns across the stage and the band plays the contemporary rock sound which cannot be differentiated from songs by the Grateful Dead, The Beatles, or anyone else. And you may try to tell me this is of God and that it is leading people to Christ, but I know better."

Despite the naysayers, Michael W. Smith became a huge star. He met Grant and was invited to become a part of her touring band. Moreover, he began writing songs with the young artist. Grant was managed by Dan Harrell and Mike Blanton. Also on their artist roster was Kathy Troccoli, for whom they had high hopes, but record labels seemed less impressed. Undeterred, they founded their own label, Reunion Records, distributed by Christian music giant Word. Troccoli's *Stubborn Love* was the label debut. The execs, impressed by Smith's songwriting skills, requested that he put together a tentative song list for an album. In two weeks, he returned with ten perspective cuts. He also enlisted a co-writer, his new wife Debbie.

Smith continued touring with Grant to ever-increasing audiences. Meanwhile, Word Records, Reunion's umbrella label, signed a distribution deal with A&M Records. Suddenly, the small market for Christian music was expanded via the major-label clout. It was perfect timing for Michael W. Smith and it was a paradigm that the label later retraced in a pact with Geffen Records in 1991, when Smith's albums reached their pop zenith.

The Christian/Gospel category of overall music sales is the sixth most popular genre, according to SoundScan's 2004 year-end report. Gospel music sales outpace sales of Latin, soundtracks, jazz, classical, and New Age genres. Christian retail stores accounted for 37.6 percent of gospel music sales, while mainstream retail outlets tracked 59 percent of all gospel music sales. Christian retailers' sales grew from 2003 by nearly one percent and mainstream sales were unchanged. Non-traditional sales—representing direct, venue and website sales—were down 18 percent.

Smith, who like Amy Grant has been negatively judged by the Christian press on numerous occasions, resists the notion of being pigeon-holed, musically or personally. "I think it's different for everybody. Everybody's got to work out their own salvation. I hate it when you get into 'styles' and this and that. My prayer every night is, 'God, I want to be the perfect conduit. I just want to be the perfect vessel and I want to stay out of the way. So you come and you do your thing and if I need to say anything, then Lord, you say it!' We have a song list but that's about it and I let it flow from there."

Still, Smith is still a pop star on many levels, but he avows, "For me, I think I can turn the corner. I think it's probably harder for the audience. They want to hear 'Place in This World.' They want to hear 'Friends' and they're gonna hear it, but I feel like I've found a way to turn the corner. I'm real comfortable with it. A lot of it I think is, 'What's my persona? How do I behave onstage? How do I even move and project and engage people?' That's 90 percent of it to me. It's almost more important than what you have to say or sing. I know that my real desire is to be a man that walks in humility, so I'm past the whole 'pop star' thing. I couldn't care less. I've had big mainstream success in the pop realm and in Christian music and the, 'Oh gosh, he's a worship leader but he's a pop guy!' I can't help it. I just happen to be both and I just scored my first movie too, so there's that other part of me. There are many facets of who I am musically, but the worship thing is the most comfortable because it just comes with ease."

Would he attribute the recent rise in Christian music to a society's search for some metaphysical truths? "That is a whole other conversation," he says flatly. "I have a hard time with that subculture. But I think it's a great medium to give people hope and people have found healing in it. That's why we do it in the first place."

RECAP: Road to the Dotted Line

MICHAEL W. SMITH

- Moved to Nashville to pursue music
- Worked as a sideman
- Signed a staff songwriting deal
- Was at the cutting edge of a new musical style

Jeffrey STEELE

Into the Heart of Nashville

"I remember being five, shaking my hips to Elvis Presley records in front of the whole family, and my brothers getting pissed and beating me up later."

Unlike many of the subjects profiled in this book, Jeffrey Steele probably is better known within the songwriting industry than to the general public. Make no mistake. If you're a country music fan, although you may not know his name, you most certainly will know his words and music. With over 300 cuts recorded in the last five years by Nashville's most bankable stars—including Tim McGraw, Faith Hill, Montgomery Gentry, Rascal Flatts, Leanne Rimes, and Diamond Rio—Jeffrey Steele is as hot as a country songwriter could possibly be. But success for this driven native Californian came only after two decades of broken dreams, busted-up bands, deals gone sour, and record executives who thought they knew more about country music than he did. "The most important thing any song-writer needs to have is that drive, an 'against all odds' instinct to keep writing through all the rejection and all the hard-ships," states Steele. "These are your stories, the stuff that turns into your songs. I think a lot of people run from these things, but they need to realize that that's what you're gonna be writing about for the next 20 years."

Independent releases sold on his website and at live shows have been, up until now, the only ways to procure Steele's solo work. But *Outlaw*, from Lofton Creek, delivers the power of Jeffrey Steele as an artist backed by the power of major distribution. To promote his record, Steele has been opening shows for Brad Paisley and Keith Urban with just an acoustic guitar. Although radio renditions of Steele's songs gleam with the studio polish and fine-tuning that Nashville affords its most bankable stars, witnessing the songwriter pounding the bejesus out of an acoustic guitar and wailing the words in his road-rough voice reveals the pure, unimpeachable conviction that glows at the core of his artistry.

"You've really got to work," he avows. "I came out for 8,000 people in Connecticut, with throngs of screaming women wanting to see Brad and Keith. I said, 'You guys have no idea who I am, but you know my songs.' The whole place was singing along. Then I did the stuff from my new record and '20 Years Ago' earned a standing ovation. But the stage manager wouldn't let me go back out for an encore, so I'm getting success and shooting myself in the foot at the same time. It's all perfect."

Beautiful Burbank
Born Jeffrey Levasseur in Burbank, CA, when he needed a country-sounding stage name, his father's occupation provided inspiration. The elder Levasseur, a metal cutter, had a shop in the San Fernando Valley just around the corner from the world-famous Palomino club where, at nine years of age, Jeffrey began performing on talent night. "I won a few times but owner Tommy Thomas got tired of me winning, so he wouldn't give me money anymore. He gave me hamburgers," he recalls fondly.

Steele's powers of perception were honed early on. "I observed my older brothers and sisters and heard all of their music." recalls the songwriter. "I was at the bottom end of the food chain, just eating that stuff up, watching and learning. Later, all of these things were there to write about." As the little brother, Steele learned how to vie for attention. "I remember being five, shaking my hips to Elvis Presley records in front of the whole family, and my brothers getting pissed and beating me up later."

One familial theme Steele has referenced in both "My Town" (Montgomery Gentry) and "20 Years Ago" is the age-old conflict between father and son. "It was my brother and my father," he says. "I'd watch them fight at the dinner table. They could never get along. Ten or fifteen years went by and they didn't talk to each other until my dad was on his deathbed in a morphine-induced state. They couldn't really make amends, but they could look each other in the eye one last time. I tell writers, 'Don't turn the other way from that. It's okay to write about it more than once, if that's a big issue in your life. It's therapy for you.'"

Bar Band Boogie

Steele spent the Eighties with a dual music career, playing in bands on the Sunset Strip and with country groups far from the center of L.A. He could make a living in the country bars, but he decided to concentrate on writing songs. Still, he couldn't resist an offer of $200 to play bass one Sunday afternoon. "I put my amp in the car and drove down to Orange Country and played the gig with Larry Parks and his brother Cary, with Hugh Wright on drums. I said, 'These guys are unbelievable.' Next thing I know, we're playing every bar in town. I started bringing my songs in and the harmonies were great. It was a once-in-a-lifetime thing." Boy Howdy's huge radio hit, "She'd Give Anything," took the band to the top of the country charts, so they moved to Nashville to be part of the hit-making machine.

The record company wanted more of the same, but the band wasn't amenable to being squeezed into the polished Nashville mold. "Boy Howdy was rowdy," Steele testifies. "When we had our first hit, the company said, 'Give us an album with ten more of these and you'll be huge.' The label wanted me to come out front and hold the mic and do the deal. They were right; we just didn't want to do that. We just had so much fun playing, but it got taken from us and that messed it up."

Steele tells of the harrowing days after Boy Howdy's demise, when he was subsequently signed to a solo deal. "I got the worst of the worst, but really no worse than anyone else. When I signed to Curb Records, I remember the guys there telling me all my songs sucked and I wasn't really that talented, but the secretary in the office thought I was cute, so they were going to give me a record deal. All of the things they say to make you feel like nothing." Meanwhile, the publishers were equally underwhelmed. "They told me my songs were nowhere near the marketplace, off by a mile. But I knew that I loved to write. It gets to a point where you either slough it off or think maybe they're right. But look at the criticism and see if it has any weight. These guys are critics, and they'll say things to discourage you. Over the years, it's become fire for me."

Words and Music

Undeterred, Steele returned to his original plan of writing with co-authors, including Al Anderson and Michael Dulaney. He marveled at the work ethic of his adopted Nashville songwriting community. "I wondered, 'How can someone sit in a room and do it everyday and not see it as a job?' These guys love finding new words to rhyme with 'love.'" Around 1998, things changed. Lee Ann Rimes cut his song "Big Deal," Kevin Sharp had a hit with "If You Love Somebody," and Diamond Rio struck gold with "Unbelievable." Says Steele, "All hell broke loose. I can't explain it and I don't want to. I just kept doing the same thing and working harder at it."

To the uninitiated, it may be a mystery why Jeffrey Steele, BMI's Songwriter of the Year and one of Nashville's most prolific talents, chooses to tour the hinterlands instead of luxuriating in town, writing songs, and checking the mailbox for what must presumably be formidable checks. He explains that touring stirs his creativity. "Particularly in the small towns, people come up and invariably tell you about their lives, about their cousins, uncles, or talk about something that happened in town. There's something to be said for playing for three hours and sitting in that autograph line for two. I always give everybody the time of day, let them tell me what they tell me. I like to say something positive, make the most of the time. They're happy to see me and I'm happy to be there. A lot of people get burned out, but I get stories and titles."

He gives this example of a song he co-wrote with Marv Green, the writer of Lonestar's hit, "Amazed." "I was on the autograph line and this guy comes up and he introduces me to his wife, this beautiful lady, and I could tell they're deeply in love. He says, 'She could have had anyone in school.' I said, 'What did you do to get her?' and he said, 'All's I did was love her.' My mental memory bank went on and we wrote the song a couple of days ago. It's about what he talked about. He never had any riches, but he promised her a life of his being there and being good to her."

Between the promotional tours for his record and production gigs, Steele tightly structures his songwriting time. "It's not unusual for me have three writing appointments a day like I'm in a doctors office. People say, 'How can you do anything artistic when you're writing that much?' First of all, I'm a freak. That answers that question," laughs Steele. If his first appointment of the day is productive, it inspires him for the next two sessions, and keeps his adrenaline running until the late hours." I know there's something wrong with me when I can't shut my brain down, when I'm getting up and writing at three in the morning. I want to keep practicing my lyric craft, get as good as I can. I want to use fewer words to say more things. Instead of having two lines, I try to get it down to two words."

Steele reveals that he's always prepared to write. "That's what anyone will say. Even if I'm an hour late to the writing session, it's because I'm at home working on an idea. I want a seed or something to go on. Putting in 30 to 40 minutes a day playing, trying to think of something, keeps you in that mode all of the time, ready to write something. Even if it's crappy stuff, you're letting your thoughts out. But I hope when a new guy comes in he's also armed and dangerous, is focused, has a bunch of stuff and wants to write hit songs." Steele shares that sometimes co-writers will expect him to, in his words, "lay a golden egg. That's the hardest part, when someone's looking at me going, 'When is it going to happen? And I'm like, 'When is what going to happen?' If I intend to lay a golden egg, I'm going to do it in the privacy of my home. I'm not going to do it in front of you, pal.'"

RECAP: Road to the Dotted Line

JEFFREY STEELE

- Was a part of a best-selling band prior to his songwriting career
- Relocated to Nashville
- Weathered an unproductive solo record deal
- Kept writing songs and creating co-writing alliances
- Writes up to three songs a day

JOSS STONE

Setting for a Sweet Soul Gem

Her immense voice fills the space in the claustrophobic confines of the Hollywood rehearsal studio. At first, teenage soul sensation Joss Stone, seated on a folding chair facing the band, is invisible. When she stands up, she is surprisingly statuesque, and as is her trademark, barefoot. How a teenaged British girl from a small village in the UK came to platinum prominence worldwide with an album of soul chestnuts is a tale of timing, intuition, and influence, but none of these successes could exist without the purity and emotion contained in one young white girl's voice.

Joscelyn Eve Stoker was born in the pastoral countryside of Dover, England. She subsequently spent her teen years in the rural town of Devon where the music that played around the house was mainly American soul—Aretha Franklin, Tracy Chapman, and Anita Baker. It was a sound Joscelyn learned to create on her own.

"When you get a chance to do something that you love, you go take it whether you're scared or not. But I was never like 'that girl.' Like in every school, there's that girl that's like the performer. That wasn't me. It was just, 'All right, I'll sing a little bit,' and then I went."

School was a chore. "I was kind of shy in school," she says, "but when I got the chance to do stuff, I would take it. I would be scared of taking it. I hated school. I hated the academic side of things. It just exhausted me. I hated getting up at seven o'clock in the morning. But when you get a chance to do something that you love, you go take it whether you're scared or not. But I was never like 'that girl.' Like in every school, there's that girl that's like the performer. That wasn't me. It was just, 'All right, I'll sing a little bit,' and then I went."

TV Tunes

She admits to being dyslexic, so learning lyrics by ear came easier than reading school textbooks. In 1999, aged 12 and still using her given name, she sent an audition tape to a British television talent show, *Star for a Night*. "I wasn't really thinking that I was going to do it," she says. "I didn't even know a whole song. I sang half of 'Amazing Grace,' half of 'Jesus Loves Me,' half of 'This Little Light of Mine.'" Apparently it was enough for the producers, who invited her to a live audition. She passed and performed on the show, winning with a version of Donna Summer's "On the Radio." Two London-based producers, the Boilerhouse Boys, Andy Dean and Ben Wolfe, saw Joscelyn's performance and forwarded the videotape to their friend and associate Steve Greenberg, president of S-Curve Records in the U.S. The Boilerhouse Boys have been at the forefront of the British music scene for over a decade—as award-winning songwriters, million-selling producers and remixers, major label A&R consultants, influential DJs, and now, innovative soundtrack composers. In December 2001, Greenberg received a call from the Boilerhouse Boys, telling him that they had just heard the greatest singer they'd ever heard from their country. He was wise to heed their enthusiasm.

Prior to founding S-Curve, Greenberg was senior vice president and head of A&R for Mercury Records from 1996 to 1999. While at Mercury, Greenberg discovered the pop/rock group Hanson and served as executive producer of their debut album, *Middle of Nowhere*, which sold over ten million copies worldwide and was nominated for three GRAMMY Awards®. He also worked on albums by a number of other Mercury artists, including Jon Bon Jovi's multi-million selling 1997 solo album, *Destination Anywhere*. Greenberg was previously responsible for the success of the Baha Men and their smash hit, "Who Let the Dogs Out?" Gritty, authentic soul and teen music may seem an unlikely combination, but Greenberg, a savvy music man, also compiled an acclaimed series of CD box sets based on the seminal Memphis soul label, Stax Records.

One of Greenberg's closest associates is New York-based producer, engineer, and songwriter Mike Mangini, who recalls Greenberg's first response to the videotape of the young British soul singer. "Steve said,

'It's got to be like Milli Vanilli. There's no way this girl sounds like this.'" Greenberg was impressed enough to bring Joscelyn to Mangini's studio in New York. "I hadn't heard her sing at that point, because she didn't have any demo tracks," recalls Greenberg. "So in the studio we downloaded some karaoke tracks off the Internet. With no preparation, she sang 'Midnight Train to Georgia' and '(Sittin' On) The Dock of the Bay,' and she just floored me. At one point, I was doubled over laughing. It was so unbelievable that she could sing like that. Joss had not only a great voice, but also the ability to put her own original stamp on classic material," he explained. "She wasn't just mimicking. She was changing and interpreting the songs, and doing it with passion and feeling. "The level of nuance was just astounding for someone who was then 14 years old."

With the Clean Up Woman
The original plans were to have Joscelyn write songs for her recorded debut. To that end, she and Mangini began working on demos. Into the mix came veteran soul legend Betty Wright, initially drafted to work with the young singer on vocals. A former member of her family gospel group, The Echoes of Joy, Wright's first recordings were as a backing singer. She later embarked on a solo career and scored a minor hit with "Girls Can't Do What The Guys Do" in 1968. Her biggest hit was "Clean Up Woman" in 1972. Her collaboration with Stevie Wonder, "What Are You Gonna Do with It?" (1981), proved to be Wright's last substantial hit, but she continued issuing albums throughout the Eighties and Nineties. She also tried her hand as a television talk show hostess and contributed back-up vocals to a wide variety of other artists such as Erykah Badu, Regina Belle, David Byrne, Jimmy Cliff, Gloria Estefan, Inner Circle, Millie Jackson, Jennifer Lopez, and Johnny Mathis. "I was given a CD of Joss's demos just one day before we met," Betty Wright remembers. "I told Steve, 'We don't know how, we don't know why, but this kind of voice is just a gift from heaven.'" Wright was the Miami connection; a former high school classmate of hers, hit songwriter and producer Desmond Child, also became connected to the project, contributing one song to the debut.

"In making *The Soul Sessions* together, I've been Joss's best friend and her worst enemy," Betty Wright admits. "By that, I mean I've made her attempt things with her voice that she couldn't even have imagined before. And Joss, for her part, has reminded me of some I things I'd forgotten—about why this kind of music is important to me and why I still enjoy creating it. We just plugged right into each other."

In the spring of 2003, Joss and her collaborators—including Greenberg, Wright, and co-producer Mike Mangini—set to work on the proposed album of original songs, co-written by Stone. But one of their first recordings, a cover of the obscure Carla Thomas song "I've Fallen in Love with You," turned their efforts in an entirely different direction. Steve Greenberg recalls, "A Carla Thomas cover didn't really fit on the album we were then planning, but Joss's performance of it was fantastic. Meanwhile, Joss's talent was evolving by leaps and bounds. So we thought we'd up the ante and have her record live in the studio with a real live R&B band, doing a whole set of classic and obscure soul songs, in addition to completing her album of new material."

Live Tracks

Greenberg came up with the idea of putting Stone in front of a live-in-the-studio R&B group and asked Wright to track down some of her Miami-based cohorts. In only a couple of days, she located musicians who had not been in the studio for years. She found guitarist Little Beaver, who had a #2 hit with "Party Down" in 1972 but was now working for Amtrak. Organist Timmy Thomas ("Why Can't We Live Together?"), who was employed as a college administrator, and keyboardist Latimore (1974's "Let's Straighten It Out") was also recruited. For four days, Stone recorded old R&B tunes with the band. She covered a version of The White Stripes' "Fell in Love with a Girl" (changed to "a Boy") in Philadelphia with The Roots. The remainder of the project was tracked at the historic The Hit Factory/Criteria Studios in Miami for what Betty Wright calls "a live soul session, just like back in the day."

Mike Mangini recalls, "We were making a little EP, a critic's thing so people could talk about her until she put out a real record." *The Soul Sessions*, the demo project, ended up selling two-and-a-half million records. "It was cut in four or five days, live, no overdubs. I'd never cut a record like that," marvels Mangini. Greenberg adds, "We did not want to do a karaoke record. We did not want to make an *American Idol* album of someone singing note-for-note copies of great records. We wanted to reinvent every song."

Greenberg suggested that Joscelyn change her name to Joss Stone. "I can't be Joss Stoker when I'm singing," said Stone, "because if I was, I'd stand by the mike, I'd have my hair right over my face." At this juncture, although she had representation in the UK, it was her mother, Wendy Stoker, who was acting as an interim manager. "It's kind of ill to have your parents on your payroll," Stone said at the time. "To employ your mum and dad is a little bit sick. They shouldn't be involved that much. I want a mum; I don't want a mum/manager. I have enough people trying to manage me and be involved. I just want her to be my mother." With the tracks completed, live showcases were set up at a 161-capacity venue, Joe's Pub in New York City—and the Troubadour in Los Angeles—to introduce the newly-christened Joss Stone to the media and potential agents.

With the success of the project, Mike Mangini relates that it was the artist herself who made it all a reality. "Joss is always amazing. It's just what version of amazing you want. She'll go in the studio for eight to ten hours in the booth—no break, no dinner. I produce the records with Betty Wright and Steve Greenberg, but Joss is her own biggest critic. In this project, I don't have to be a dictator. *The Soul Sessions* was truly a live record. The band played live and we didn't manipulate it at all. And all of Joss's vocals were live takes. She just went and sang it a few times, a take was picked, and that was it."

RECAP: Road to the Dotted Line

JOSS STONE

- Broke through on a national television show in the UK
- Was introduced to a U.S. label through local connections
- Sent only a videotape to gain label interest
- Was hooked up with a mentor, Betty Wright

Phil VASSAR

Go for the Gold

Distinct parallels can easily be drawn between the high-pressure worlds of sports and entertainment. In music—with careers measured by album sales, chart positions, and concert grosses—competition will always be a determining factor. The concept of teamwork is equally vital in both professions. Whereas in sports, trainers, coaches, and managers prevail, so do the components of a music business team—managers, agents, and record executives—supply similar support and expertise.

But whether it's winning the Super Bowl or selling a million copies of a record, the ultimate goal in both professions is victory. For Nashville-based songwriter and artist Phil Vassar, an upbringing of playing football and running track-and-field prepared him well for the hard knocks he encountered on his ten-year trip to the top of the country charts.

"Sports was a good teacher for me," says Vassar. " It taught me about getting up after being knocked down. You're not going to win every day, and the harder you work it's going to pay off eventually, hopefully. In a perfect world it does, anyway. But I think that's what sports did for me, taught me discipline and that you have to sweat a lot to get where you're going. I was way into sports in high school, and it took me to college on a scholarship. I was glad, but it was putting off the inevitable, getting into the music industry, which my dad tried to talk me out of so many times. What can you do? It's in your heart and your soul and in your blood, and you can't do anything about it." To appease his father, who was trying to steer him toward a more conventional career, he majored in business in college. Ironically, it was in college that he started on a path that mirrored his father's. Indulging his love for music, he took courses in music theory, music history, and music business.

When Vassar first moved from his home in Lynchburg, VA to Nashville, he spent his first nights in a Motel 6 on Harding Way, wondering if he'd made the right decision. Then he took the timeworn route up and down Music Row. "I knocked on some doors," he laughs, "and said, 'I'm a singer and a songwriter." They went, 'Yeah, so is everyone else.' But it was great. I wouldn't trade it."

His first job in Nashville was as a bartender. Eventually he began performing in clubs as well, up to six different clubs a week. He later narrowed it down to one or two, which enabled him to consolidate his crowd, pack the room and earn a substantial income—all without benefit of a record or publishing deal. "I think I probably played in front of every kind of crowd—sober, not sober, men, women, softball teams, bachelorette parties. It's a billion things. It's a good experience." He relied on a decided balance of discipline and focus to exist as a club performer at night and a serious songwriter woodshedding with his craft by day. "I probably did things a little differently," he explains, "I tried to make a living and I approached music that way. I kind of stayed away from the publishers and the industry part of it. "I'd gotten doors shut in my face and I was like, 'Look, I'm going to go over here, on this side of town, and make a living and make money and write songs and do whatever. I'd have songs I'd written and a lot of people said, 'You need to be in L.A., not in Nashville. You'll never get these songs cut here.' I didn't for a while, but eventually the songs they said wouldn't get cut became #1 songs for someone and hopefully for myself, too. You sort of have to find your niche and your place."

Club Dates
Phil then bought his own club. "I had nightclub and a restaurant for four years," he explains. "I had a great following in Nashville and I had the opportunity to open up this place. It was like 'I'm going to do it. I've got my own club to play in and I can't get fired!'" In addition to performing his original songs, Vassar played covers by Warren Zevon,

Billy Joel, James Taylor, and Jimmy Buffet. "I would do anything," he laughs. "I would always want everybody to sing with me. It was like a fraternity party every night." For Vassar, the concept of performing in front of a live audience was one key to his eventual success. He learned from his club experiences what made the audience move. "If you're an entertainer or an artist and you don't do clubs, you're missing out," he says.

Owning a club delivered another perspective. "I always took a very business approach to things. I think a mistake a lot of musicians make is to think the club owner is doing something for them just by letting them play there. Take the approach of 'Look, I'm playing here and I'm bringing people in. You're making money, so you're going to pay me for that. Otherwise, I'm going to go somewhere else and do it.'"

A patron of the club asked Vassar to send him a tape of a couple of his songs. He sent a demo that included "Once in a While," which he had written with another bartender. The song became his first cut when the patron's father, Engelbert Humperdinck, recorded it. Suddenly, things began to swing upward. He collaborated on a song with noted Nashville writer Skip Ewing ("Mary Go Round") and began working with other well-known Nashville songwriters who frequented his club to perform. That attracted music industry professionals, including publishing executive Greg Hill, who eventually signed Vassar to a publishing deal with EMI.

Penning hits for Alan Jackson ("Right on the Money"), Collin Raye ("Little Red Rodeo"), Tim McGraw ("For a Little While" and "My Next Thirty Years"), and Jo Dee Messina ("I'm Alright" and "Bye, Bye"), Vassar was named ASCAP's songwriter of the year in 1999. It was the entrée to an artist deal. "Every song I've ever written has been for me as an artist, so they just ended up getting recorded before my records," avows Vassar. "I went through a lot of sleepless nights when somebody wanted to record a song. I was like, 'Man, I don't know if I want to let that go or keep it,' but it worked out perfect every time. I don't regret giving away any songs to anyone. I kept what I wanted and I kept the songs that are more me and even made a little bit of money in the meantime. It's been the best of both worlds. "

"Writing hits for others before beginning an artist career is a venerable tradition, but many things about Phil Vassar are markedly atypical. For instance, he's a front man who plays the piano. Although it can often be heard of in the background of hit records, the piano is not an instrument one generally associates with country music. A short list of players notwithstanding—Ronny Milsap, Charlie Rich, Con Hunley, and cousins Jerry Lee Lewis and Mickey Gilley—it is generally many notches below the guitar in ranking as an instrument that a front person would play while performing. "For so long, people would come see me play and they'd say, 'Yeah, you're OK, but you're a piano player. We don't do that here.' It just took time for everyone to realize, 'You know what? Maybe this is interesting that you're a piano player.' Being a piano player is part of what I do, part of my writing style. A lot of people didn't want to write with me, either. Once people say 'He's a piano player,' they automatically think 'ballad.' I think I write ballads just fine, but up-tempo songs are my forte, with real aggressive, internal rhymes. That's how I like to write. I think it took having some hits for people to realize that, too, but it's not their fault."

Mentoring the Muse

Another turning point in Phil's career came when he was introduced, through friends, to his first mentor, songwriter and producer Linda Hargrove. Hargrove has been a powerful presence on Nashville's Music Row since the early Seventies. She immediately heard the vast potential in Vassar's songs. Vassar points to the Nashville legacy of mentors. "In Nashville, that's wonderful thing," he explains. "People pass down knowledge to up-and-coming writers."

He hopes to repay the creative favor: "People did it for me and I hope I can do that for someone someday. I think it's great. If everyone did that, it would sure help a lot of people. You meet someone and you feel they have a talent, but maybe it's a little rough and could be honed in a little bit. Linda helped me do that. She got me to a point where when we weren't working together anymore, I was ready to go and do something else. I think it takes that. As long you're in Nashville, you always have something that takes you to another step. When that crashes and burns, something's there to take you on to another step. Sometimes it doesn't happen. People leave and go home. I was always lucky enough to have something going."

"It took ten or eleven years to really have success, which I think takes a while. I've known artists who have come in and gotten a record deal in six months. It takes some people longer than others. It was about the journey. A lot of great songs came out of that time, being excited and up and down and every other emotion you can fathom."

First and foremost, Phil Vassar reserves his highest respect for the creators of songs. "People in the industry tend to forget it, but I've been in meetings where I've said, 'Look at this building. It's all because some songwriter busted his ass and wrote a great song and you're making the money on it.' It's the minutest of all details, but it all comes down to the art. Smoke and mirrors will only get you so far."

RECAP: Road to the Dotted Line

PHIL VASSAR

- Studied music business in college
- Applied business principles to a music career
- Was at the center of a burgeoning scene
- Parlayed his visibility and friendships into co-writing relationships

Rufus Wainwright

MOTHERS, FATHERS, AND SONS

If you believe all of the press generated by Rufus Wainwright in his relatively short career, you might envision him as some jaded, latter-day Oscar Wilde, cruising the neon streets of Manhattan's Chelsea district with a thesaurus in one hand and a hit of Ecstasy in the other. The reality is, of course, substantially more grounded. Still, with his nakedly theatrical voice, exquisite taste for lyrical detail, and brave, confessional stance, Rufus Wainwright has designed his own filigreed niche high above the clouds of contemporary music—his own ornate alcove, high in the tower of song.

With the delivery of his self-titled 1998 debut album, Wainwright arrived seemingly full-blown onto the music scene. The Canadian-born scion of an illustrious song-writing family (his father is Loudon Wainwright III and his mother is Kate McGarrigle), he was first introduced to the record-buying public as an infant, courtesy

"If you can go and fill a small coffee-house and get $500 at the end of the night, you've made it. You never know when times are going to change, but as long as you can get a gig, it's the way it should be."

of "Rufus Is a Tit Man," a song his father wrote about his voracious oral appetites.

It wasn't long after weaning that Wainwright himself was in the spotlight. At six, he was playing piano and by age 13 he was performing in concert with his mother. A year later, Wainwright was nominated for a Juno (the Canadian equivalent of a GRAMMY®) as Most Promising Young Artist, while his "I'm A-Runnin'" was concurrently nominated for a Genie (the Canadian counterpart to an Oscar) for Best Song in a Film.

"For a long time, I listened to classical music," he recalls. "It was really more of a disease than anything. Sometimes I hate the fact that most of my teenage years were spent with the headphones on listening to Verdi's *Requiem* in the dark. But the one thing I did learn from it, aside from the fact I'd be alone a lot because no one wanted to hear it, is you get better as you get older. The best stuff you write is right before you die. It's the best music because it's going to be a long journey. And that's something in pop and rock that is so lost and something I'm trying to bring into my career because nobody strives for that as much. I'm young now, it seems exciting, but who knows what it will be like in a few years. There's brief shelf-life for a pop singer, so I'm trying to follow that classical ethos: you get better as you get older." This immersion in the arias of Verdi coincided with the more personal drama of growing up gay. Wainwright related more to the "damned ladies" of opera than to the pursuits that society would have a teenage boy embrace. "Opera was an escape from the fear and frustration I was feeling."

He was enrolled as a student at the prestigious Millbrook School in upstate New York. "It was a beautiful, pastoral setting," Wainwright remembers fondly. "I really thought it was *Brideshead Revisited*. It was the greatest thing that ever happened to me. I knew where I fit in. I was the little Mozart guy, playing the piano and singing, that old McGarrigle thing, 'Let's put on a show!' I sort of regained my innocence."

For a brief time, he studied music at Montreal's McGill University, eventually turning away from classical performance toward pop and rock. "I thought I'd do all these wonderful things and there'd be all these creative people," he recollects, "but it was like going to engineering school. There were great moments, like finally singing the *Requiem* with an orchestra, but the academic setting was ultimately a dead end for me." It was then that he decided not to limit himself to classical music because, he claims, "All the cute boys were doing rock."

Family Business

So is the cliché true, that songwriting is quite literally in his blood? "I took to it early and naturally," Wainwright affirms. "My mother recognized from a very early age that I was going to be a ham, that I was much more comfortable onstage, that I was a natural. Since she was in the same business, she realized I needed to get my chops together and was always very tough on me and very honest with what I should do, that I had to work very hard and essentially if I didn't take it seriously right away then I wouldn't get anywhere. I think she knew what I was going to do was different, that I wasn't going to be a pop singer, that I had my own idea. I think in a weird way she wished I was a pop singer, that I wasn't so interesting, because these days it's tough in this business to be different. And in her career I think maybe she wishes she hadn't been such an individual. They might have made more money. I'm trying to saddle both of those desires." How does Wainwright himself feel about being so different, distinctive, and instantly identifiable? "It's both a blessing and a curse," he confirms.

Unlike pop stars, Wainwright observes that songs don't need Botox and face-lifts. "A great song is a great song," he insists. "Certain Cole Porter songs or old cowboy songs, they never age, no matter in what format they're presented. I think the act of great songwriting, which I'm trying to perfect for myself, is high and above technological trends. You're dealing with the immortal if you can get there. I'm more interested in that format."

Canadian Bridges

Wainwright departed his hometown of Montreal for New York, where he was unsuccessful in locating a record company who understood his art. "I went to New York in the early Nineties and failed. When I first arrived in New York, it was the era of Jeff Buckley and Nirvana. Jeff Buckley, I remember him being at the height of his power. There was this one club, Cafe Sine, where he'd played, and they refused my tape three times. I hated Jeff Buckley. I resented him. I was jealous, whatever. I guess my wish was fulfilled, unfortunately. Years later, after his tragic demise, I heard him. I listened to him without that feeling and realized it was a great loss."

"I was working in a movie theatre. It was incredibly hard to play anywhere. I failed and left and went back home. I decided perhaps I should attempt my launch in a more hospitable environment, so I went to Montreal." Back home, he played mainly at Cafe Sarajevo, a club frequented by refugees from the Yugoslavian wars. He spent most days at the home he shared with his mom, writing. "And my mom allowed me to do this, as long as I was writing songs. She said, 'As long as you're seriously working on music, I'll support you. Don't get a job, because if you work, it will crush you.'" Becoming a fixture on the Montreal club circuit, Wainwright recorded with producer Pierre Marchand, who had worked with the McGarrigle Sisters and was a trusted family friend.

Pass It On

Wainwright opines that he wasn't that ambitious. His family connections paid off, though, when his father passed a tape to legendary songwriter/producer Van Dyke Parks. Parks in turn passed it on to Lenny Waronker, who was president of DreamWorks Records. "My initial response to Rufus's music was, 'How could a 21-year-old be writing this stuff?' It was amazing. But when I met him, I saw immediately that he was very much a kid of his generation. Still, he's doing something no one of his generation is doing, which is why I think other artists appreciate him so much."

Signed to DreamWorks, Wainwright was given a rental apartment at The Oakwood, an industry encampment near Universal City. "I ended up in a very expensive studio playing everything I'd written since I was 12," he recalls. "In retrospect, it's great I have those recordings and they exist. I had written a lot and it was good that I got it out. I probably should have done it at home on a four track, and I wouldn't say all of them are worthy of recording. They're there nonetheless, just me and guitar and piano. And this was after a good 17 years of working on material." Wainwright worked with Marchand and producer Jon Brion (Aimee Mann, Jellyfish), recording enough songs to fill a vault. "Sixty-two rolls of tape, fifty-six songs," he reports. "It basically drained my life's blood! It took a lot of time and resources, but Lenny didn't care how long it took, as long as we were doing good work."

City of the Fallen Angels

Wainwright, when not ensconced in The Oakwood or the studio, took to L.A. nightlife. "I had a real traumatic experience in California in a lot of ways. I never expected to work or live in L.A. or have any L.A. connections. I thought I'd be singing in Holiday Inns for a while. I had no idea what L.A. really was. One thing that's funny is once you're signed and have clout, everything swings open immediately, especially if you're connected to Lenny Waronker. I was bombarded by this West Coast lore where it's meeting Lance Loud or hanging out with Van Dyke Parks and all these people. I loved it at first and very much felt at home, but like any great drug there was a crash I experienced. There's so much schmoozing and drinking and people blowing a lot of smoke up my butt. I've got to watch it. There's a double-edged sword, this town. I've learned to handle it now.

Having grown up around the music industry, Wainwright harbors few illusions. "In this business there's no money. Don't do it. My parents, what's great about their careers is that they really stuck to their guns in terms of their music. But they paid a price. They had to stay in motels and play crappy clubs and tour endlessly, especially my father. They're fine now, but they were struggling. For me, it gave me a sense that the business is not a rock star thing. It's not about glamour or money or you're here today, gone tomorrow. A lot of the myths were dispelled quite early for me. I think often one's parents' mistakes are the greatest learning thing for the child, not mistakes but events."

"I just learned the only thing—if you can go and fill a small coffee-house and get $500 at the end of the night, you've made it. You never know when times are going to change, but as long as you can get a gig, it's the way it should be."

RECAP: Road to the Dotted Line

RUFUS WAINWRIGHT

- Began performing as a young teen
- Developed a unique sense of songcraft
- Returned home to Montreal after unsuccessful years in New York
- Was signed on the basis of a well-produced demo

Gretchen WILSON

Pride of Pocahontas

"Each man creates his own destiny. It's up to you what you're going to do with your life. It's not up to anybody else."

From Pocahontas, IL to the world, Gretchen Wilson is a hard-rocking, tobacco-chewing, self-proclaimed Redneck Woman whose ringing authenticity has crowned her a new favorite in modern country music. She's also a record-setting artist, having entered the history books with a debut single, an album, and a video all topping their respective charts. As a female member of Nashville's Musik Mafia—a loose affiliation of artists led by Big & Rich and including James Otto and prototypical country rap artist Cowboy Troy—she is the embodiment of a new rebel spirit.

Pocahontas, Wilson's hometown, is a hard-scrabble community 36 miles due east of St. Louis, a rural enclave where abundant trailer parks are clustered alongside verdant cornfields and pungent pig farms. When Gretchen was born, her mother was all of 16 years old. By the time she was two, her father had moved on. Her dad picked around on the guitar and had a quiet voice. And Gretchen, who made it a point to meet him for the first time when she was 12, relates that he had musical bloodlines. "His family, I'm told, had a little traveling band. I think it was a gospel band."

Whenever the family couldn't make rent, they packed up what little belongings they owned and moved down the road to another trailer. With a working mother and no father for support, Gretchen turned to her grandmother for parenting. It was a support system that also helped Wilson after she took on the responsibility of raising her baby brother at the age of ten. She says she went to more than 20 different schools by the time she finally dropped out in the eighth grade. At 14, she joined her mother cooking and tending bar at Big O's, a rough-and-tumble bar five miles outside of town. Big O's was owned by Mark Obermark. Over the years, Obermark became something of a father-figure to Wilson. He and his bar helped support Wilson's family during the tough times, and it wasn't an easy bar to manage. A year later and living on her own, Wilson was managing the roughneck joint with a loaded 12-gauge double-barrel shotgun stashed behind the bar for protection. Long before Karaoke machines, she got up onstage every night at Big O's with a microphone and sang along to various CDs for tips, an extra $20 that came in handy when it was time to put food on the table.

Honky Tonk Heroine
Eventually, singing to CDs was a thing of the past, and so was serving drinks, when Gretchen began fronting a cover band, Sam A. Lama & the Ding Dongs, at age 16. She followed that experience by joining her first country band, St. Louis-based Midnight Flyer. For the first time, she felt like maybe there was a life for her outside Bond County. "Each man creates his own destiny," she believes. "It's up to you what you're going to do with your life. It's not up to anybody else." Taking control of her own destiny, Gretchen Wilson had bigger plans than spending the rest of her life slinging drinks or singing in a cover band. She had a goal of moving to Nashville.

Singers like Tanya Tucker, Loretta Lynn and, of course, Patsy Cline, influenced Gretchen Wilson. "I could feel the pain," she says, "and I could only imagine what it was like to have an abusive husband and all the different things that she sang about."

Nashville Skyline
At 23, Gretchen moved to Nashville with typically high hopes. "I just thought it was gonna be go in, play some music, and get a record deal," says Wilson. Somewhat discouraged after a brief encounter with a local musician, whom she happened to recognize at a Nashville music shop, she thought long and hard about how to go about realizing her dream.

"I looked at him," she recalls, "and said, 'I'm brand new to town. What's my first step? How do I do this?' He pretty much laughed at me and said something that didn't make sense. He said, 'Well, you have to create a buzz.' I thought, 'What the hell good does that do me?'"

It would take her four long years to figure out what he meant and, in the meantime, she did the one thing she knew how to do in order to make ends meet—she got a job concocting cocktails and drawing beers down in Printers Alley at the Bourbon Street Blues & Boogie Bar where she'd sit in and perform with the house band. She didn't have the glamorous country-diva look of Shania Twain or Faith Hill. "I was a bit too old," she notes. "I was a few pounds too heavy." None of this, of course, impacted her supple powerhouse of a voice. By 1999, Wilson, now with a daughter of her own, was supplementing her club income by singing demos for songwriters and music publishers. "I was paying the bills and I was working in the music industry. I felt like I had already made it in Nashville."

With her romantic partner, Mike Penner, and her daughter, Grace, Wilson rented a small house in Mt. Juliet. The demo gigs brought anywhere from $200 to $1,200 a week, but she often didn't get paid for sessions for at least six months. "We were living demo job to demo job," Wilson recalls. "We were freaking out to try to come up with the rent. Every six months, I'd take a day off to call publishing companies and ask where the money is." In the past, she says, she's filed bankruptcy with no legal representation. "I've struggled and fought my whole life just to keep $100 in my bank account. It was always so stressful. And then having a child as I did, the stress got worse and worse wondering how I'm going to provide for her future. I'd have days where I'd sit around thinking, 'I'm just a demo singer. I've got nothing in my future to offer this child.'"

Muzik Mafia Uncorked

It is closed now, but Pub of Love will stay forever open in country music legend. With its maritime decor and thrift-store sofas, the two-story hole-in-the-wall perfectly fit its grungy Gulch surroundings. On most nights, the action was upstairs. Mondays featured up-and-coming musicians of all genres, from jam-band to punk. The vibe changed on Wednesdays, when Pub of Love hosted puppet shows, performance art, and spoken word under the moniker "Poetry, Etc." But it was Tuesday nights when two Nashville musicians without record deals, Big Kenny Alphin and John Rich, would take over the club to play music with their friends at the Pub of Love in a loose aggregation know as the Muzik Mafia.

Boom had gone bust in Nashville by the early 21st century. Palatial office buildings, opened in country's mid-Nineties heyday, were boarded up and vacant. Clearly, Nashville needed a rejuvenating shot of energy, and Big and Rich—spearheads of the Muzik Mafia—were about to deliver it.

It was a Friday night when Big Kenny and John Rich walked into Bourbon Street Blues & Boogie Bar. They were there to "have a few cocktails" and thus got to hear Gretchen Wilson belt out a couple of tunes with the house band. Wilson remembers their initial encounter. "John followed me up to my little cubby-hole bar upstairs with his trench coat and cowboy hat and I think his exact words were, 'Hey, how come you ain't got a record deal yet?' I looked at him in disgust and threw him a business card and a little homemade demo and said, 'I'm busy. I'm working right now.'"

For months, John tried getting in touch with her. For months, Gretchen ignored his calls, until someone finally said, "Look, you should really return his call. He might be able to help you out." He introduced her to his circle of friends—"they started to use me singing on some demos"—but he also taught her how the Nashville song-writing community really works, "how they write, break for lunch, and then come back, how they come up with ideas and how to contribute to a songwriting session." Gretchen also became a member of the loose-knit group of singers, songwriters, and musicians who get together to jam —and party—every Tuesday. It was in front of her very honest peers, that she honed her songwriting style.

Oh Brother to Oh Sister
Enter John Grady, a Sony executive who had a creative hand in the marketing, promotion, and sales of dozens of top-selling artists, including Whitney Houston, Kenny G, Bonnie Raitt, MC Hammer, and many more. Between 1993 and 2002, John was senior vice president of Sales, Marketing and Promotion for Mercury Records in Nashville, where he helped launch the career of Shania Twain as well as break the multi-million selling movie soundtrack *Oh Brother, Where Art Thou?* (2000). The worldwide success of *Oh Brother...* propelled Grady into a partnership in DMZ Records and CBS Records, with movie producers, The Coen Brothers, and platinum guitar icon T-Bone Burnett. In 2002, former boss and mentor Don Ienner, president of CBS, offered the presidency of Sony Music in Nashville to John Grady. Relates Grady, "The guy who hired me, Don Ienner, taught me how to walk through walls for something I believe in. *Oh Brother, Where Art Thou?* was about belief, when nobody else believed. I think maybe that's what I did better than anybody else, believe."

With her less-than-glamorous image, at an age when many execs would have overlooked Gretchen Wilson, Grady saw something in the raw power and earthy songwriting of the tough-talking tobacco-chewing woman. He believed, signed Wilson to a record deal, and was rewarded with an across-the-board success. Wilson's lead-off single, "Redneck Woman," struck an immediate chord in country music listeners, registering the highest-charting debut for a country album ever—her *Here for the Party* entered the *Billboard* charts at #2

"What I'm doing has definitely been done before, it just hasn't been done in a long time," Gretchen says. "It's not perfect and it's not glamorous. I had to struggle here," she continues, "and all the people who did turn me down and the all the things that happened, it couldn't have worked out more perfectly. 'Redneck Woman' is not just about me, but my mom and my grandmother and probably every other woman in Pocahontas."

Gretchen was named Female Vocalist of the Year at the 39th annual Country Music Association Awards, held at New York City's Madison Square Garden in November 2005. Her career continues to soar.

RECAP: Road to the Dotted Line

GRETCHEN WILSON

- Began singing live to karaoke machines
- Moved to Nashville
- Made a living as a demo singer
- Hooked up with two soon-to-be-prominent scenemakers
- Was signed on the strength of a new musical trend

Lee Ann WOMACK

The Perseverance Prize

Despite the alluring rags-to-riches mythologies of country music, there really are no overnight successes, just artists who grow up so marinated in the music and the writing and performing of it that their career paths seem predestined. Lee Ann Womack is one such artist, a diminutive woman whose steely determination transported her from the dusty plains of Texas to GRAMMY®-winning success. Like a classic country song, hers is a saga is steeped in romance, betrayal, and divorce, with stardom as the ultimate prize.

Unlike many country singers of her generation, pop music didn't make much of an impact Lee Ann Womack. From her earliest years in the small Texas town of Jacksonville, Womack absorbed the sound and culture of country music. Her father was a part-time disc jockey who frequently took her into the studio with him and let her choose records for him to play. (Bob Wills,

"I spent a lot of time feeling in the dark and had some curves thrown me. I waited in Nashville for ten years before I had a record deal or anything."

Ray Price, and Glen Campbell were her favorites.) "My dad also worked at an AC/soft rock station but I can't tell you who the artists are," she affirms. She credits her father with exposing her to hard country. "I think it had to do with being a Daddy's girl and wanting to listen to what he did. It was a huge influence on me. I don't know why I didn't rebel, like in high school, but I never went through a period of time where I listened to rock music or anything. I listened to country music from the time I was little till now."

"In college, I was a huge Ricky Skaggs fan and he worked with James Taylor, so I started listening to him. It progressed into listening to pop a little bit, but I still don't listen to it a lot. My strongest influences are Willie Nelson, Ray Price, and Hank Thompson." At home, if weather conditions were favorable, she would lie between the stereo speakers to hear the music beaming in on radio waves from Nashville, from the Grand Ole Opry. "Strangely enough, in high school I loved Vern Gosdin, George Jones, and Merle Haggard, guys who were singing about terrible things they went through and then sang it with such emotion you knew they'd been through it. You could feel it. I don't know why I was drawn to those sorts of things as a child, but I was. From a commercial standpoint, I've got to watch it. But you've got to do what works for you." she declares.

The Road to Nashville

"I grew up as this weird kid that wanted to have a career in music. I knew from a very early age exactly what I wanted to do with my life. I always felt like somewhat of a misfit. I was always the shortest kid, not the brightest or the prettiest, and I think that's made me work really hard." Nashville was a city that she had to conquer. She first visited when, instead of taking her senior trip with the rest of her class, she bargained with her parents for a visit to tour Music Row. She began formulating a strategy for a permanent move. After graduation, Womack studied music at South Plains College in Levelland, TX, one of the first schools to offer a degree in bluegrass and country music. She became a member of the school band, Country Caravan, and toured with them throughout the Southwest and Southern California.

Lee Ann knew she had to get to Nashville, so she enrolled in Belmont University's music business program. "The Mike Curb College of Entertainment and Music Business combines classroom study with internship experience and extracurricular activities to prepare men and women for operational and administrative, as well as creative and technical positions within the music and entertainment industry," reads the school's promotional information. Colleges with music business programs have increased in significant numbers in recent years. Specialized schools like the Berklee College of Music in Boston and Musicians Institute in Hollywood offer hands-on education, not only for musicians and technicians, but also for budding executives and entrepreneurs. For Womack, it was evident that being just a few blocks away from the epicenter of country music afforded tremendous access.

Nashville's reverence for the song form cannot be overstated. These days, it's not just country in Music City, either. Christian, pop, rock, gospel, alternative—and especially alt.country and Americana—are also viable forms. Nashville is a city of surprises. The rumpled-looking gentleman sitting next to you at a coffee shop could be a major songwriter, executive, or record producer. Certain parts of town near Music Row are similar to a college campus in that many of the patrons in the restaurants are in the music business. Nashville respects longevity and credibility, with personal relationships especially important in this friendly, song-oriented town. Most of the major music publishers have offices, and many smaller boutique companies exist, too. As part of Belmont's curriculum, students are given the opportunity to intern at major record labels, music publishing and management firms, and talent agencies. Womack's internship was at MCA Records, a label that, coincidentally, became her second recording home.

Publishing, Demos, and Matrimony

A funny thing happened on the way to the Opry. Just like a good country song, matters of the heart threatened to overshadow a budding career. Lee Ann fell in love and married another aspiring singer and songwriter, Jason Sellars. With the birth of their daughter Aubrie, Lee Ann took time off to be a mom. But ambition still burned deep. Womack tells tales of traversing Music Row on foot with the baby in a stroller, going from door to door to drop off copies of her demos at music publishing firms.

With her authentic Texas inflections and unadorned, straight-ahead vocal style, Womack's voice was pitch perfect for projecting the words and melodies of other songwriters. More importantly, singing demos kept her imbedded in the tight community of songwriters, publishers, and record company A&R. Interestingly, it wasn't Womack's voice that led to her first formal contract with the industry. It was her own abilities as a songwriter. With characteristic determination, she booked herself into songwriter showcases, Nashville institutions. A representative from Tree Publishing, a well-established Music City firm, heard her live and asked for a tape. Eventually, producer and songwriter Don Cook, chief creative officer and senior vice president of Nashville's Sony/ATV/Tree Music Publishing, signed her to the firm.

As a staff writer at Tree, Womack widened her contacts and experience considerably, working with legendary Opry star Bill Anderson, Sam Hogin, Ed Hill, and a collaborator who became her producer, Mark Wright. In early 1996, Womack signed as an artist with Decca

Records, the legendary label of Ernest Tubb, Patsy Cline, Webb Pierce, Loretta Lynn, and many of her musical heroes.

With the signing came a career conundrum—what to do about her name? At just about the time Womack joined Decca, LeAnn Rimes was making her media breakthrough and there was the question of whether two country singers with identical sounding first names might needlessly confuse fans. Womack was philosophical about the whole matter. "I was not opposed to changing my name," she says. "I suggested we go with Lu, since that had always been my nickname. But the label didn't want Lu because they thought it sounded too masculine, so we stayed with Lee Ann. The one who actually decided that I should keep my name was my manager, Erv Woolsey. He said that when he started managing George Strait, there had been some pressure for George to take a different name, on account of George Jones. Erv said, 'George Strait kept his name, and it worked. You should, too.'"

But four months after the release of her second album in 1999, Decca Records closed its doors. Ultimately, the album sold respectably, and Womack moved over to MCA. Husband Jason Sellars's career never exceeded a promising start, and he and Womack parted ways in 1996. She subsequently married record producer Frank Liddell, Decca's director of A&R who ultimately produced her breakthrough records for MCA. "I spent a lot of time feeling in the dark and had some curves thrown me," Womack declares. "I waited in Nashville for ten years before I had a record deal or anything. And of course I'd spent my whole life before that growing up in East Texas, wanting to do this, and not knowing if I'd ever make it. Just because you get a record deal and have a hit or two doesn't mean you're going to have a long career. That happens; there are ups and downs in everything. It's how you learn from your mistakes and learn how to handle that that really makes you the person that you are." Womack laments record company changes she has been forced to deal with during her career. "Everytime I put out a record since I started, the label shut down, or they fire everybody. You get a little more thick-skinned."

"I Hope You Dance," penned by Tia Sillers, was the song that arced her career into the stratosphere. "You can't really predict commercial success. There are too many people involved in the process between my recording it and getting it out to the people, either to the radio stations and the listeners or to the stores and the buyers. I can't control any of that. I knew it was a special song and I knew if people heard it, it would really touch them. I didn't know how many or on what level."

Womack is at the forefront of a legion of female artists who dominate the country charts. Has she noted similar advances for women in the ranks of record executives or producers? "I'm not seeing them producing anymore, unfortunately," she responds. "But I shouldn't say 'unfortunately' because I don't care. I never really look at somebody's sex as a musician or writer or producer or whatever. I figure if they're good enough, they're going to make it. I'm not one of those people who goes around saying, 'We need more women producing records.' Allison Krauss produces some great stuff and I don't really think of her as a woman; I think of her as a musician and a great producer. As far as the executive and business side of things, I'm not enough a part of that environment to comment on that. But again, I don't think being a woman is going to hold anyone back, not in this day and age. On the artist side, we have no complaints—Shania, Faith, the Chicks. And my current record is selling really well. We're taking up most of the Top 10. We're doing our part."

In November 2005, the Country Music Association Awards named Lee Ann's *There's More Where that Came From* Album of the Year. Its single, a song about yielding to temptation called "I May Hate Myself in the Morning," won Single of the Year. Womack also shared an award with George Strait for Musical Event of the year, their collaboration on "Good News, Bad News." Backstage at the Madison Square Garden event, Lee Ann quipped, "Last year I watched the CMAs on my couch in my pajamas. This year I'm in Alexander McQueen in the front row."

After almost a decade in Nashville, Lee Ann Womack's hard work had paid off.

🟦 RECAP: Road to the Dotted Line

LEE ANN WOMACK

- Grew up with a father in the broadcast business
- Studied music and music business at two colleges
- Learned the business by interning at a record label
- Made contacts as a songwriter and a demo singer
- Endured ten years in Nashville, never leaving the business

ABOUT THE AUTHOR

Acknowledged as one of the American media's foremost authorities on popular music, Dan Kimpel contributes to a dizzying variety of print and electronic mediums: books, interactive CDs, magazines, web sites, videos, and new media. If you've flown on United Airlines you've probably heard Kimpel's audio interviews with recording artists worldwide on The United Entertainment Network.

The author of *Networking Strategies for the New Music Business*, the follow up to his best-selling title, *Networking in the Music Business*, Dan conducted a weeklong master seminar for five years at Sir Paul McCartney's Liverpool Institute for Performing Arts (LIPA) in the U.K. Stateside, he lectures at colleges, universities, and conferences across the U.S. and Canada; this year he joined the faculty of Musician's Institute in Hollywood, CA.